LITERATURE AND JOURNALISM IN ANTEBELLUM AMERICA

LITERATURE AND JOURNALISM IN ANTEBELLUM AMERICA

THOREAU, STOWE, AND THEIR CONTEMPORARIES RESPOND TO THE RISE OF THE COMMERCIAL PRESS

Mark Canada

palgrave
macmillan

LITERATURE AND JOURNALISM IN ANTEBELLUM AMERICA
Copyright © Mark Canada, 2011.

First published in 2011 by PALGRAVE MACMILLAN® in the United States – a division of St. Martin's Press LLC, 175 Fifth Avenue, New York, NY 10010.

Where this book is distributed in the UK, Europe and the rest of the world, this is by Palgrave Macmillan, a division of Macmillan Publishers Limited, registered in England, company number 785998, of Houndmills, Basingstoke, Hampshire RG21 6XS.

Palgrave Macmillan is the global academic imprint of the above companies and has companies and representatives throughout the world.

Palgrave® and Macmillan® are registered trademarks in the United States, the United Kingdom, Europe and other countries.

ISBN 978–0–230–11094–6

Library of Congress Cataloging-in-Publication Data

Canada, Mark.
    Literature and journalism in antebellum America: Thoreau, Stowe, and their contemporaries respond to the rise of the commercial press/ Mark Canada.
        p. cm.
    Includes bibliographical references.
    ISBN 978–0–230–11094–6
    1. American fiction—19th century—History and criticism.   2. Journalism and literature—United States—History—19th century.   3. Press and journalism in literature.   4. Journalism—United States—History—19th century.   5. American newspapers—History—19th century.   I. Title.
    PS374.J68C36 2010
    810.9'39—dc22

                                                                2010037605

A catalogue record of the book is available from the British Library.

Design by MPS Limited, A Macmillan Company

First edition: April 2011

10 9 8 7 6 5 4 3 2 1

Printed in the United States of America.

A version of "Stowe's Abolitionist Exposé" in Chapter 6 originally appeared in the Ignatius Critical Edition of *Uncle Tom's Cabin* (Mark Canada, "News of Her Own: Harriet Beecher Stowe's Investigative Fiction," *Uncle Tom's Cabin*, ed. Mary R. Reichardt [San Francisco: Ignatius Press, 2009], 635–53.). Used with permission.

Cover Image
Reading Room of the Astor House
Painting by Nicolino Calyo
Museum of the City of New York

For my family
You are with me always

CONTENTS

TABLE

ACKNOWLEDGMENTS

Appearing on *60 Minutes* after his retirement from the *Washington Post*, Ben Bradlee was asked about Janet Cooke, the *Post* reporter who won the Pulitzer Prize for her series "Jimmy's World" and then lost it when it turned out she had made up parts of the story. Bradlee, though penitent, offered one explanation. Cooke, he said, "wrote like an angel." If I had been in the room with Bradlee, I might have told him what I told my wife at the time—that it's easy to write well when you're making up the material. Facts are to the experienced writer what power lines are to the landscape photographer—in a word, inelegant. Oh, to be free of them! What sentences one could write!

I could say that this book began with that interview, and saying so would make for a good story, although probably not a true one. The truth is that the origins of this study of literature and journalism are, like the origins of most things, difficult to pinpoint. They are, I suspect, bound up with my life, which has at one time or another included training to be a journalist, writing and editing newspaper copy, writing fiction, and studying and teaching literature by American authors, including many who themselves trained to be journalists, wrote and edited newspaper copy, and wrote fiction. Such experiences, perhaps inevitably, led me to thinking about the intersections of writing fact and writing fiction.

Easier to identify are the people who shaped my experience and ultimately helped turn it into something concrete. One of the first was my high school journalism teacher, Julie Kukolla, whose invaluable lessons on the First Amendment and more have remained with me to this day. During and after graduate school at the University of North Carolina at Chapel Hill, I have been the beneficiary of other outstanding mentors: Joseph Flora, Richard Rust, Connie Eble, and Philip Gura. I thank them all for their wisdom and support.

The catalyst for this book was my institution, the University of North Carolina at Pembroke, which granted me directed academic leave to work on this project in the spring of 2007. That spring and the following summer, I traveled to several academic libraries around the country, read as many books and poems and articles as I could, presented my work at scholarly conferences, and drafted the first version of this book. This invaluable opportunity, one that led to an enormously rewarding experience, is only one form of support I have received from an institution that has done much more for my career.

Several librarians have helped me tap their holdings of microfilm, books, manuscripts, and more. I am especially grateful for the assistance of my UNCP colleague Michael Alewine, whose assistance I have sought—and received—on countless occasions, not only for this project, but for others, as well. I cannot imagine anyone more generous with his time and expertise than Michael has been with his. In the final stages of production, I received a great deal of additional assistance from my department's research assistant, Marri Brooks, who has a fine eye for detail.

The people who deserve the most thanks are those closest to me, my family. My parents, Alan and Frances Canada, have been a source of endless support, from my earliest years to my tenure on my high school newspaper to the summer days I spent working on this book in their home. The work that went into this book has occasionally come at the cost of my children's playtime, I'm sure. Essie and Will, thank you for donating some of your time so that I could complete a project that meant a lot to me. I hope that you both have the opportunity to enjoy a similar labor of love in your own lifetimes. Finally, I can only begin to thank Lisa—my wife, my best friend, my foundation. On her love and support rest this book, my career, and many more things besides.

INTRODUCTION

A SIBLING RIVALRY IN AMERICAN LETTERS

One might have guessed that his star had blazed and faded. Dead for more than two decades, his best-known book little more than a memory, Truman Capote, it seemed, had gone the way of Rachel Carson. Then, seemingly out of nowhere, director Bennett Miller resurrected the reputation of the one-time literary celebrity, turning the story of his research for *In Cold Blood* into one of the most acclaimed films of 2005. Another film by another director followed, as did a new edition of his best-known novel. Just like that, Capote was back.

A few years earlier, another writer had seen his reputation travel in the opposite direction. In the late 1990s, Stephen Glass watched his star blaze as he published articles in *The New Republic*, *Rolling Stone*, and *George*. Then, in 1998, the truth came out: Glass had made up much of his material. After he was exposed, Glass told his story on *60 Minutes* and published a novel, *The Fabulist*, but his career as a star journalist was over. Just like that, Glass was gone.[1]

Aside from its moral about the fluid nature of literary celebrity, this tale of two writers points to a central issue in American writing. The nonfiction novelist rose and the imaginative journalist fell largely because they challenged Americans' notion of genre, crossing the line between literature and journalism. Capote, who wrote as an author, was hailed as an innovator; Glass, who wrote as a journalist, was dismissed—literally—as a fraud. One man's transcendence was another's transgression. In the years between Capote's triumph and Glass's demise, America saw a number of similar instances of genre confusion. In the 1960s and 1970s, Tom Wolfe pioneered something he called the "New Journalism," a conflation of journalism and literature. On the heels of his successes, journalist Janet Cooke won and lost the Pulitzer Prize for "Jimmy's World," which she admitted to fictionalizing. The confusion has only increased in recent years. Americans have fallen in love with the "fake news" of Jon Stewart and Stephen Colbert, but Jayson Blair's fake news led to a resignation from the *New York Times*. Other supposed truth-tellers—from the journalists Jack Kelley and Patricia Smith to the memoirists James Frey and Matt McCarthy—also have come under fire. Meanwhile, Lasse Hallström, Christopher Guest, and other filmmakers have turned lies into entertainment, not only by documenting the famous fabrications of Glass and Clifford Irving in *Shattered Glass* and *The Hoax*, but also by dressing up their own lies as truth in mockumentaries such as *Best in Show* and *Borat*. In some circles, it would seem, facts are crucial; in others, they are negotiable. In still others, they can even be sexy. Witness the rise of reality television, blogs, Facebook, YouTube, and Wikipedia.[2]

Americans want the truth. They just can't agree on who should tell it—and how it should be told.

As new as it might seem to modern Americans, this quandary over truth-telling has its roots in the early nineteenth century, at the dawn of another information age. In the decades leading up to the Civil War, new developments in printing technology, including the development of steam-powered rotary presses, provided publishers with an enormous boost in productivity. Meanwhile the dramatic expansion of railroads facilitated the movement of products, including books and periodicals, across the expanding nation. Publishing trade associations and publications, periodical depots, and newsboys all promoted the sale of reading material. Aided by these forces, as well as developments in youth and adult education, America was becoming a nation of readers.[3] As is the case in our own day, these readers were faced with a variety of choices. Two were especially significant.

On September 3, 1833, a twenty-something printer named Benjamin Day launched a newspaper, the *New York Sun*, which sold on the streets for a penny a copy. The first successful penny paper, the *Sun* was a sensation in more ways than one. It sold phenomenally, reaching a circulation of 8,000 by the time it was six months old, and excited readers with sensational news of violence, elopement, and more. Following the *Sun*'s lead, James Gordon Bennett founded the *New York Herald* and pioneered both newsgathering and news reporting, leading his newspaper to far greater circulations—77,000 by 1860. With help from Bennett, journalism began to develop a new set of conventions in content and methodology. In this period, the newspaper gradually began to take its modern shape as a vehicle for reporting timely information on politics, crime, business, sports, and human-interest subjects for a mass audience.[4] Almost simultaneously, American literature was experiencing a revolution of its own. In 1837, Ralph Waldo Emerson delivered "The American Scholar"—or, as Oliver Wendell Holmes put it, "our intellectual Declaration of Independence."[5] Over the next two decades, Emerson and other American authors produced what would become some of the most important literature in the nation's history: *Narrative of the Life of Frederick Douglass* (1845), Nathaniel Hawthorne's *The Scarlet Letter* (1850), Herman Melville's *Moby-Dick* (1851), Harriet Beecher Stowe's *Uncle Tom's Cabin* (1852), Henry David Thoreau's *Walden* (1854), Walt Whitman's *Leaves of Grass* (1855), and scores of other novels, short stories, poems, and essays by James Fenimore Cooper, Sara Willis ("Fanny Fern"), Edgar Allan Poe, Rebecca Harding Davis, Emily Dickinson, and others. During this era, which literary scholar F. O. Matthiessen famously dubbed "The American Renaissance," American authors developed their own sense of purpose and identity.

As journalism and literature grew, they grew apart. The once peaceful, almost monolithic world of American letters, characterized by author-journalists such as Benjamin Franklin and Philip Freneau, was undergoing a revolution. What began as a world of "letters"—words combined, often artfully, to convey information about the world—emerged in the nineteenth century as two distinct disciplines, each with its own set of aims, conventions, and practices, as well as, most significantly, its own sense of truth.[6] For journalists, truth was largely a matter of information about the material world: "news" about markets, elections, crimes, and disasters. Reporters and editors served their readers by selecting and collecting this information, packaging it for easy consumption, and delivering it in a timely fashion. Although they were equally concerned with truth, America's authors conceived of it differently. Following the precepts and examples laid down by generations of poets and philosophers before them, Emerson, Thoreau, Poe, and their contemporaries looked for truths beneath or beyond the facts: spiritual principles, psychological motivations, and other material not adequately covered by their counterparts in journalism. They found these truths in real people and events, but also in ponds, the wind, and their own minds, and they reported them in their own ways and at their own pace. While they did not always agree on what these truths were, they agreed that literature—not journalism—was the appropriate medium for exploring and conveying them. In short, while journalists and authors continued to employ the same means—that is, language—they were using it in different ways and for different ends. The result was a sibling rivalry in America's literary marketplace.

As Bennett's *Herald* and thousands of other newspapers became many Americans' reading matter of choice and even, in Thoreau's words, their "Bible," the nation's authors—most of them considerably less successful—responded with countless critiques of journalism, which they characterized as an inferior and inadequate form of truth-telling. Furthermore, in several acts of one-upmanship that anticipate the work of Capote and Wolfe, some of these authors adapted and challenged journalistic conventions to create a variety of hybrid genres—some of them earnest, others sarcastic—in which they offered alternatives to the stories readers were finding in their newspapers.[7]

Perhaps because of its implications for understanding the current state of American writing, this story of the sometimes intimate, sometimes stormy relationship between literature and journalism in the United States in the nineteenth century is drawing increasing attention. In recent years, Karen Roggenkamp and Doug Underwood have produced studies of the various ways the two fields have interacted. These scholars and several who preceded them have shed light on some important ways that journalism has shaped American literature, particularly as a training ground and as a source to be adapted for literary purposes. Underwood, Shelley Fisher Fishkin, and Edgar Branch, for example, have explored the impact of journalistic experience on Whitman, Twain, and other writers, often portraying early work on newspapers as a kind of "apprenticeship" for a literary career. The experience of gathering news and packaging it for mass consumption, often on deadline, dramatically shaped such writers' worldviews and literary techniques, leading Underwood to make a compelling case for the role journalism has played in shaping the course of both American and British literature. A few scholars have looked beyond the apprenticeship model, illuminating other aspects of the relationship between journalism and literature. In *Beneath the American Renaissance*, for instance, David Reynolds exposes the ways that writers such as Hawthorne and Melville employed the subversive materials they encountered in penny papers and other sensationalistic publications. Michael Robertson's *Stephen Crane, Journalism, and the Making of Modern American Literature* examines the transitional role that Stephen Crane played in the reunion of journalism and literature around the turn of the century. In *Narrating the News*, Roggenkamp has looked at hybrid genres, such as the literary journalism of Nellie Bly and Richard Harding Davis.[8] While it draws on the work of these and numerous other scholars, this book explores another dimension of the relationship between the two disciplines. Many American authors wrote journalism, but even more wrote *about* journalism. Indeed, a survey of scores of novels, short stories, poems, and essays by these authors reveals the pervasive presence of journalism in the literature of the era and points to a different kind of influence. If journalism left its stamp on those who produced it, it also dramatically affected those authors who had little or no experience in the field. As critical readers or beleaguered subjects of newspapers, even Emerson, Thoreau, Dickinson, Stowe, Cooper, and Melville felt the influence of journalism, which was becoming the most powerful presence in America's literary market-place even while these writers were spearheading a renaissance of their own. In this sense, journalism became a counterpoint for authors' conceptions of truth-telling. In examining the sibling rivalry that emerged in American letters between 1833 and 1861, *Literature and Journalism in Antebellum America* shows American writers respond-ing to the *phenomenon* of journalism, developing their own sense of truth-telling in opposition to journalism's example, and crafting their own "news" about the world. In so doing, it exposes the role that journalism played in shaping some of the era's best-known works, including *Walden* and *Uncle Tom's Cabin*. Finally, because it examines alternative forms of truth-telling during a media revolution similar to the one we are currently witnessing, it provides a context for answer-ing the questions that confront modern readers and writers: Whom should we trust to tell us truths about our world and ourselves? How should they tell them? Where will this new revolution take us—or where should we take it?

*   *   *

Any study of the vast and various world of antebellum American letters is fraught with complexity. The world of journalism comprises not only a wide variety of publications, but also such diverse figures as the savvy businessman James Gordon Bennett and the idealistic missionary Horace Greeley. Likewise American literature ranged from Poe's romances to Davis's realism, from Bryant's conventional lyrics to Whitman's revolutionary free verse, from Stowe's impassioned activism to Dickinson's remote ruminations. To attempt a study of a scene so diverse and complex is to run the risk of oversimplification. As Jerome McGann has noted, when one attempts any kind of synthesis in a monograph or an essay, such as F. O. Matthiessen's *American Renaissance*, one inevitably has "falsified" something. Still, McGann is right to point out that synthesis is a literary scholar's legitimate work.[9] In this case, a close analysis of news articles, novels, short stories, poems, and essays by numerous leading journalists and authors turns up several basic principles underlying the relationship between journalism and literature in the early nineteenth century.

Part I examines the intimate relationship between journalism and literature in the antebellum era, as well as the critiques that grew out of this relationship. Chapter 1, for instance, explores the numerous commonalities at the core of each discipline's purpose and practices: the pursuit of stories and truths, the writer's role as a mediator between reality and the reader, the writer's dependence on "material," similarities in execution, and the need to find an audience. Drawing on observations by scholars and the writers themselves, this chapter shows that journalism and literature not only share both a means and an end, but also employ some similar rhetorical devices and tap into many of the same sources of interest, including conflict, novelty, and irony. Chapter 2 traces the various ways that the era's leading authors encountered journalism—that is, as readers, subjects, and writers. As this chapter shows, these writers' experiences provided them with insights and attitudes that helped to shape their war on journalism. Chapter 3 examines the critiques that grew out of these encounters. Although some writers occasionally faulted journalists for merely human failings—incompetency and bias, for instance—some also took aim at the purposes, audiences, criteria, and conventions of journalism, showing how such considerations interfered with the press's pursuit of truth.

Part II explores the various ways that authors sought to replace journalism with "news of their own." Chapter 4, for example, shows that both Thoreau and Dickinson set up their literature in opposition to conventional journalism. Borrowing language from the world of newspapers, both writers offered what might be termed "dispatches from the fringe" as alternatives to a press that they considered misguided or insufficient. Chapter 5 examines a particularly interesting hybrid genre, the hoax, which Poe presented as an alternative form of journalism, one that tells truth through fiction. Finally, Chapter 6 explores attempts by Poe, Stowe, and Davis to fill the gaps they perceived in journalism with something we might call "investigative fiction."

If this study tells us where we have been, it may also help guide us to where we ought to go. Like Day, Bennett, Poe, Thoreau, and their fellow journalists and authors, we stand on the threshold of a new age in information and communication. While the ultimate demise of traditional journalism is all but certain, what is less clear is the future that lies beyond this demise. Philip Bennett, former managing editor of the *Washington Post*, has noted that journalists "need to find a new way to tell stories."[10] New Journalism is no longer new, but the next wave has not yet arrived. Over the last decade, Americans have seen plenty of contenders offering their own versions of stories and truths: bloggers and Wikipedia contributors who operate without training or editors, veteran journalists who fictionalize their articles, comedians whose trade is "truthiness," mavens of the new social media, e-mail purveyors of urban legends, and both professional and amateur producers of memoirs, creative nonfiction, mockumentaries, and reality television. Who will be crowned as the next Capote? Who will be expelled as the next Glass? As we wait for answers, we will continue to marvel and cringe at the exploits of innovators and fabricators as we seek the best ways to tell stories and truths.

PART I

ENCOUNTERS AND CRITIQUES

CHAPTER 1

THE STORY AND THE TRUTH

For more than three centuries, America's journalists and authors have been after the same things: the story and the truth. Writers of both news and literature, in fact, have commonly used these terms for their products and purposes. Whether they go out and get it or sit down and write it, a story has long been something familiar to both reporters and authors. Furthermore, whether they have painstakingly assembled it from facts or woven it out of their imaginations, both frequently have insisted that they were delivering the truth. Former reporter David Simon refers to journalists as "truth-tellers"; however, to tell his own version of the truth, Simon created a fictional television series, *The Wire*.[1]

The commonalities in journalism and literature go well beyond terminology. In each realm, writers seek to capture some aspects of reality and convey them to an audience through the medium of language. Once they have collected it, whether it consists of facts or impressions, both reporters and authors must give to this raw material some kind of form, often turning to many of the same tropes and conventions, including metaphor, imagery, plot, and characterization. Along the way, they employ similar stances and methods, generally remaining detached observers while they go foraging for "material" in the world around them. In the end, they must produce something that will appeal to an audience, at least if they are going to make a living or any kind of impact. These commonalities in the areas of purpose, product, method, and audience, which are the subject of this chapter, are important because they helped lay the groundwork for the sibling rivalry that eventually developed in the world of American letters in the early nineteenth century.[2] Authors came to see themselves in competition with journalists, who were also seeking to capture truth in language, but were achieving a new prominence in American culture.

ORIGINS

Although both can be traced back hundreds of years, formal journalism is much younger than literature. After some early forms of governmental reporting in China and Rome, news sheets became common in Europe in the early seventeenth century. In 1665, England produced a publication that conformed to a definition of a "newspaper" used by modern journalism historians: the *Oxford Gazette*, which later became the *London Gazette*, appeared two times a week and reported relatively current information for a general audience. The Puritans who settled in New England in the early seventeenth century set up a printing press in 1638, but the first real newspaper did not appear in the colonies until 1704, when postmaster John Campbell began publishing the *Boston News-Letter*, a small publication that carried shipping news, reports of governmental affairs, and other information for a relatively small audience. A number of similar papers followed, so that by the time of the American Revolution, journalism was playing a major role in reporting and shaping colonial affairs. The journalism practiced by Campbell and those who followed him was, in some respects, a distinctive endeavor. As the name of Campbell's publication implies, it involved the collection and delivery of timely information, or "news." This information, furthermore, was largely factual material—proclamations, accounts of foreign conflicts and coronations, lists of ships arriving and departing—and was thought to be of general significance. James and Benjamin Franklin, Isaiah Thomas, and other editors who followed Campbell fit Edwin and Michael Emery's definition of a "journalist" as "one who acts as the transmission belt carrying ideas, information, and inspiration to the general public, which is dependent on such resources for rational opinion." These journalists, however, did not restrict themselves to the publication of news. A substantial portion of the contents of colonial newspapers, in fact, belonged to the realm of literature. Essays in the tradition of English publications such as the *Tatler* and the *Spectator* were especially common. Furthermore, some items in these papers combined fact and fiction. Indeed, as Elizabeth Christine Cook has shown, British literary works—particularly *Cato's Letters* and the *Spectator*—shaped much of the material that appeared in colonial newspapers. In short, although something modern historians can recognize as journalism was emerging, it had not developed a firm set of conventions and criteria. Instead, colonial journalism might be said to belong to the mixture of news and novels, facts and fiction common in British literature in the sixteenth, seventeenth, and eighteenth centuries. In *Factual Fictions: The Origins of the English Novel*, Lennard Davis has suggested that ballads and other forms carrying "newes" constituted a "news/novel discourse" and that journalism and novels would develop out of this "undifferentiated matrix." In the eighteenth century, however, the world of letters was still just that—a realm in which authors such as Daniel Defoe, James Boswell, and Benjamin Franklin combined facts and fiction in diverse formats, as Doug Underwood has noted.[3]

As we will see, a separation would begin to occur in the United States in the antebellum era, when journalists such as James Gordon Bennett and authors such as Ralph Waldo Emerson carved out distinctive identities. Still, a number of commonalities in purpose, position, and technique have remained in place, leaving practitioners of journalism and literature to battle over which discipline is better equipped to tell the truth.

THE SEARCH FOR TRUTH

Edward Jay Epstein has noted that modern journalists "almost invariably depict themselves not merely as reporters of the fragments of information that come their way, but as active pursuers of the truth." The Society of Professional Journalists gives voice to this goal in its Code of Ethics, where the top item is "Seek Truth and Report It." Fred Brown, a former president of the SPJ, has written, "Telling the truth is a journalist's overriding duty."[4] Throughout the antebellum era, journalists returned repeatedly to their mission of conveying the truth. The inimitable James Gordon Bennett, editor of the *New York Herald* during the heyday of the penny press in the 1830s, put it this way:

> Ignorance and prejudice are fast disappearing under the action of the cheap newspaper press. Formerly no man could read unless he had $10 to spare for a paper. Now with a cent in his left pocket, and a quid of tobacco in his cheek, he can purchase more intelligence, truth and wit, than is contained in such papers as the dull Courier & Enquirer, or the stupid Times for three months.

Samuel Bowles, editor of the *Springfield Republican*, wrote of the effort "to speak the exact truth," and a writer for the *Southern Quarterly Review* argued that editors should obey the "law" of "THE TRUTH."[5]

America's authors used similar language in discussing the aims of their own discipline. Noting that "all men live by truth, and stand in need of expression," Ralph Waldo Emerson argues in "The Poet" that articulating this truth is the poet's work. Returning to this subject in his essay on Goethe in *Representative Men*, Emerson says that the writer has a "burden on his mind,—the burden of truth to be declared, . . . and it constitutes his business and calling in the world, to see those facts through, and to make them known." Just such a writer is the protagonist of Herman Melville's *Pierre*. Like his creator, Pierre becomes an impassioned writer and declares, "Henceforth I will know nothing but Truth; glad Truth, or sad Truth." Rebecca Harding Davis, writing of the fictional pieces she was sending to James T. Fields in the early 1860s, noted that they were "*true*—in all essential points."[6]

The crucial question, of course, is what one means by "truth." *The Oxford English Dictionary* contains more than a dozen definitions, including "Conformity with fact; agreement with reality; accuracy, correctness, verity (of statement or thought)" and "That which is true, real, or actual (in a general or abstract sense); reality; *spec.* in religious use, spiritual reality as the subject of revelation or object of faith."[7] The first of these definitions is the easier to grasp and to measure; it concerns the world humans encounter with their senses, what might be called "objective reality" or "factual reality." The second definition of *truth* requires an appreciation of an invisible reality. Plato's and Aristotle's works refer to ideals, or "forms," that lie behind the physical world and constitute the real truth. In his famous "allegory of the cave" in *Republic*, Plato likens ordinary humans to people who have been chained in a cave, where they can see only shadows, not the objects they represent. Only the philosopher, like a former cave inhabitant who has been freed from the chains and observes the real objects as illumined by the sun, knows the real truth. On a less abstract level, this second conception of truth might also apply to general principles or theories, which explain the occurrences of specific factual phenomena, or even ideas of how things "should" or "could" be. In his *Poetics*, Aristotle explains that "it is not the function of the poet to relate what has happened, but what may happen—what is possible according to the law of probability or necessity."[8] A typical poem or novel contains details that exist only in the author's imagination; however, if these details help to illuminate basic principles of human motivation or to delineate the true nature of existence in a philosophical or religious sense, then they can be said to represent "abstract" truth, if not "factual" truth.

At different times and in different ways, American journalism and American literature have pursued both forms of truth; however, each discipline has come to be associated with one of these two kinds of truth-telling, particularly as the two fields diverged in the early nineteenth century.

The "abstract" truth—that is, a theoretical framework for understanding the world—has sometimes been part of the journalistic endeavor. A devotion to God and a passion for delivering "his truth" were behind William Lloyd Garrison's *Liberator*, as David Nord has noted. Andie Tucher has argued, furthermore, that rival papers covering the murder of Helen Jewett in New York in 1836 capitalized on the archetypes of the "Poor Unfortunate" and the "Siren" to provide readers with a framework for making sense of their world. Bennett himself, furthermore, told readers that he sought to provide the "philosophy of commerce."[9] For journalists, however, truth usually involves the reporting of facts—that is, incidents, numbers, and other "information," which can be observed, documented, and verified.[10] Philip Patterson and Lee Wilkins have traced the journalistic emphasis on facts back to the "'correspondence theory' of truth," which emerged during the Enlightenment. Today, factual accuracy is often characterized as the central principle in journalistic ethics. "There is always the hope that new information can spur changes, create reforms, and curb abuses of power," investigative journalists David Weir and Dan Noyes explain. "But first, investigating the powerful requires getting the facts straight."[11] Checkered though it may be, the emphasis on factual accuracy in American journalism stretches at least back to the 1830s, as Michael Schudson has noted. By the middle of the century, journalism historian Hazel Dicken-Garcia explains, newspapers were following an "information model." Newspapers sometimes referred explicitly to their roles as bearers of "facts" and indeed came to be regarded as accurate, reliable sources of factual reality. When Theodore Weld sought to show the reality of slavery, he presented facts he had collected from thousands of newspaper articles. Truth in factual detail has even been a legal defense for journalists accused of sedition or libel. In 1734, in a case still cited by journalism historians, attorney Andrew Hamilton defended John Peter Zenger, editor of the *New York Weekly Journal*, against a charge of sedition by arguing that what Zenger reported was true. In 1804, Alexander Hamilton employed a similar defense, arguing that the press had "the right to publish with impunity truth, with good motives, for justifiable ends, though reflecting on Government, Magistracy, or individuals."[12] The message emanating from both journalists and attorneys, then, is that the journalist's primary charge is to illuminate objective reality.

In some cases, authors' conceptions and definitions of truth parallel those of their journalistic counterparts. Such was the case during the era of realism, when James, Howells, and others eschewed fantasies, ideals, and stereotypes and strove to capture the "real thing," a phrase that appears not only in the title of one of James's best-known stories, but also in Rebecca Harding Davis's 1861 story "Life in the Iron-Mills," in which the narrator tells the reader, "I want you to hear this story. There is a secret down here, in this nightmare fog, that has lain dumb for centuries: I want to make it a real thing to you." As Sharon Harris has noted, Davis provided readers with "an illusion of actual experience." Many of America's authors, however, were after "abstract" truth in addition to or even instead of factual reality, particularly during the romantic era. Hawthorne's distinction between the novel and the romance is instructive here. In his preface to *The House of the Seven Gables*, he refers to "the truth of the human heart," which a writer of romances could approach without maintaining a "fidelity, not merely to the possible, but to the probable and ordinary course of man's experience." Melville makes a similar point in *The Confidence-Man*:

> And as, in real life, the proprieties will not allow people to act out themselves with that unreserve permitted to the stage; so, in books of fiction, they look not only for more entertainment, but, at bottom, even for more reality, than real life itself can show. Thus, though they want novelty, they want nature, too; but nature unfettered, exhilarated, in effect transformed. In this way of thinking, the people in a fiction, like the people in a play, must dress as nobody exactly dresses, talk as nobody exactly talks, act as nobody exactly acts. It is with fiction as with religion: it should present another world, and yet one to which we feel the tie.

For Emerson, in fact, objective reality was merely emblematic of a latent truth and required decoding, as John Irwin has explained: "The sense of the people and things that Emerson writes about is that their real meanings are hidden, that to confront them is necessarily to involve oneself in a process of interpretation whereby the surface is penetrated and inner necessity revealed." To do less, to be content with bare facts, was, in Emerson's eyes, to miss something essential. "In the street and in the newspapers," he argues in "Experience," "life appears so plain a business, that manly resolution and adherence to the multiplication-table through all weathers, will insure success. . . . Power keeps quite another road than the turnpikes of choice and will, namely, the subterranean and invisible tunnels and channels of life." Had they spoken with one voice to their journalistic counterparts, who largely limited themselves to objective facts, America's authors might have quoted a line from *Hamlet*: "There are more things in heaven and earth . . . / Than are dreamt of in your philosophy."[13]

All of this is not to say that authors as diverse as, say, Emerson and Poe always agreed on what those "things" were. If Emerson and Thoreau were intent on unearthing basic and original principles in nature, Dickinson and Poe pursued other sorts of truths—those that lay behind human actions, for example, and those that might lead to future innovations in science. Still other writers, notably Stowe and Davis, sought to expose hidden facts—that is, the same kinds of material covered in newspapers—but argued implicitly and sometimes explicitly in their fiction that journalists were missing some of these crucial facts. For these writers, reporting the truth meant telling "the rest of the story." In any case, as we will see in Part II, many of these authors frequently adapted journalistic conventions to report "news of their own." Their commitment to truth, then, has long linked journalists and authors, but their sometimes different conceptions of truth have made for tension. Specifically, the "information model" of the press, together with the constraints of certain news values such as "timeliness" and the need for brevity, helped to drive a wedge between journalists and their literary counterparts.

THE MEDIA

As the modern term *media* suggests, both journalists and authors occupy a middle ground between the truth and their readers. Since no one can be everywhere at once, readers depend on journalists to observe reality in various places and to report back to them. As National Public Radio anchor Robert Siegel put it in a 2009 promotion, reporters are the "eyes and ears" for the rest of us.[14] Authors, too, can expose us to personalities, experiences, and ideas that we have not yet encountered, but that may hold value for us.

For both journalists and authors, however, the role is more complex than simply collecting and relaying reality. As countless theorists of journalism, literature, and linguistics have recognized, various factors intervene to limit the writer's account of reality. On the most basic level, writers cannot collect all of the information about a given event, phenomenon, or subject. The briefest, simplest, most contained incident—a minor traffic jam, for instance—involves a host of causes, consequences, and psychological impressions, many of them unknown even to the people involved, much less to detached observers such as reporters and authors. Of course, these writers often address events that are much longer and more complex than traffic jams: elections, wars, economic depressions, race riots. Even if they were able to collect all of the scores or thousands of details surrounding such small or large events, writers would have to select which of these details to relay to their audiences. Ishmael, the narrator of *Moby-Dick*, recognizes the challenge, which he notes is especially great when it comes to "a large and liberal theme," such as the whale—or, for that matter, all that it represents in Melville's grand and symbolic novel. Ishmael says:

> Friends, hold my arms! For in the mere act of penning my thoughts of this Leviathan, they weary me, and make me faint with their outreaching comprehensiveness of sweep, as if to include the whole circle of the sciences, and all the generations of whales, and men, and mastodons, past, present, and to come, with all the revolving panoramas of empire on earth, and throughout the whole universe, not excluding its suburbs.

Even a Melville—or the most dedicated investigative reporter with the most supportive editor—cannot possibly "get it all in." The crunch is especially great for journalists, who, as Epstein notes, work under limitations of space, money, and time. "Under these conditions," he explains, "it would be unreasonable to expect even the most resourceful journalist to produce anything more than a truncated version of reality." Journalists often must settle for what Bob Woodward once called "the best obtainable version of the truth."[15] Working with small staffs or even by themselves, without tape recorders or press conferences, antebellum journalists, in fact, faced even greater obstacles than their modern counterparts, especially when they were attempting to encapsulate their cities, nation, and world in a few pages.

There are linguistic restraints, as well, as Poe lamented time and time again in his fiction. Reacting to Roderick Usher's striking paintings, one of his narrators confesses that he "would in vain endeavor to educe more than a small portion which should lie within the compass of merely written words." Similarly, after referring to his lover's "*expression*," the narrator of "Ligeia" laments, "Ah, word of no meaning! behind whose vast latitude of mere sound we intrench our ignorance of so much of the spiritual."[16] The difficulty—indeed, the impossibility—of capturing truth in language has been a theme in discussions of language and literature at least since the days of Plato.[17]

Language, after all, is not reality, but merely a means of representing reality—and an imperfect means at that. In his influential *Essay Concerning Human Understanding*, John Locke argues that words mean nothing on their own, but rather are merely arbitrary signs humans impose on the ideas within their own minds in order to convey these ideas to others. In this model, communication is subject to ambiguity and ultimately to confusion.[18] As Philip F. Gura has shown, the ongoing conversation about the ability of language to capture truth had reached a turning point in the early nineteenth century. Responding directly to Samuel Taylor Coleridge's book *Aids to Reflection*, theologians such as James Marsh and Horace Bushnell had come to appreciate the value of figurative language as a means of expressing divine truths. Bushnell, for instance, had argued that words were not exact representations of reality, but mere "hints or images" that could, in Gura's words, "help one *toward* the comprehension of some fact or thought."[19] Gura explains: "Language in theology, then . . . could be seen only as 'an instrument of suggestion' rather than as one of 'absolute conveyance of thought.'"[20] Furthermore, the Swedenborgian Sampson Reed, whose Harvard commencement address in 1821 had a powerful impact on Ralph Waldo Emerson, had said that humans could "make a language out of nature," and philologist Charles Kraitsir had stirred Henry David Thoreau's thinking about the ways that studying words' etymologies could unearth their original, spiritual meanings.[21] The result, as Gura shows in his careful analysis of this crucial historical moment, is that leading American authors came to espouse three central principles in the relationship between language and reality. First, nature, as the endpoint of divine creation, is itself a kind of language. Second, the work of the poet is to read this natural language and to translate it for the rest of humanity. Third, because truths reside in nature and in the words that represent those natural phenomena—water, leaves, mountains—poetic language naturally will consist of highly symbolic language. As Gura explains, Thoreau, Hawthorne, and Melville all took Emerson's philosophy of language a step further than Emerson had; instead of assuming that reading nature would help humans to approach a single truth, they remained open to multiple truths, thus their fascination with ambiguity.

In short, authors such as Hawthorne, influenced by both a long literary tradition and a current religious controversy over the capacity of language to capture spiritual truth, were not to be satisfied with the language of journalism, which generally reported facts in literal language. Instead, they believed in the value—indeed, the necessity—of indirect, symbolic, ambiguous, suggestive language: the language, that is, of literature.

TO CRAFT A STORY

Imperfect though it may be, the conversion of reality into language is the work of both journalists and authors, work that results in products that share many common elements, as well as a common term. Like *truth*, the word *story* is ambiguous. Over its long history—its first recorded appearance in English comes from 1225, and it goes back to the Latin word *historia*—*story* has generally referred to a narrative; however, like *itch* and *bill*, it is among a handful of English words that can carry opposite meanings—in this case, something that is definitely true or something that definitely is not. In the nineteenth century, it was used to refer to "A person's account of the events of his life or some portion of it" and "A narrative or descriptive article in a newspaper; the subject or material for this." As early as 1834, however, *story* could also mean "A lie," a meaning it retains in our own time, as in a sentence such as this one: "He said he was late because he got a flat tire, but I think he's telling me a story." In the nineteenth century, furthermore, the word also could be used to refer to a fictional tale. Behind this identical terminology exists a number of parallels in values, structure, and language. Modern observers, in fact, often emphasize the link between the stories found in journalism and those found in literature. "Telling the news usually means telling stories," the authors of one modern journalism textbook explain, noting that "journalists often use the techniques of other storytellers, such as novelists and screenwriters."[22] Such borrowing was common in the antebellum era. Whether they were writing a news account of the murder of Mary Rogers or a literary "Mystery of Marie Roget," a column about life in New York or a "Song of Myself," both journalists and authors have prized many of the same elements, such as conflict, novelty, and irony.

Journalism experts commonly refer to several basic criteria, or "news values," that reporters and editors use to determine whether an event is newsworthy: timeliness, proximity, impact, prominence, currency, conflict, and novelty. The last two, which were common features of news stories of the nineteenth century, are also common components of literature. Noting that conflict "has been a driving principle of U.S. news since colonial times," Norma Green notes that trials and sports provided Bennett with "drama" for his *New York Herald*. In supplying their readers with descriptions of conflicts, Bennett and his fellow journalists were capitalizing on a central component of literature—one, in fact, that the ancient Greeks employed thousands of years earlier and that Melville, Stowe, and other antebellum authors employed in their novels and tales. Bennett and Benjamin Day, furthermore, capitalized on readers' appetites for novelty: stories of a man whose mouth spoke after his head was removed, a man who took galvanic shocks to remove seven demons from his body, and a woman who accidentally returned to the wrong hotel room, where she had an experience that left her "almost bereft of her sense." Curiosities were also a specialty of the "illuminated jumbo" papers, which Isabelle Lehuu has likened to P. T. Barnum's shows. As Poe famously declared in "The Philosophy of Composition," novelty—or, as he put it, "originality"—is "a source of interest" for the author, as well.[23]

Many journalism experts also frequently refer to the criterion of "human interest," which might be considered as a synonym for "novelty" or as a general term for novelty, prominence, and currency. In any case, what counts as human interest often consists of elements common to drama and fiction. Irony, a central feature of literary works ranging from *Oedipus Rex* to O. Henry's "The Gift of the Magi," has often given news stories much of their appeal, as well. It can be found, for example, in an account of a preacher who impregnates a parishioner in an 1843 issue of the *Brooklyn Daily Eagle*. Equally appealing, though exactly opposite, is the stereotype. If humans like to be surprised by irony, they also like to recognize the familiar in a stereotype; there is, perhaps, some comfort in knowing—or, at least, thinking—that one will find just what one expects to find in people and situations. An examination of human-interest stories will turn up an ample supply of stereotypes. Indeed, as Jack Lule has argued, "archetypal myths," including some of the same ones that figure prominently in literature—the victim, the hero, the good mother—play a major role in American journalism. On a broader level, Schudson has argued that literary conventions shape news coverage in general, suggesting that news "is in ways both intentional and unintentional a fiction" and that "news is a contrivance for giving form to experience—as is a poem, a novel, a history book, or a fairy tale."[24] In the antebellum era, such myth-making characterized Bennett's journalistic storytelling. Tucher notes that Helen Jewett, a prostitute murdered in New York in 1836, became, for journalists such as Benjamin Day, the figure of the "Poor Unfortunate." For Bennett, Tucher says, she was "the latest incarnation of a painfully tragic and appallingly familiar figure, the frail, flawed female undone by sex"; Tucher compares her to Helen of Troy, Clarissa Harlowe, and a host of other literary figures.

Yet another element with "human interest" appeal is a conflation of irony and stereotype, what we might call the "conventional twist," a characteristic of both journalism and popular literature; thus, an 1845 item called "Ups and Downs" identifies numerous people who went from rags to riches or from riches to rags and ends with a question: "What are the fictions of romance writers, compared to some of the realities of human life?"[25]

In writing their stories, furthermore, journalists of the antebellum era often employed a narrative approach common to fiction. Eventually, the "inverted pyramid" style—in which details appear roughly in the order of importance—would take over in American news reporting; however, before the Civil War, journalists frequently narrated events chronologically, as in reporting congressional deliberations in an 1834 issue of the *New York Mercury* and a riot and an account of Daniel Webster's death in 1852 issues of the *New York Herald*. Journalists also routinely borrowed stylistic devices from literature, treating their human subjects as characters and employing imagery and figurative language to evoke scenes. William Huntzicker has noted that Bennett's coverage of the Jewett murder took the form of a "morality play" and "the tragedy of a young woman led astray and murdered." "The penny press personalized victims and criminals in cases that unfold like serialized fiction or drama and offered new acts every day," Lehuu explains. "Criminals were perceived as 'actors' in 'domestic tragedies,' and the scene of the crime resembled the stage of a theater." Writing of one item in the penny press, Dan Schiller says, "The boundaries between news and literature were indeed thin."[26]

If there were similarities in the ways that journalists and authors chose and crafted their stories, however, there were also key differences. For one thing, many of the criteria that shaped the contents of newspapers were challenged or ridiculed by serious authors, as we will see in Chapter 3. What good is timely news for a writer such as Poe, who reveled in worlds "Out of Space—out of Time"? Poe seems to mock the fascination with breaking news in "The Unparalleled Adventure of One Hans Pfaall," in which a bellows-maker complains that others are obsessed with keeping up with the news.[27] Prominence, furthermore, was of little or no concern to Davis, who sought to explore and expose the commonplace. Even the journalists' obedience to criteria more closely associated with literature, particularly those appealing to "human interest," drew fire from numerous authors, who argued through their writings that journalists' determination to produce a good story inhibited their ability to tell the truth. In striving to fit their material into the prefabricated formulas of conflict, irony, and stereotypes, as well as sensationalism, journalists ran the risk of neglecting or minimizing contrary details or simply failing to report on more important matters.

MATERIALS AND METHODS

If they are to tell any kind of stories or truths about the world, writers first must discover facts or impressions that will serve as the substance for their journalism or literature. Reporters, columnists, poets, novelists, and dramatists, along with every other writer who ever sought to fashion some aspect of reality into a story, depend on what they commonly refer to as "material." Although he was targeting television journalists in his 1981 song "Dirty Laundry," Don Henley expressed a dilemma common to all writers when he sang, "I make my living off the Evening News/Just give me something—something I can use."[28] This dependence on material, then, constitutes more common ground for journalists and authors. As numerous accounts from the nineteenth century testify, these writers were hungry for something they could "use," and they often employed specific, even extreme strategies to collect it.

For both kinds of writers, America was a rich vein that needed only to be mined to turn up valuable material for journalistic or literary "stories." Emerson said as much in "The Poet" when he called for someone to give voice to the poem that was America:

Our logrolling, our stumps and their politics, our fisheries, our Negroes, and Indians, our boasts, and our repudiations, the wrath of rogues, and the pusillanimity of honest men, the northern trade, the southern planting, the western clearing, Oregon, and Texas, are yet unsung. Yet America is a poem in our eyes; its ample geography dazzles the imagination, and it will not wait long for metres.

When Walt Whitman came out with *Leaves of Grass* in 1855, he echoed this sentiment in his preface, saying, "The United States themselves are essentially the greatest poem." Whitman's book, in fact, can be read as a response to Emerson's invitation. Here he "reports" on a suicide, a runaway slave, blacksmiths and other workers, a massacre, a battle at sea, and countless other people and events. As a journalist, Bennett recognized the value of American material, as well, writing: "If a Shakspeare could have taken a stroll in the morning or afternoon through the Police [Office], does any one imagine he could not have picked up half a dozen of dramas and some original character? The bee extracts from the lowliest flower—so shall we in the Police Office."[29]

Whitman gave memorable expression to the act of trolling for material when he wrote, in one of his best-known poems, "Once I pass'd through a populous city, imprinting my brain for future use with its shows, architecture, customs, and traditions. . . ." As Fishkin explains, Whitman actually employed an approach similar to the one described here when he was editing the *Aurora* in the 1840s. After going on walks through New York, he would write up what he encountered in a column for the paper. Fishkin argues that Whitman drew on the same kind of material, the facts of the world around him, for his poetry: "The world of contemporary realities out of which he made his newspapers was the same world out of which he would make his poems, not only in 1855 but throughout his career." According to an account he published in his *Marginalia*, Poe took a more unusual approach to cultivating his material, turning inward to his mind's own creations instead of outward to the city around him. Here he describes his ability to wake himself from the hypnagogic state between wakefulness and sleep and then to examine what he has encountered in this state. The surreal quality of "The Pit and the Pendulum," "The Masque of the Red Death," and other works suggests that Poe may have tapped this source for his literary output.[30]

The dependence on material and the strategies that writers employ to collect it form another point of connection between journalism and literature. Just as both news people and authors sought to capture and deliver some version of the truth to their audiences, they owed their truth-telling to material that they had to discover or create.

THE COMPETITION FOR AUDIENCE

In the end, whatever truths the writers of journalism or literature glean from their material and package for consumption are all but meaningless if they do not reach an audience. Newspapers, furthermore, must turn a profit to justify their existence as business enterprises, and profits depend on readers; the greater a paper's circulation, the more appealing it is to advertisers. Authors, too, derive an income from the sale of their work, either to periodicals or directly to readers. The pressure to please an audience was especially great in a young republic, where, as Stephen Railton has noted, "Americans generally subscribed to the democratic belief that the majority was not just the most equitable body for determining political questions, but the final arbiter of all moral, cultural, and even aesthetic ones. . . . To the extent that he [the American writer] called himself a democrat, he had to be prepared to accept the public's judgment of his work."[31]

Table 1.1   A timeline of antebellum literature and journalism

	Journalism	Literature
1833	United States has about 1,200 newspapers.[a] Day launches *New York Sun*.	
1834		
1835	Bennett launches *New York Herald*. *New York Sun* publishes moon hoax. New steam presses facilitate large press runs.[b]	Poe publishes "Hans Phaall—A Tale."
1836	Jewett murder story becomes sensation. *Herald* claims circulation of 20,000. Bennett raises price of *Herald* to 2 cents.[c]	
1837		Emerson delivers "The American Scholar."
1838	Whitman launches *Long Islander*.	Cooper sues editors for libel.
1839		
1840	The United States has 1,631 newspapers, including 138 dailies.[d] The press is called the "fourth estate" in print.[e] Rival editors stage "Moral War" against Bennett.	Poe publishes *Tales of the Grotesque and Arabesque*.
1841	Greeley launches *New York Tribune*. New Yorkers follow Rogers murder story.	Emerson publishes *Essays*.
1842		"The Mystery of Marie Roget" begins to appear in *Ladies' Companion*.
1843		
1844	Morse telegraphs message from Washington, D.C., to Baltimore	Poe's balloon hoax appears in *New York Sun*.
1845		Douglass publishes *Narrative of the Life of Frederick Douglass*. Thoreau moves to house on Walden Pond.

(Continued)

Table 1.1 Continued

	Journalism	Literature
1846	Whitman begins writing for *Brooklyn Daily Eagle*. *Philadelphia Public Ledger* begins using Hoe's "lightning press," which will revolutionize newspaper printing.[f]	Journalists challenge authenticity of Melville's *Typee*.
1847	Douglass launches *North Star*.	
1848		
1849		
1850	U.S. has 2,526 newspapers, including 254 dailies; total U.S. newspaper circulation is nearly 500 million copies.[g]	Hawthorne publishes *The Scarlet Letter*.
1851	Raymond launches *New York Times*.	Melville publishes *Moby-Dick*.
1852		Stowe publishes *Uncle Tom's Cabin* in book form.
1853		
1854	Greeley's *Tribune* employs 14 reporters, as well as 10 editors.[h]	Thoreau delivers "Slavery in Massachusetts" and publishes *Walden*.
1855		Whitman publishes *Leaves of Grass*, and Willis publishes *Ruth Hall*.
1856		
1857		
1858		Dickinson begins corresponding with Samuel Bowles, editor of *The Springfield Republican*
1859	Douglass launches *Douglass' Monthly*.	
1860	U.S. has about 3,000 newspapers.[i] *Herald's* circulation is near 77,000.[j]	
1861		Davis publishes "Life in the Iron-Mills."

a. Huntzicker, *The Popular Press, 1833–1865*, 170.
b. Huntzicker, *The Popular Press, 1833–1865*, 166.
c. Emery and Emery, *The Press and America*, 144.
d. Nord, *Communities of Journalism*, 94.
e. Dicken-Garcia, *Journalistic Standards in Nineteenth-Century America*, 47.
f. Emery and Emery, *The Press and America*, 167–68.
g. Nord, *Communities of Journalism*, 94.
h. Emery and Emery, *The Press and America*, 263.
i. Huntzicker, *The Popular Press, 1833–1865*, 170.
j. Emery and Emery, *The Press and America*, 144.

In the early nineteenth century, America's reading public was substantial. Indeed, as Ronald Zboray has shown, the United States was becoming a nation of readers. Public education, together with Sunday schools and home education, helped children develop basic literacy, and other institutions, such as libraries and mechanics' clubs, helped adults to augment their basic skills. Meanwhile, the cost of newsprint fell, and new presses, such as the Hoe "lightning press," dramatically increased production, from 200 to 20,000 pages an hour. The spread of railroads, furthermore, facilitated the sale of books through the commission system while providing a new venue for both selling and reading books and periodicals.[32] The United States, in short, contained a vast audience for reading material and a greater capacity for producing and delivering this material, but the question remained: what would Americans read?

The answer is that they read a variety of materials ranging from cheap sensational pamphlets about sordid crime to high-brow poetry and fiction. More than anything, however, they read newspapers. The reason may have been at least partly economic: beginning in the 1830s, a newspaper could be purchased for a penny, whereas a typical paperback or hardback book cost 12 to 125 times that amount. As Zboray has noted, improvements in printing technology did not put books in the hands of a vast number of working-class Americans. Books were especially hard to acquire for rural Americans, who could not find a wide selection at bookstores—if, indeed, they had bookstores.[33] As bearers of factual information about politics and business, furthermore, newspapers may have held an edge over fiction in the eyes of many antebellum Americans. "All the institutions promoting literacy operated under a system of values maintaining that knowledge must be useful first and entertaining second or not at all," Zboray explains. "This utilitarian attitude toward knowledge preached not only by the lyceum but by other antebellum literary institutions as well probably little encouraged the public taste for American-authored fiction."[34]

Whatever the underlying reasons, journalism, as we will see in the next chapter, became one of the most conspicuous, pervasive, and powerful institutions in America in the nineteenth century. Meanwhile, Henry David Thoreau was left with most of the original copies of his first book still on his hands, Herman Melville fumed over the lukewarm response to *Moby-Dick*, and most of Emily Dickinson's letters to the world turned out to be letters to herself. In 1857, Russian traveler and author Aleksandr Lakier noted, "'Literature little profits from the 3,754 newspapers published in the United States (613 in

New York alone)."[35] Margaret Fuller, herself a central literary figure, as well as a columnist for Horace Greeley's *New York Tribune*, made a similar observation: "The Newspaper promises to become daily of more importance, and if the increase of size be managed with equal discretion, to draw within itself the [audience] of all other literature of the day." Lehuu, in fact, has argued that the jumbo papers and other carnivalesque aspects of the popular press presented a kind of "parody of the official book culture." Accentuating the competition was the juxtaposition of journalism and literature in the marketplace. Both in periodical depots and on trains, readers could choose between newspapers and books. Such competition further helps to explain why virtually all of the century's significant authors, even writers as different as Cooper and Thoreau, waged war on journalism, as we will see in future chapters.[36]

One might wonder whether these authors really needed to worry about competition from the popular press. After all, were they really aiming at the same Americans who were reading sensationalistic coverage of sex and violence in the *Sun* and the *Herald*? Determining who was reading what is a tricky endeavor, but the short answer is that, at least in some cases, they were. Lehuu may be correct in arguing that the explosion of periodicals in antebellum America led to "the creation of new 'textual classes,' the building of new associations around common uses of print." Still, newspapers appealed to readers of various classes. Bennett pioneered coverage of Wall Street in the *Herald* and boasted of his paper's popularity among the "business, educated, and intelligent classes." Furthermore, however "literary" their works were, American authors did not write only for high-brow readers. In a famous passage from *Walden*, Thoreau addresses readers who are struggling to make a living. Hawthorne, David Reynolds has argued, incorporated juicy bits into stories such as "Wakefield" to appeal to readers accustomed to newspaper copy. As we will see in the next chapter, Melville actively sought to control newspaper coverage of his first novel because he was concerned that doubts about the novel's veracity would undermine the book's reception. Terence Whalen has argued that even the elitist Poe sought acceptance by a mass audience, the same kind of readers who read newspapers. For these authors, newspapers were rivals for readers' attention and respect.[37]

*   *   *

Despite a fair amount of common ground in purpose, product, and method, then, America's truth-tellers and storytellers were developing separate conventions, practices, and identities in the nineteenth century. Authors' experiences as critical readers, beleaguered subjects, and crossover writers of journalism, the subjects of the next chapter, deepened their knowledge of this competing genre and, in many cases, deepened their hostility toward it. Together, these commonalities, differences, and encounters laid the groundwork for a sibling rivalry that erupted in two ways. In scores of short stories, novels, and essays, virtually every major American author—from Poe and Thoreau to Dickinson and Davis—took journalists to task not only for personal transgressions, such as inaccuracies, but also for their conventions and practices. Although some of these writers acknowledged the promise of the press, the vast majority condemned it as a failed medium. At the same time, many of these same writers substituted various kinds of "news of their own," often playing their dispatches from nature, truthful hoaxes, and investigative fiction against journalistic foils to show up the flaws of journalism and demonstrate the superiority of literature. Siblings they were; rivals they became.

Chapter 2

Encounters with the News

If we were to borrow a metaphor from Henry James and imagine American literature as a "house of fiction," we might see a newspaper on the front step. Journalism was in the air in the nineteenth century, and authors put newspapers everywhere else. Readers of antebellum fiction and poetry would have found newspapers in a variety of places—in the lap of Poe's narrator in "The Man of the Crowd," in a volume in Hawthorne's sketch "Old News," in the living rooms of Senator Bird and Augustine St. Clair in Stowe's *Uncle Tom's Cabin*, in the welcoming hands of a "Snow-Bound" family in Whittier's famous poem. Journalists are here, as well, appearing in works ranging from Cooper's *Home As Found* to Davis's "Life in the Iron-Mills."

Journalism's presence in the era's literature reflects its presence in American culture. After the appearance of the *Boston News-Letter* in 1704, countless printers added weekly news sheets to their business, and readers responded. By 1850, the United States was home to thousands of newspapers, published in both large cities and frontier towns. The total yearly circulation of these papers was close to 500 million copies.[1] Even a virtual hermit, such as Emily Dickinson, would have had difficulty ignoring such a pervasive institution. In fact, as the prevalence of newspapers and newspaper people in the era's fiction and poetry suggests, the phenomenon of journalism left an impression on the era's authors, who came into contact with it in a number of ways. Many of these authors would have encountered newspapers in the same places their fellow Americans saw them; indeed, they surely would have noticed that their own books sometimes competed with newspapers at periodical depots and on trains. Some authors, such as Hawthorne and Dickinson, were regular newspaper readers, and both Cooper and Melville became the subjects of news coverage. Finally, in the most intense relationship with the mass media, Douglass, Bryant, Poe, and other authors of the era were producers of journalism at one point or another in their careers, working as editors, reporters, or columnists. In short, all three corners of the rhetorical triangle—audience, subject, and producer—were occupied by authors in the nineteenth century. Such contact brought ample opportunity for the era's authors to know journalism as both outsiders and insiders. Their experiences as critical readers, beleaguered subjects, and crossover writers helped to shape their rejection of the press as an inferior medium.

THE PROMINENCE OF JOURNALISM

"Remote from civilization and poor as he may be," Hungarian Sandor Farkas wrote after his travels in America, "every settler reads a newspaper."[2] In the early nineteenth century, many of these papers looked much the same: the first and fourth pages consisted primarily or entirely of small line ads for everything from cigars and hats to schools and plays to a lost cockatoo. In between, on the second and third pages, were transcripts of speeches, copies of legislative acts, brief accounts of fires and shipwrecks, notes on the arrivals and departures of ships, reports of wars and other events in Europe (always months old because of the time ships required to cross the Atlantic), letters to the editor, and items reprinted from other newspapers, as well as poems, anecdotes, historical narratives, advice, and home remedies. Indeed, the contents of the newspapers from the first third of the nineteenth century could be summed up by a heading that sometimes appeared in these papers: "Miscellany." Except for the occasional tiny picture of a ship or small heading, there were virtually no images or headlines—just column after column of text printed in small fonts. Later, thanks largely to Bennett's innovations in newsgathering and Samuel Morse's invention of the telegraph, Americans could read news that was only days instead of months old and were finding much more local news, more "human-interest" material, and generally more detailed coverage of their world. Images and headlines became more common, as well.[3]

Readers loved it. Some subscribed to their local newspapers, paying from $4 to $10 for annual subscriptions to papers such as New York's *Columbian* and the *Independent Chronicle and Boston Patriot*. Other Americans read papers—or listened to others read them—in taverns, reading rooms, and workplaces.[4] The centrality of the American press only escalated in the 1830s, when New York printer Benjamin Day introduced the country's first successful penny paper, the *Sun.* "The consequences of the scheme," Poe observed, "in their influence on the whole newspaper business of the country, and through this business on the interests of the country at large, are probably beyond all calculation."[5] In 1835, two years after Day launched his paper, Scottish immigrant James Gordon Bennett came out with the first issue of the *New York Herald,* which would become the country's most popular newspaper. Unlike party and mercantile papers such as New York's *Courier and Enquirer* and *Journal of Commerce,* which cost six cents an issue, the penny papers were affordable to the working classes. Over the next three decades, the "mass" in "mass media" would grow dramatically. By 1840, the *Herald* was reaching some 50,000 readers, more than ten times the number reached by the top-circulating newspaper of the early 1830s. At the dawn of the Civil War, the *Herald* claimed a circulation of 77,000.[6] Thousands of other urban and rural newspapers, including Horace Greeley's influential *New York Tribune* and Henry J. Raymond's *New York Times,* followed. There were specialty papers, as well, including abolitionist publications such as William Lloyd Garrison's *Liberator* and Frederick Douglass's *North Star,* religious papers such as the *New York Evangelical,* and papers aimed at Native Americans, businesspeople, and farmers. By the middle of the century, Americans could choose from some 3,000 papers.

The reach of this diverse press was tremendous, as mass and specialty papers extended the influence of journalism to all classes and segments of the population. Although the low cost of the newspapers of the 1830s undoubtedly drew thousands of working-class readers to journalism, Bennett went after other audiences, as well. Bennett boasted, "No newspaper establishment, in this or any other country, has ever attained so extensive a circulation, or is read by so many of the business, educated, and intelligent classes." Dan Schiller argues that the primary audience for the penny papers consisted of skilled workers, such as mechanics. Furthermore, once the newspaper entered the home, one contemporary writer observed, it circulated through the family, from the father to the mother to the children: "Thus the important visitant passes from hand to hand, till every member of the family has gratified his . . . curiosity, down to the little children, who ask permission to look at the ships, the houses, or the pictures of the wild beasts that are for exhibition in the menagerie."[7]

Even in our own information age, modern Americans may not appreciate the pervasive presence of newspapers and magazines in the nineteenth century, when such printed matter did not have to

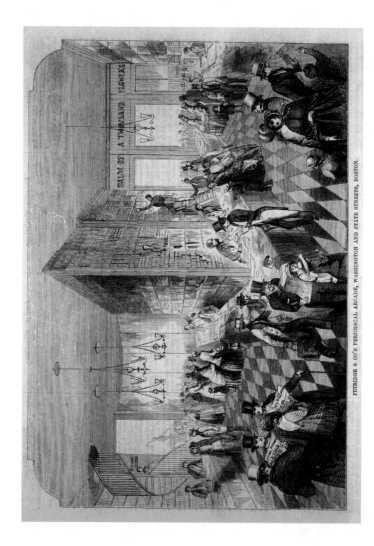

FETRIDGE & CO'S PERIODICAL ARCADE, WASHINGTON AND STATE STREETS, BOSTON.

Note: *War News from Mexico*, Richard Caton Woodville, 1848, oil on canvas, 27 x 25 in. (68.6 x 63.5 cm). Courtesy Crystal Bridges Museum of American Art, Bentonville, Arkansas.

share the stage with radio, television, or the Internet. Beginning in the 1830s, Bennett and others began emphasizing individual sales over subscriptions, and urban Americans could hear newsboys calling out the latest stories on the streets. They could purchase newspapers from these newsboys, hear them read by other workers while they were at work, browse the latest issues at periodical depots such as W. P. Fetridge's Periodical Arcade in Boston, or buy them on trains, where they were favorite companions for the noisy, boring journeys.[8] As Thomas Leonard has noted, Americans even used newspapers to stay in touch with one another, mailing them to acquaintances in place of personal letters or greeting cards. Alexander Mackay commented on the ubiquity of the newspaper in the account of his travels in the United States:

> In connection with American newspapers, the first thing that strikes the stranger is their extraordinary number. They meet him at every turn in all sizes, shapes, characters, prices, and appellations. On board the steamer and on the rail, in the countinghouse and hotel, in the street and the private dwelling, in the crowded thoroughfare and in the remotest rural district, he is ever sure of finding a newspaper.

Periodicals dominated the U.S. mail in the 1830s, constituting all but about 5 percent of its weight. In the 1850s, Samuel Bowles, editor of the *Springfield Republican*, argued that the telegraph and other technological developments had "made neighborhood among widely dissevered States." Bowles added, "The mind accustomed to the gossip of nations, cannot content itself with the gossip of families." Leonard notes, "A hunger for print journalism has often seemed to set Americans apart from the lands they came from. This New World was frequently defined by its obsession with a page of news." The word "obsession" may not be too strong if one woman's attitude toward the newspaper is representative: "My wife grows nervous when I give her waste paper lest she is burning holy writ, & wishes to read it before she puts it under her pies." Perhaps Emerson, who made this note in his journal, wondered whether his wife would treat his own writings as equally sacred.[9]

This obsession may owe something to the changes that were taking place in the country. As more and more Americans found themselves residents of cities instead of small communities, newspapers took over for other instruments and helped build a sense of community, as Nord and Lehuu have both argued. Reading the newspaper, Lehuu explains, gave Americans the opportunity to engage in a kind of "mass ceremony," and the "human interest" and crime stories they found there served as surrogates for both gossip and the spectacles Americans once encountered in public executions and the like. Furthermore, Schiller has argued that the commercial press "cultivated a new social role through its declaration of protection of the public good."[10] More than a commercial enterprise or a popular source of entertainment, the press was becoming an instrument and an institution, a force that played a role in the daily lives of Americans.

CRITICAL READERS

The prominence of American newspapers was not lost on America's literary class. "Happy are the editors of newspapers!" says the narrator of Hawthorne's sketch "Old News." "Their productions excel all others in immediate popularity, and are certain to acquire another sort of value with the lapse of time." Indeed, in an age when periodicals were as prominent as television or the Internet is today, it was almost easier to read them than to ignore them. "Today I read in Mr. Birney's [*Philanthropist*]," Stowe noted in a letter to her husband. "Abolitionism being the fashion here, it is natural to look at its papers."[11] As carriers of the zeitgeist, as well as a major component of it, newspapers were an integral part of Americans' worlds, whether these Americans liked it or not. Authors came to know journalism in other ways, as well. Dickinson, for instance, not only read the *Springfield Republican*, but also maintained a close friendship with its editor, Samuel Bowles. A survey of these encounters reveals the exposure that informed authors' critiques of journalism, as well as their attitudes toward its value for them. As it turns out, many of these authors treated newspapers as sources of material that they then could transform into their own poems and tales. For these writers, journalism was not always a bearer of truth in its own right, but merely a starting point for the exploration of truth in imaginative literature—a storehouse of facts akin to the farm that Thoreau describes in *Walden*. A farmer draws from the land physical objects that can be sold for profit, but Thoreau explains that the poet seizes "the most valuable part of a farm": "Why, the owner does not know it for many years when a poet has put his farm in rhyme, the most admirable kind of invisible fence, has fairly impounded it, milked it, skimmed it, and got all the cream, and left the farmer only the skimmed milk" (82–83). Like the poet who observes a farm, authors such as Melville and Poe often "skimmed" literary material from the newspapers they read.

Among the era's major authors, the most diligent—even obsessive—reader of newspapers was Hawthorne. A regular reader of the *Salem*

Gazette and a friend of the editor, Caleb Foote, he was also, in Reynolds's words, "a lifelong addict of popular newspapers." A letter from 1840 shows that he regularly read the *Boston Post* during his stint at the Custom House. Later, while living in Liverpool in the 1850s, he even arranged for someone to mail him packets of American newspapers. Julian Hawthorne explained that his father found "pleasure and relaxation" in imaginative works such as poems, "but if study were his object, he would resort to the newspapers and magazines." More than a source of recreation or even a place to find information vital to a democracy, journalism was for this literary giant a kind of encyclopedia of the human experience and thus an endless source of material. A clue to the use to which Hawthorne put contemporary journalism can be found in the opening to his story "Wakefield," in which the narrator recalls "a story, told as truth, of a man . . . who absented himself for a long time, from his wife." In a revealing piece of phrasing, Hawthorne does not call the original news account a "factual account" or even a "news item," but rather deems it a "story, told as truth," as if the account were merely masquerading as the truth. In fact, the article serves the author as a detail to set his own imagination into action. It could serve a similar purpose for the reader, as the narrator notes. "If the reader choose, let him do his own meditation;" he says, "or if he prefer to ramble with me through the twenty years of Wakefield's vagary, I bid him welcome." In either case, the value of the story is to be found in the reflection and interpretation, not in the bare details—or, as the narrator puts it, "Thought has always its efficacy, and every striking incident its moral." He underlines this principle when he poses the question "What sort of a man was Wakefield?" and answers, "We are free to shape out our own idea, and call it by his name." When Wakefield reenters his home at the story's end, the narrator refuses to follow him, noting that he has provided "food for thought."[12]

This explicit treatment of a news story as the seed for imaginative literature dramatizes a process that Hawthorne and other authors frequently employed in producing their fiction. Melville read Bennett's *New York Herald*, and Poe's letters show that he was familiar with a number of publications, including the *New York Evening Star*, the *New York Evening Post*, the *New York Express*, and the *New York Courier and Enquirer*. Whitman, as we will see, himself worked for a number of newspapers, including the *Aurora* and the *Brooklyn Daily Eagle*. As Reynolds has shown, penny newspapers and other sensationalistic organs, such as crime pamphlets, found an audience among these authors, who transformed the characters, themes, and images they found there into fiction and poetry of universal value. An understanding of these sensational sources can help to illuminate much of the strange material we find in these and other writers' works. Whitman told Emerson that *Leaves of Grass* had grown out of his reading of, among other things, "popular newspapers of every variety." Reynolds emphasizes, however, that authors transformed the material they found in journalism and elsewhere, likening, for example, Poe to "the landscape gardener of 'The Domain of Arnheim,' who uses the artistic imagination to convert an untamed wilderness into a garden possessing both wildness and cultivation, both novelty and order."[13]

Other authors mined newspapers for literary material, even if they did not always initiate the specific transformative process Reynolds describes. Emily Dickinson, whose timeless and ethereal poetry might seem to have come from a poet detached from everyday events, actually was exposed to a number of publications, including *The Hampshire and Franklin Express, The Amherst Record, The Atlantic Monthly, Harper's New Monthly Magazine,* and *Scribner's Monthly.* She also read *The Springfield Republican* "every night," according to one of her letters. In this same letter, she recounts reading the paper out loud as her sister sewed. Biographer George Whicher has suggested that the *Republican* was second only to the Bible in terms of its influence on her early in life. This daily paper, Whicher argues, exposed Dickinson to native humor and struck a chord with the young writer, who set out to compose her own attempts at comic writing. Years later, it was the *Republican* that published seven of the ten Dickinson poems that made it into print during her lifetime. In his study of her reading, Jack L. Capps has argued that Dickinson's encounters with periodicals also deepened her understanding of the world and allowed her to learn about aspects of it without experiencing them firsthand. Most tellingly, she seems to have drawn heavily on these encounters in crafting her poetry, even storing newspaper clippings for future use and attaching them to copies of her poems.[14] Joan Kirkby has suggested that Dickinson entered into conversations with poems she encountered in newspapers, perhaps responding to poems such as "The Unwilling Bride" and "Love, Honor and Obey" with her own poems about marriage, and Capps identifies some poems, such as "I Like to See it Lap the Miles," that appear to contain material adapted from the periodical press.[15]

Dickinson experienced journalism on another level, as well, since she was close to two journalists, Josiah Holland and Samuel Bowles. Holland wrote for the *Springfield Republican* and later launched

Scribner's Monthly. Dickinson maintained a friendship with him and his wife, Elizabeth, and regularly read his published work. As editor of the *Republican*, Bowles was one of the leading newspapermen in the country. For Dickinson, biographer Richard Sewall argues, Bowles was at least two other things: a possible means to publication and the love of her life. He may even have been the inspiration for the mysterious "Master" letters. Sewall writes that she "was deeply in love with him for several years and never ceased loving him, at a distance, for the rest of her life." In both capacities—those of potential publisher and possible lover—he disappointed her. Of the some 50 poems she sent to him or his wife, his newspaper published but a few; his love, furthermore, was not hers to have. By visiting the homes of Dickinson's parents and brother and sister-in-law, however, Bowles did serve as a bearer of the zeitgeist for the poet and her family; as such, he was a kind of newspaper himself. Dickinson's relationship with Holland and Bowles surely provided an additional intimacy with journalism, one that exerted a powerful influence on her poetry, as we will see in Chapter 4.[16]

Although he actively avoided journalism, Thoreau occasionally read newspapers, even becoming obsessed with the story of John Brown's raid at Harpers Ferry. Leonard has argued that Thoreau's reading of this coverage served as a kind of catalyst for his own thinking on slavery. He quotes a passage from a journal entry in which Thoreau describes the "smothering" of "four millions under the hatches" and ironically alludes to a newspaper editorial that merely calls for "the quiet diffusion of the sentiments of humanity." Leonard writes, "The journal shows us that the function of press opinion was often to inspire such provocative passages, that he saved items and copied the public prints to answer journalism with a higher language." Like his friend Emerson, furthermore, Thoreau was an acquaintance of Greeley and exchanged letters with him in 1848.[17] As we will see, Thoreau drew on his reading of newspapers to issue a scathing critique of them in "Slavery in Massachusetts."

Although he shared Thoreau's disdain for journalism, Emerson seems to have been less averse to reading newspapers. His journals contain references to the *Boston Daily Advertiser*, the *Boston Transcript*, the *Boston Times*, the *Boston Daily Chronotype*, and the *New York Tribune*, and he stored clippings from newspapers such as the *Tribune* and the *Boston Atlas* in a notebook called *Dialling*. Emerson also knew Horace Greeley, talking with him frequently in the 1840s and even sharing living space with him in 1856 when the two of them were on the lecture circuit. He also apparently knew journalists Charles A. Dana and Thomas McElrath, whose names appear in his journals.[18] Such encounters must have shaped the critiques Emerson aimed at journalism.

Similarly, both Stowe and Davis drew on their encounters with journalism when writing their investigative fiction, as we will see in Chapter 6. While living in Cincinnati, Stowe frequently read the *Western Monthly Magazine* and probably also read at least one newspaper, the *Cincinnati Journal and Western Luminary*. After moving to Maine in 1850, she subscribed to the *New York Independent*, which her brother Henry Ward Beecher edited. As a girl growing up in rural Virginia, Davis saw little journalism. In her memoir *Bits of Gossip*, she recalls receiving news by means of "a man on a galloping horse." Although she explains that no one in her town "was in a hurry to hear the news," the presence of this recollection in the opening paragraphs of her book points to the author's own interest in news reporting.[19] Later, as we will see, Davis went to work for her town paper and eventually pioneered a form of realism akin to investigative journalism.

These authors' encounters with journalism provided a foundation for their widespread, impassioned reactions to the press. Furthermore, the accounts of their experiences as readers show that Hawthorne, Emerson, and their fellow authors were not passive receptors of the material that appeared in America's newspapers and magazines, but active respondents. Newspapers may have provided material, but authors provided the imagination that transformed this raw material into literature. Especially as both journalists and authors developed their own separate identities, authors took care to establish their own pursuit of truth as an endeavor apart from—and superior to—the efforts of their journalistic counterparts. As we will see in future chapters, the results included both penetrating critiques and a variety of alternatives to traditional journalism, such as truthful hoaxes and investigative fiction.

BELEAGUERED SUBJECTS

Two authors of the era, Cooper and Melville, experienced another kind of encounter with journalism, one that shaped their attitudes toward the press. By 1830, Cooper was, along with Washington Irving, one of the country's two most prominent authors. In what would become a pattern in American journalism, this fame brought with it more scrutiny of the subject's personal affairs. As Stephen Railton has noted, Cooper's problems were compounded by his politics, which made him a target of Whig journalists. Cooper came to believe that the public had turned on him and, as Railton explains, "succumbed to a mild form of paranoia, feeling that there was a secret journalistic conspiracy that schemed to embarrass and annoy him." "Unfortunately," Railton writes, "Cooper's name must be included on the list of American authors—Brown, Poe, Melville, Twain, James—whose imaginations were permanently affected by what they perceived as America's rejection of them." Cooper got into deeper trouble with the press and its audience after he used a Cooperstown newspaper to warn his neighbors not to trespass on land that had belonged to his father. As might be expected, some citizens took offense, a story that journalists in three Whig publications were more than happy to report. In a series of actions practically scripted to draw even more antagonism from press and public alike, Cooper filed libel suits against the papers and blasted the masses and news organs in writings such as *The American Democrat*. Indeed, he confessed that "it was precisely on account of this affair that Homeward Bound and Home As Found were written." Fiction, he explained, was a vehicle by which he could "defend" himself. "It was not easy, however, to make a book out of this one transaction, but it could be introduced as an incident of an ordinary tale, so as to answer all my purposes." Thus, this encounter with journalism helped shape not only one author's attitude toward the press—particularly the power that it derives through publicity—but the kind of critiques that he incorporated into his own writing. The oppressive, judgmental press may have reminded Cooper, on an unconscious level, of his domineering father, Judge William Cooper, as Railton has argued.[20] On another level, one explicitly addressed in *The American Democrat* and *Home As Found*, Cooper joined the press and the public as two tyrannical forces, as we will see in the next chapter.

Melville's troubles with the press are legendary. Occasionally strident, the reviews of his fiction had a profound impact on the author, as Hershel Parker and Brian Higgins have noted. They write that the "disastrous reception" that greeted *Pierre*—a reception that included some of the nastiest reviews in the history of American literature—"dealt Melville's reputation a blow from which it never recovered, temporarily then all but permanently halting his career as a book-publishing author." Even before Melville turned to ponderous and peculiar novels such as *Pierre* and *Moby-Dick*, however, he had run-ins with journalists, particularly those writing for Christian publications. Indeed, Parker and Harrison Hayford have argued, "More than any other single factor, Melville's defiance of the religious press cost him his career as a writer."[21] Much of the animosity he encountered came in the form of negative reviews, a hazard of the profession. The attacks on Melville, however, deserve special attention in this study of the sibling rivalry between journalism and literature. More than mere critiques questioning the quality of his writing or his ability as an author, the assault on Melville by American journalists constitutes a challenge on the subject of truth-telling.

As Higgins and Parker have documented, Melville's first novel, *Typee*, initially drew positive responses from both British and American reviewers in early 1846. Gradually, however, questions emerged about the authenticity of the book, which had been marketed as a faithful account of the author's adventures in the Marquesas Islands after he and a fellow sailor had jumped ship. In telling his story, one reviewer wrote, Melville "makes some statements respecting the social condition and character of the tribe with which he was domesticated, of so remarkable a character that we cannot escape a slight suspicion that he has embellished the facts from his own imagination, in other words, that there is an indefinite amount of romance mingled with the reality of his narrative." The reviewer wavers between expressing his "suspicion" and recognizing the book's "verisimilitude," and is generally favorable, if somewhat doubtful. The identity of the reviewer is significant: it was Charles A. Dana, who would become one of the leading journalists of the day. Years after he wrote this review for the *Harbinger*, Dana wrote that his *New York Sun* gave readers "a daily photograph of the whole world's doings in the most luminous and lively manner." As his language here suggests, Dana espoused a common journalistic view of truth—that of objective, visible reality. To be true according to this view, an account would need to be factual. Other reviewers expressed similar doubts about the veracity of *Typee*. Far more suspicious and less forgiving than Dana, a writer for the *New York Morning Courier and New-York Enquirer* wrote:

> It may be that the author visited, and spent some time in, the Marquesas Islands; and there may be foundation for some portions of the narrative. But we have not the slightest confidence in any of the details, while many of the incidents narrated are utterly incredible. We might cite numberless instances of this monstrous exaggeration; but no one can read a dozen pages of the book without detecting them.

Christian publications questioned the book's authenticity, as well, but sometimes added a charge that Melville was misrepresenting Protestant missionaries at work with natives on Pacific islands. A writer for the *New York Evangelist* said that *Typee* contained "slurs and flings against missionaries and civilization," adding, "When the author alludes to, or touches matters of fact at the Sandwich Islands, he shows the sheerest ignorance, and utter disregard of truth." Not all of the reviewers focused on transgressions regarding factual truth. Indeed, a lengthy discussion of the novel in the *Christian Parlor Magazine*, although accusing Melville of "errors of general fact," concedes that his book probably is a "narrative of real events." Nevertheless, the reviewer claims to "present the other side of the case to the public, with the hope of rendering at least a little service to the cause of truth." For this reviewer, it seems, the truth has less to do with facts and more to do with general values of civilization. "But whether true or false," the reviewer writes, "the real or pseudonymic author deserves a pointed and severe rebuke for his flagrant outrages against civilization, and particularly the missionary work." Years later, a writer for another Christian publication, the *New York Independent*, seems to have had a similar conception of higher truth in mind, noting in a review of *Moby-Dick* that the author had talent, but was misusing it. This reviewer suggested that Melville could serve sailors well if only his mind would "turn on the poles of truth." At the beginning of his career as a novelist, then, Melville faced challenges from the press over the factual and philosophical truths of his narratives.[22]

Melville's response to these challenges is revealing. In a move that points to his recognition of the power of the press, Melville wrote and solicited defenses of his novel in the press. After his companion in the South Pacific, Richard Tobias "Toby" Greene, whom Melville believed to be dead, turned up and confirmed the truth of his story, for example, Melville orchestrated a publicity campaign to draw attention to Greene's vindication of his own account in the book. Instead of ignoring the press, he tried to turn its influence to his advantage. Both before and after the appearance of "Toby," however, Melville was in a strange position of arguing for the veracity of a novel, a genre that by definition is not entirely true. As Higgins and Parker note, the suggestion that he had fabricated material infuriated him—even though he knew that he had done so. For one thing, he had spent only three weeks, not four months, in the Marquesas. Nevertheless, in a queer kind of apology for truth in fiction, he set out to defend the veracity of his novel. In response to the *Courier and Enquirer*, he wrote an item for the *Albany Argus*, arguing that his book was "a true narrative of events which actually occurred to him." Later, he ghost-wrote a note in which a supposed reader expresses his faith in the book. He described the ruse in a letter to Alexander Bradford: "I have endeavored to make it appear as if written by one who had read the book & beleived it—& moreover—had been as much pleased with it as most people who read it profess to be." He added,

"I feel confident that unless something of this kind appears the success of the book here as a genuine narrative will be seriously impaired."[23] In short, Melville crafted a fiction in support of the truth of a fiction. The notion that truth could be stranger than fiction had emerged in the various reviews of *Typee*, but here was another kind of belief—that is, that fiction could be truer than truth. It is a belief that would pervade the literary responses to journalism throughout the era.

CROSSOVER WRITERS

A few of these same authors, as well as a host of others, experienced even closer encounters with journalism. Given the need to make a living, the choice of many writers to put their pens to work for newspapers and magazines is no surprise, especially during the advent of what Ronald Weber has called "America's Golden Age of Print." If the decision is not surprising, it is significant. As Underwood and Fishkin have noted, journalism helped shape the literary careers of some American authors by providing them with training, material, and an outlook on the world. Indeed, most scholars who have examined the intersection of journalism and literature in the nineteenth century have examined newspaper work as a kind of "apprenticeship" for writers such as Whitman and Dreiser.[24] The experience of working for newspapers and magazines gave these writers something else, however. As reporters, columnists, correspondents, and editors, budding authors were developing an insider's knowledge of what they eventually would view as a competing genre. It is fair to say, in fact, that American authors, as a whole, knew more about journalism than they knew about politics, science, law, ministry, or any other field. As a result, at the same time that it was putting food in their mouths and skills into their literary arsenals, journalism was putting ideas into their heads, ideas that, in some cases, ultimately would drive them away from journalism or help build their case against it. Journalism was turning its practitioners into some of its harshest and most penetrating critics.

As is still true today, journalism was not an especially well-paying career in antebellum America. Nevertheless, a writer generally could expect to make a better living by landing a steady job with a newspaper or magazine than by writing, say, a poem about an ominous talking bird. For "The Raven," one of the few literary sensations he achieved during his lifetime, Poe reportedly made no more than $20. He earned, Weber writes, "perhaps no more than $6,200 for his entire career as a writer, magazine editor, and literary lecturer." In other words, in current dollars, the author of "The Tell-Tale Heart," "Annabel Lee," and a dozen more of the best-known poems and short stories in English was averaging less than $11,000 a year, about $7000 below the poverty level for his three-person household. Among serious American authors, only a few, including Cooper and Irving, could depend solely on their income from book sales. The Panic of 1837 made a literary career especially precarious, as Aleta Feinsod Cane and Susan Alves have noted:

> The depression in the book industry that followed the panic was caused, in part, by the lack of copyright laws, which allowed the pirating of materials from England so cheaply that American authors could not compete. Many American writers turned to the periodical press, which paid them from four to twelve dollars a page for their work.

When a man who aspired to make a living as a writer in New York announced his ambition to Greeley, the editor responded, "You do not realize how little the mere talent of writing well has to do with success or usefulness. There are a thousand at least in this city who can write very good prose or verse . . . while there are not fifty who can earn their bread by it." If Greeley thought fewer than one in twenty good writers could make a living with their pens, his contemporary George Tucker was even less sanguine about an author's prospects. "But of all the intellectual labors, those of authors are, in general, the worst rewarded," Tucker wrote in *Political Economy for the People.* "Now and then, indeed, a popular writer receives a liberal remuneration; but, for one of this description, there are probably fifty failures, and perhaps twenty who do not receive for their efforts in this way the pay of a common laborer."[25] In a country largely without patrons, most writers of literature had to have another source of income. Some, such as Henry Wadsworth Longfellow and Oliver Wendell Holmes, had regular jobs as professors or doctors. Others, such as Emerson and Hawthorne, lectured or worked in government positions. Many others turned to journalism.[26]

In the eighteenth century, the turn had not been all that sharp. For Benjamin Franklin, in fact, it was not a turn at all. Apprenticed to his brother James, a Boston printer and publisher of the *New England Courant,* Franklin became familiar with the colonial newspaper as a venue for literature, particularly satirical essays, as well as straight news reporting. Franklin published his first noteworthy literary works, his Silence Dogood essays, in his brother's newspaper. After taking over the *Pennsylvania Gazette* in 1729, Franklin continued to treat newspapers as a venue for essays and satires, writings that modern readers would consider literature, but that Franklin and his contemporaries would have considered perfectly appropriate material to appear alongside news reports of trials and political matters. In the decades around the turn of the century, Philip Freneau, Susanna Rowson, and Charles Brockden Brown also worked in journalism.

In the nineteenth century, as journalism and literature grew into separate disciplines, however, the turn became sharper and, for some writers, crueler. For Bryant, journalism was a necessary evil, something akin to a low-brow patron who stingily provides a living while exacting tedious work from the artist. Trained in the law, he began editing the *New-York Review and Atheneum Magazine* in 1825. The following year, he went to work as an editorial assistant to William Coleman, editor of the *New-York Evening Post*. Two years later, he borrowed money and bought an interest in the newspaper; the $1,000 he made from this investment each year was twice what he had made in law. By 1829, he was editor-in-chief of the newspaper. Bryant would edit the newspaper for approximately half a century, becoming a leader in the field. A staunch Democrat who later became a Free-Soiler, Bryant wrote vigorous editorials, including one in which he warned, "If the tyrannical doctrines and measures of Mr. Calhoun can be carried into effect, there is an end of liberty in this country; but carried into effect they cannot be." James Boylan writes, "Even under the self-imposed handicap of forswearing sensational news and mass circulation, Bryant built the *Evening Post* into a paper to which the leaders of the nation paid close attention for decades, and which was profitable enough to confer on Bryant modest wealth." Bryant, in short, devoted most of his life and much of his energy to journalism and became one of the most successful editors of his era. Despite his success, the experience of working in journalism did not make him sanguine about the influence of the profession on a writer. Rather, it seems to have left him disappointed by the constraints the work placed on his career as an author. Newspaper work, he wrote, "fills the mind with a variety of knowledge relating to the events of the day, but that knowledge is apt to be superficial, since the necessity of attending to many subjects prevents the journalist from thoroughly investigating any." He continued, "In this way it begets desultory habits of thought, disposing the mind to be satisfied with mere glances at difficult questions and to dwell only upon plausible commonplaces."[27]

In his heart, Bryant was not a journalist, but a poet. Years before going to work for his first newspaper, he had written what would become his most famous poem, "Thanatopsis." Throughout his career as an editor, he published "To the Fringed Gentian," "The

Prairies," and other poems, literary works that would help make his reputation as a poet, but that would not make him the kind of living that journalism provided. Asked about dealing with politics, a mainstay for journalists, Bryant responded, "I do not like politics any better than you do—but . . . you know politics and a bellyful are better than poetry and starvation." Indeed, Bryant resented his dependence on journalism and fantasized about reducing this dependence or leaving it entirely behind him. In a letter to his brother, he wrote, "I have been employed long enough with the management of a daily newspaper, and desire leisure for literary occupations that I love better." He toiled on, however, even after the 1837 recession made his *Post* less profitable. Unable to sell his part of the paper or keep up with payments, he felt, in his words, like a "draft horse harnessed to the wain of a daily paper."[28]

Bryant may have spoken for a number of his literary contemporaries when he expressed his resentment of producing journalism for a living. By the middle of the 1830s, his fellow poet Poe already had published two books of poetry and a prize-winning story, "MS. Found in a Bottle." Poe's financial prospects were not promising, however, and he took a position as editor of the *Southern Literary Messenger* after the deaths of his foster father and grandmother. For $10 a week, he churned out some 176 reviews and other pieces and carried out much of the regular business of the magazine. Over the next decade, Poe continued to depend on journalism for a meager income, taking on jobs with *Burton's Gentleman's Magazine* and other publications. After leaving one of these publications, *Graham's Magazine*, he complained, "To coin one's brain into silver, at the nod of a master, is to my thinking, the hardest task in the world." Nevertheless, Poe became adept, if not comfortable, with such exploitation of his mind's products, as Terence Whalen has noted. Indeed, the experience of working in journalism may have helped shape his ability in this area, since news was appreciated for its pecuniary value. Even Thoreau, who never successfully made the transition to journalism, found the field disappointing. In an attempt to secure an income from the products of his pen, he approached periodicals such as *Brother Jonathan* and *The New York Mirror*, but was discouraged by both the low pay and the deluge of competition.[29] Whether he was more principled—or merely less flexible or less desperate—than Bryant and Poe, Thoreau never became a fulltime journalist. The experience of seeking and failing to coin his own mind into silver may have left its mark. As we will see, no one issued more scathing condemnations of newspapers than Thoreau.

Not all of America's crossover writers were as quick to dismiss journalism as a necessary evil. Margaret Fuller, who edited the Transcendentalist journal *The Dial* before working as a contributor to Horace Greeley's *New York Tribune*, once referred to the periodical as an "efficient instrument." Other women of the nineteenth century shared this attitude. For these women, Cane and Alves argue, magazines and newspapers were tools for a variety of ends, including reform. Perhaps the most successful of these women, at least in terms of popularity and income, was Sara Willis, or "Fanny Fern." As an adolescent and a young woman in Boston, Willis wrote and edited material for *The Recorder* and *The Youth's Companion*, two newspapers established by her father, Nathaniel Willis. Like most women of the era, however, Willis eventually married and confined her work to homemaking and childrearing. Finding herself destitute after her husband's death in 1846, Willis made small change through needlework and tried unsuccessfully to become a teacher. As she later recounted in her autobiographical novel *Ruth Hall*, journalism became a way out of poverty:

> A thought! why could not Ruth write for the papers? How very odd it had never occurred to her before? Yes, write for the papers—why not? She remembered that while at boarding-school, an editor of a paper in the same town used often to come in and take down her compositions in short-hand as she read them aloud, and transfer them to the columns of his paper. . . . She would begin that very night, but where to make a beginning? who would publish her articles? how much would they pay her? to whom should she apply first?

For both Ruth and the real Sara Willis, journalism eventually provided more than bread and milk for her and her daughter. After getting by on six dollars a week from her contributions to a couple of weeklies, the *Olive Branch* and the *True Flag*, Willis, now writing under the pseudonym "Fanny Fern," secured a more lucrative position with the New York *Musical World and Times* in 1852. The following year, she published a collection of her columns, *Fern Leaves from Fanny's Portfolio*, which sold some 100,000 copies in the United States and England. Because she chose to collect royalties on the book instead of selling the rights to it, Willis made nearly $10,000 on the book. The one-time resident of boarding houses bought a home in Brooklyn and again took control of her other daughter, whom she had left with her in-laws while she was still in the depths of poverty. In 1855, she negotiated for an agreement that would pay her $100 per column. The first female columnist in the United States, Willis was now making more money writing for a newspaper than anyone else in the country. She would write for the *Ledger* until her death in 1871. Like many of her contemporaries, she wrote both journalism and literature. In addition to *Ruth Hall*, which appeared in 1854, she published the novel *Rose Clark* in 1856.[30]

Journalism provided Willis with both a substantial income and a powerful vehicle for her ideas on womanhood, marriage, altruism, and a host of other subjects. Willis is a prime example of a woman who used journalism, in the words of Cane and Alves, "for the critique of gender roles and expectations." Writing in a bold, satirical style, Willis said the things that many women probably wanted to say, but were perhaps afraid to say, at least to their husbands. In "Family Jars," for instance, she imagines a husband and a wife who trade jobs for the day: Jeremiah, who has told his wife how difficult his job is, agrees to stay home with the children while she tends to his store. Before the day is done, the beleaguered homemaker-for-a-day is so rattled by his experiences that he sets up the children with a pile of sugar and escapes to a bar, eventually running off to California. In other columns, such as "Women's Salaries" and "Dull Homes in Bright Places," Willis championed women's financial independence and encouraged hard-working wives and mothers to "take a little comfort" and "look after No 1." "Her ideal woman," Joyce W. Warren explains, "was independent, vital, and energetic, not bound by convention and not limited to marriage as a goal. . . . Writing fearlessly on subjects then considered taboo, particularly for women, she deplored the social double standard, approved divorce if necessary, and urged family planning." Willis clearly was thinking of herself when she wrote that her alter ego, Ruth Hall, "had the courage to call things by their right names, and the independence to express herself boldly on subjects which to the timid and clique-serving, were tabooed." As Warren notes, Willis used her columns to address poverty, disease, and other issues, as well.[31] Willis's attitude toward the value of journalism can be seen in *Ruth Hall*, where Ruth has appreciated the "Household Messenger" partly because its editorials "were fearless and honest, and always on the side of the weak, and on the side of truth."[32]

Journalism, in short, provided Willis with a unique opportunity to tell the truth as she saw it. Perhaps for this reason, she was highly critical of journalism that hid or distorted the truth for readers. In *Ruth Hall*, she goes out of her way to expose the "puffery" and other forms of bias that characterized much of the era's literary criticism and other journalism. In a chapter that strays from the novel's narrative,

Willis presents the ruminations of Horace Gates, an editor who works under Ruth's brother Hyacinth Ellet on his newspaper:

> Well, well, it's no use wondering, I must go to work; what a pile of books here is to be reviewed! wonder who reads all these books? Here is Uncle Sam's Log House. Mr. Ellet writes me that I must simply announce the book without comment, for fear of offending southern subscribers. The word "slave" I know has been tabooed in our columns this long while, for the same reason. Here are poems by Lina Lintney—weak as diluted water, but the authoress once paid Mr. Ellet a compliment in a newspaper article, and here is her "reward of merit," (in a memorandum attached to the book, and just sent down by Mr. Ellet;) "give this volume a first-rate notice." Bah! what's the use of criticism when a man's opinion can be bought and sold that way? it is an imposition on the public. . . . Heaven forgive me the lies I tell this way on compulsion.[33]

Willis may have drawn on a variety of sources for this indictment of journalistic "lies." By the time she wrote *Ruth Hall*, she had been not only a journalist herself, but also the daughter, sister, and friend of journalists. The fictional Gates, in fact, was based on James Parton, who worked for her brother Nathaniel P. Willis, the inspiration for the superficial and heartless Hyacinth in the novel, and eventually married Sara Willis in 1856. In any case, her exposure to journalism helped her to develop an appreciation for both its power and its failings.

Like Willis, Rebecca Harding Davis found the periodical an "efficient instrument." Before publishing her breakthrough story, "Life in the Iron-Mills," in 1861, she had contributed reviews and other material to the *Wheeling Intelligencer*, the most widely circulated newspaper in western Virginia. After entering the literary scene with a kind of journalistic fiction, one that exposed the underbelly of industrial America, Davis went on to write a number of other reformist stories and essays in the decades after the Civil War. In 1869, she joined the staff of the *New York Tribune* as a contributing editor. In the short story "The Yares of Black Mountain," Davis sketched a female journalist who tells an acquaintance, "If you earned your bread by your brains, as I do, you'd want as much bread for a penny as possible." Davis knew what it meant to earn her bread with her brains. The need for income, in fact, may have been part of what attracted Davis to journalism. It certainly was on her mind when she was offering material to the *Atlantic Monthly* in the early 1860s. In a letter to the editor James Fields, she wrote, "Money is enough a 'needful commodity' with me to make me accept with a complacent smile whatever you think the articles are worth." She revealed her dependence on writing for income in other letters, as well, even making a "horrid" request that Fields pay her earlier than they had arranged. "May I change my mind, and ask you—if it is all the same to you—to send the remaining $160 now?" she asked. "I want to buy something and haven't money enough, and thought I would rather ask you than run in debt." As a woman, Davis had open to her far fewer careers than were available to Twain, Whitman, or any of her other male counterparts. As the experiences of Sara Willis, Lydia Maria Child, and numerous other women showed, writing was one that could prove profitable. In her essay called "Women in Literature," Davis notes, "Increase of population will compel more of my sex to earn their living, and literature (or journalism) will always be, as now, an easy, respectable way of doing it."[34]

As this comment suggests, journalism was not, for Davis, the burden that it was for Bryant. In addition to finding it "easy" and embracing it as an opportunity to advocate reform, she shared its appreciation for facts. In "Two Methods with the Negro," she notes that "facts are facts, and to ignore them fatally weakens any cause." In her memoir *Bits of Gossip*, she criticized Ralph Waldo Emerson and others for their ignorance of reality. The conversation that she encountered among such figures "left you with a vague, uneasy sense that something was lacking, some back-bone of fact," she writes. "Their theories were like beautiful bubbles blown from a child's pipe, floating overhead, with queer reflections on them of sky and earth and human beings, all in a glow of fairy color and all a little distorted." In her own writings, such as "Some Testimony in the Case" and a review of the book *Undistinguished Americans*, Davis quoted real people on the race issue and praised an author for presenting stories of real, average people.[35] In short, journalism held much that appealed to Davis: a means of making a living, a grounding in reality, and the opportunity for effecting reform. Between her stint on the *Intelligencer* and her work for the *Tribune*, however, Davis issued an important critique of journalism in "Life in the Iron-Mills," as we will see in the final chapter.

Like Willis and Davis, Walt Whitman was exposed to journalism at an early age, working as a printer's apprentice while he was still a boy. In 1838 he launched a newspaper, the *Long Islander*. Over the next 17 years, the years leading up to his publication of *Leaves of Grass* in 1855, Whitman worked for several newspapers, including the *New York Aurora* and *New York Statesman*. He did some of his most noteworthy journalistic work as editor of the *Brooklyn Daily Eagle* from 1846 until 1848. Throughout this period, Whitman was writing poetry and fiction, as well. He wrote a number of traditional poems, as well as a temperance novel called *Franklin Evans*. Still, the sheer length of time he devoted to journalism suggests a certain level of commitment to the field. He clearly valued journalism, particularly as a vehicle for reform. As a writer for the *Daily Eagle* and other publications, he wrote numerous editorials on free trade, the living conditions in prisons, and other topics. Writing for the *Sunday Dispatch* in 1850, he called on the federal government or the individual states to provide land for "patriot exiles" who fought despotism in Europe. In 1854, he advocated for the repeal of restrictions on the operation of rail cars and other activities on the Sabbath. Whitman often took advantage of the medium of a newspaper, with its capacity for quickly and cheaply conveying ideas to a wide audience, to call attention to wrongs and suggest correctives. In articles such as "Is there any Hope?" and "The Poor Wretches," as well as others he wrote for the *Daily Eagle* and other newspapers, he called for reforms that would improve the lives of prisoners, "the masses of the old world," and others in need of help. More than a mere source of income, journalism was a meaningful career for Whitman. Fishkin argues that the career and the writer were a perfect match. Showing a number of similarities in characters, "concrete details," "the catalog technique," and theme—especially the importance of firsthand experience—Fishkin even goes so far as to argue that Whitman's journalism and literature were two sides of the same coin: "Whitman spent his years as a journalist absorbing the world around him and then reflecting that world, in all its richness and fullness, in articles, editorials, and sketches. His project as a poet is largely the same, but with a key difference: it is the triadic relationship of the writer, his world, and his work, rather than the world alone, which is his main concern."[36]

At the same time that Whitman was using his position in journalism to advocate reforms in free trade and the treatment of prisoners, another crossover writer was producing a different brand of reform journalism. In a reversal of the usual order of things, Frederick Douglass became a fulltime journalist only after *Narrative of the Life of Frederick Douglass* made him a well-known author. In 1847, he launched his own newspaper, the *North Star*. Under this title and a new one, *Frederick Douglass' Paper*, this paper featured accounts of atrocities, news of legislation related to slavery, announcements of rallies, and other material related to slavery and the abolitionist movement. Later, he worked on two other periodicals: *Douglass' Monthly* and the *New National Era*. Douglass's career path followed naturally on his own experience as a newspaper reader. While he was still a slave, newspapers served as a text during his early attempts to learn to read, as he explains in his 1845 slave narrative. After he secured his freedom, he saw newspapers not only as educational tools, but also as vehicles for reform. In New Bedford, he subscribed to Garrison's *Liberator* and became enamored, even obsessed with the abolitionist work it did:

> The paper came, and I read it from week to week with such feelings as it would be quite idle for me to attempt to describe. The paper became my meat and my drink. My soul was set all on fire. Its sympathy for my brethren in bonds—its scathing denunciations for slaveholders—its faithful exposures of slavery—and its powerful attacks upon the upholders of the institution—sent a thrill of joy through my soul, such as I had never felt before!

For Douglass, the motivation of reform overrode any desire to realize his potential as a literary author. For this reason, journalism was a natural outlet for Douglass, whose slave narrative itself can be read as a kind of investigative journalism, written to expose the destruction that slavery wreaked on slaves' families, bodies, and minds. By the time Douglass's narrative and newspaper appeared, American newspapers already had established themselves as vehicles for reform, as Whitman's editorials demonstrate. In the prospectus that Douglass published in the inaugural issue of the *North Star*, he alluded to his own reformist ambitions:

> We are about to assume the management of the editorial department of a news paper devoted to the cause of Liberty, Humanity and Progress. The position is one which we have, with the [purest] motives, long desired to occupy. It has long been our anxious wish to see, in this slave-holding, slave-trading and negro-hating land, a printing-press and paper permanently established, under [the] complete control and direction of the immediate victims of slavery and oppression.

In this prospectus, particularly in the reference to a "cause," one can see Douglass's belief in the power of the press. Running his own newspaper may have appealed to Douglass on another level, as Wilson Moses has argued, noting that the orator-turned-author-turned-journalist "achieved a measure of escape from the role assigned to him by the white abolitionists of the 1840s by founding his newspaper and taking control of his own literary destiny." In any case, Douglass demonstrates a commitment to journalism rare among American authors. In addition to writing and editing the *North Star*, he deliberated on what should constitute the contents of a newspaper. In a brief essay called "Hints on Journalism," he lays out the various departments a new journal should have: "a department devoted to the politics or the state of the union," summaries of "the news of the week," "belles-lettres or polite literature," and so on. Douglass not only wrote as a journalist, he thought like one.[37]

Whether they valued or begrudged their time in journalism, some of these crossover writers could be critical—sometimes brutally so—of journalism, as we will see in the next chapter. Their insiders' knowledge of the field sometimes provided them with distinctive insights into obstacles that often came between journalists and the truth.

THE "NEWSPAPER INSTINCT"

The experiences of Bryant, Willis, Whitman, and other crossover writers of the antebellum era would be repeated later in the century in the careers of Mark Twain, William Dean Howells, Theodore Dreiser, Stephen Crane, and Rebecca Harding Davis's famous son, Richard Harding Davis. By the late 1890s, the crossover writer was not only common, but noteworthy. "It is a remarkable fact that some of the best and most popular novelists of the day are active journalists," noted a writer for the *Boston Herald* in 1897. This writer goes on to say, "It looks as if journalism was a good school for literature, as it clearly is for its descriptive features, and the instances above cited prove that the two professions work harmoniously together." Another journalist, writing for the *Boston Journal* the same year, remarks, "If Rudyard Kipling, Stephen Crane and Richard Harding Davis all get to the front before the Greeks and Turks finish fighting, the war ought not to be without its share of picturesque chronicles." Some of the journalists who commented on the latest group of crossover writers, however, heard more discordant notes than harmony. One, writing for the *New Bedford Standard*, complains that "Mr. Crane, in attempting fine writing, has simply produced balderdash fit only for sensational third rate novel" and adds, "Of the real forces which predominated in the battle, the strategy which caused it to be fought at that particular spot, and the concentration of a superior force on the part of the Turks, he doesn't appear to have had the slightest conception." Taking a similar line, a writer for the *San Francisco Argonaut* says:

> We think we are entirely warranted in saying that it is impossible for any one, no matter how carefully they may be read, to gain any coherent information from these letters. There is a ludicrous attempt to make out that the Greeks were holding the Turks in check, which is contradicted in every alternate line. There is no attempt made to tell the truth, and these "special letters" are a mere farrago of "fine writing" [and] "scenes and incidents" which Mr. Crane might just as

[well?] or even better have written while sitting in a cafe in Athens. In fact he may have done so.[38]

An article in the *Syracuse Standard* suggests that reading the "slop work" that came from writers such as Crane was "a pure waste of time" and added that "the way to get the news is unknown to them." A writer for the *Rochester Post Express* highlights "the hyperbolic point of view of the impressionable novelist, to whom every incident, every emotion in the tragedy and comedy of life is so much copy" and complains of Crane's detachment, saying, "From a distance it was like a game to the novelist, no blood, no horror, only the movements of 'a tiny doll tragedy.'" A writer for the *Los Angeles Express* characterizes Crane as an outsider in the field of journalism:

> Stephen Crane, the novelist, badly disguised as a newspaper war correspondent at Athens, has published a letter chiefly made up of abuse of a western newspaper man who succeeded in getting an interview with King George. If Stephen had ever been in a "scoop" race before he would not make the mistake of calling attention to a rival's success by abusing him. Mr. Crane's dispatches, by the way, are pretty specimens of fair English, but as far as their information-values go, have the disadvantage of being one or two days behind the news dispatches sent from the seat of war.

As merely a writer of "pretty specimens of fair English," Crane, in the eyes of this writer, is out of his element in journalism, which calls for reporting timely, factual information. Still another journalist, writing in the *Brooklyn Eagle*, calls Crane and Kipling "shining failures of this war" and predicts: "This is the last time newspapers will send novelists into the field to get news for them."[39] The argument in all of these condemnations is twofold: authors are not journalists, and their stories are not journalism. "A man has to be born with the newspaper instinct to be a success in journalism," argues a writer for the *Brockton Enterprise*. "The men who make a hit in that business are born, not made after they have reached manhood's stage. Kipling and Davis have been away from active newspaper work too long to fit readily into the harness." Similarly, a writer for the *Boston Herald* says, "Neither Rudyard Kipling, Richard Harding Davis nor Stephen Crane has yet distinguished himself at the seat of war. They are all graphic writers, but it takes other qualifications to be a great war correspondent. They will all find that out before they get home."[40] Being a good journalist, some of the articles argue, means more than simply writing good prose; it involves an appreciation of what makes news, an ability to ferret out this news, and the skill of reporting this news economically. If literature consists of "fine writing" done at a distance by detached authors looking for good "copy," this argument suggests, journalism is sparse prose collected on the ground by hard-nosed reporters bent on finding the truth and the reasons behind it.

The attacks on Crane and his fellow crossover writers in 1897 show how much the world of American letters had evolved over the course of the nineteenth century. At the beginning of the century, this world was still the largely monolithic one that readers had known in the colonial era. Although Benjamin Franklin, the greatest man of letters of the eighteenth century, had died in 1790, successors such as Freneau and Bryant were, like him, writers of both journalism and literature. Throughout the nineteenth century, furthermore, newspapers continued to publish "fine writing," including poetry, satire, and essays. As this chapter has shown, journalism and literature continued to cross paths, but a separation was gradually developing, leaving observers, such as Crane's critics, to remark on the novelty of an author in journalism. As we will see in the next chapter, this growing separation can be traced in a myriad of literary critiques aimed at journalism by many of the era's leading authors.

CHAPTER 3

LITERARY CRITIQUES OF JOURNALISM

Reflecting on how far journalism had come during the era of the penny press, James Gordon Bennett boasted of the press's new influence. "I have shown, in eighteen months," he wrote in his *New York Herald* in 1837, "that a daily newspaper conducted with power, knowledge, industry and genius, can be made the most powerful instrument of civilization and of improvement the world ever saw." With characteristic bravado, he continued, "Shakespeare is the great genius of the drama—Scott of the novel—Milton and Byron of the poem—and I mean to be the genius of the daily newspaper press." The same year, a rising author and lecturer wrote with similar enthusiasm for the future of American literature. "Who can doubt, that poetry will revive and lead in a new age," Ralph Waldo Emerson asked, "as the star in the constellation Harp which now flames in our zenith, astronomers announce, shall one day be the pole-star for a thousand years?"[1]

Over the remainder of the century, journalists and authors returned repeatedly to the roles or promise of their respective endeavors, often in similar terms, such as "truth" and "real." Indeed, as we saw in Chapter 1, journalism and literature share a common purpose: each, in its own way, attempts to capture and represent the truth of the human experience. More to the point of this chapter, these parallel manifestos point to two disciplines in competition. Just as the rise of science elicited responses from Poe, Hawthorne, and Whitman during this era, the growth and high aspirations of journalism provoked pointed critiques by a number of American authors.[2] While some, such as Douglass, recognized the promise of the press, most regarded it as an inferior and inadequate vehicle for their conception of the truth. In dozens of works, ranging from *Home As Found* to "Slavery in Massachusetts," Cooper, Emerson, Thoreau, Poe, Davis, and other authors deplored the enormous power of the press, chronicled its abuses and shortcomings, and warned of the consequences of investing so much power in a flawed instrument.

The sheer number and variety of these critiques are dizzying. Authors took journalists to task for every imaginable failing: pride, hypocrisy, simplicity, stupidity, inaccuracy, bias, conformity, and more. Some of these authors' hostility toward journalism may have derived from their own negative experiences with it. As we have seen in the previous chapter, Cooper's experience as a beleaguered subject clearly shaped his attitude toward journalism and even inspired some of his fiction. Other authors, such as Poe and Thoreau, may have resented the need to seek work in journalism, which was clearly winning the battle for readers' attention. On close inspection, however, the literary war on journalism in the antebellum era comprises a complex collection of penetrating critiques targeting each component in the rhetorical triangle: producer, audience, and text. First, as an instrument managed by erring humans, the press, these critiques argued, was prone to bias, conformity, and other human failings. Furthermore, since their audience consisted of humans with their own weaknesses, among them vulgarity and an excessive curiosity about others' affairs, newspapers tended toward stories of little or no consequence to serious writers. Finally, the most interesting and revealing of these critiques addressed the very nature of journalism—specifically, the criteria and conventions that gave shape to the texts journalists produced. At the heart of the literary war on journalism lay a concern for truth. Although both journalists and authors claimed to be delivering it to their readers, authors insisted that constraints at all three corners of the triangle left newspaper readers with false representations of reality.

To delineate authors' critiques of journalism is not necessarily to endorse them. It is worth remembering that, as we have seen in Chapter 1, journalists and authors have different conceptions of the truth. Furthermore, the authors themselves did not always agree on what constituted truth. For some, as we will see in the next two chapters, truth entailed natural and spiritual principles not adequately covered by mainstream journalism, or, alternatively, it comprised the possible and not just the factual. For others, exposing the whole truth meant reporting psychological perceptions, larger forces, and other factors that often did not make it into journalistic accounts of people and events. We need not side with authors or journalists in this contest over which better captured or delivered the truth. Rather, our goal should be a thorough understanding of authors' conceptions of journalism, since these conceptions help to illuminate not only their own attitudes toward truth-telling, but also the "news of their own" that grew out of their responses to journalism. Whatever authors believed about the nature of truth, many seemed to agree that journalism was not the best vehicle for telling it. Along with their cases against journalism, some of these authors presented arguments showing why literature was the superior truth-teller, as we will see at the end of this chapter.

One must be careful, of course, when suggesting that a group of diverse people over the course of nearly three decades spoke with a single voice. American writers of the early nineteenth century, however, were not isolated individuals, but parts of a literary network of readers, writers, critics, and correspondents. Furthermore, since some of them—Thoreau and Emerson, for instance, and Hawthorne and Melville—were friends who stayed in touch with one another, they had the opportunity to influence one another's attitudes. In her memoir *Bits of Gossip*, Davis recounted her interactions with several literary figures, including Emerson, Hawthorne, and Louisa May Alcott. Even Dickinson, who of course lacked such personal intercourse, would have encountered her fellow authors' ideas in their writing. In one of her letters, she reveals that she wishes to borrow her sister's copy of *The Atlantic Monthly* because she is interested in Davis's story "Life in the Iron-Mills," which features a critique of journalism.[3] As we will see, some of Emerson's and Thoreau's pronouncements on news were so similar that we might guess that they grew out of their conversations on the subject. Through casual conversations, correspondence, and the practice of reading one another's work, writers such as these exchanged perspectives and, one can assume, influenced one another's attitudes, especially about the world of letters. Such interactions help to explain the remarkable parallels in the critiques that emerged from the literature of these and other writers.

Just as America was home to a variety of authors, it was home to a variety of newspapers. As we have seen in the previous chapter, antebellum American journalism comprised not only the mainstream press, but also abolitionist weeklies, religious papers, and other specialty publications. Thoreau, Emerson, and Poe occasionally singled out specific newspapers for criticism, but many of the literary critiques of journalism did not distinguish among the various forms. In *The American Democrat*, for instance, Cooper lumps all of American journalism under the heading of "the press." In some cases, it may be safe to assume that authors who wrote of "the press" or "newspapers" were thinking of mainstream publications, such as Bennett's *New York Herald* and Greeley's *New York Tribune*; however, since some of the same conventions and criteria were common to both the mainstream and the specialty press, authors' complaints about timeliness and other limiting factors would have applied to journalism as a whole. Among all of this variety and complexity, we can see that America's literary class staked out a clear position on journalism. Despite its promise for educating and civilizing readers, it ultimately did not and could not deliver the sorts of truths that authors thought stories should be telling.

THE PROMISE AND PERILS OF THE PRESS

With the arrival of a mass medium often come enthusiastic predictions about its potential for improving the lot of the human race. Before Americans of the twentieth century gushed over the possibilities of television and the Internet, commentators of the early nineteenth century celebrated the promise of the press, which allowed for the wide distribution of facts and ideas. As Alexis de Tocqueville noted in *Democracy in America*, "Only a newspaper can deposit the same thought in a thousand minds at once." Both contemporary and modern observers have recognized the potential of the press to enlighten the American public and to right wrongs. Among these observers were a number of authors, including Douglass, Whitman, and Davis.[4]

Enlightenment was the theme of the century in which the American newspaper took its early development. Perhaps it should come as no surprise, then, that journalism came to be associated with both the spread and the positive use of information. Near the end of the eighteenth century, Thomas Jefferson had expressed his faith in "the good sense of the people" and predicted that journalism could help to steer them in the right direction when they lost their way:

> The way to prevent these irregular interpositions of the people, is to give them full information of their affairs through the channel of the public papers, and to contrive that those papers should penetrate the whole mass of the people. The basis of our government being the opinion of the people, the very first object should be to keep that right; and were it left to me to decide whether we should have a government without newspapers, or newspapers without a government, I should not hesitate a moment to prefer the latter.

Years later, Hungarian traveler and author Sandor Farkas credited newspapers with "spreading useful knowledge, learning, and culture simply and cheaply." In the 1820s, journalism historians Edwin Emery and Michael Emery explain, Americans turned to journalism for "the information, inspiration, agitation, and education of a society often unable to keep up with its need for schools." The explosion of newspaper readership in subsequent decades only increased the audience for this inspirational and educational material. No one better represented this spirit of enlightenment than Horace Greeley, editor of the *New York Tribune*. "To him," J. Herbert Altschull explains, "a newspaper was not so much an instrument of potential profit as it was a tool to be used to educate the people, to provide for them not merely information but also instruction in the virtuous life, an instrument with which to lead the new Americans . . . to a new and brighter future."[5]

The journalists themselves, of course, were quick to boast of the benefits their medium bestowed on the American public. No one issued greater boasts than Bennett, who asked, "What is to prevent a daily newspaper from being made the greatest organ of social life?" With characteristic bluster, he continued:

> Books have had their day—the theatres have had their day—the temple of religion has had its day. A newspaper can be made to take the lead of all of these in the great movements of human thought and human civilization. A newspaper can send more souls to heaven, and save more from hell, than all of the churches or chapels in New York—besides making money at the same time. Let it be tried.

Bennett's chief competition, the *New York Sun*, crowed that "the penny press, by diffusing useful knowledge among the operative classes of society, is effecting the march of independence to a greater degree than any other mode of instruction."[6] As Schiller has explained, Bennett and his fellow journalists were the carriers of objective facts to the people, providing them with the raw material on which to exercise their sense of reason. If the *Herald* and the *Sun* played this role for New York's working classes, specialty publications could do the same for other Americans looking to rise economically and socially. An 1837 issue of *The Colored American* called for this kind of paper, saying, "Such an organ can be furnished at little cost, so as to come within the reach of every man, and carry to him lessons on industry and economy—until our entire people, are of one heart and of one mind, in all the means of their salvation, both temporal and spiritual."[7]

Education and enlightenment were only part of the equation. Both by exposing wrongs and by advocating solutions, Greeley and

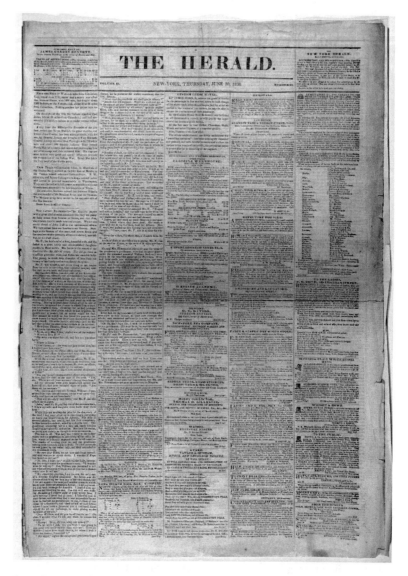

Source: Front page of James Gordon Bennett's *New York Herald*, June 30, 1836. Courtesy, American Antiquarian Society.

other reform-minded journalists played an important role in a culture obsessed with improving itself. Investigative journalism, which can be traced back to some of America's earliest news sheets, was a significant part of the journalistic mission in the antebellum era, as we will see in Chapter 6. Editors such as Garrison and Douglass, furthermore, used their newspapers to promote abolition, free speech, labor organization, and other causes. Whitelaw Reid wrote that his *New York Tribune* helped drive the movement against slavery, and Dana noted the capacity of journalism for "moving public opinion," a capacity that enabled it to be "the greatest influence in a free country." As editor of the *New York Post*, Bryant became known for his editorials on a range of issues. In an 1836 editorial, he referred to the "trust" that his paper had taken on as a watchdog of public affairs. Elsewhere, he wrote, more colorfully, "You can't imagine how difficult it is to make the world go right."[8]

Bryant was not the only author to appreciate the promise of the press. In *Papers on Literature and Art*, Fuller says, "The means which this organ affords of diffusing knowledge and sowing the seeds of thought where they may hardly fail of an infinite harvest, cannot be too highly prized by the discerning and benevolent." As we have seen, Douglass used journalism to educate himself as a slave and later, after establishing his own publications, his fellow Americans. Indeed, Eric Sundquist has suggested that his work in journalism did more to influence and spread his contributions than his autobiographies. "When a great truth once gets abroad in the world," Douglass says, "no power on earth can imprison it, or prescribe its limits, or suppress it." Newspapers such as his *North Star* could be a powerful means to send truth abroad. Noting that control lay with the public, Douglass wrote of the project of "abolitionizing public sentiment." Whitman, too, recognized and employed the power of the press to fight wrongs, as evidenced by his editorials in the *Brooklyn Daily Eagle* and the *Brooklyn Evening Star*. Even Cooper, one of its harshest critics, wrote in *The American Democrat* that the press "is the lever by which the thrones of tyrants and prejudices are the most easily overturned" and that it could serve as "the instrument of elevating man to the highest point of which his faculties admit." The problem, as Cooper also argued, is that it could be destructive, as well.[9]

The pervasive and powerful presence of the press in antebellum America inspired a backlash among some observers, not all of them literary figures. As Lehuu has argued, these observers deplored the practice of pleasure reading, which deprived workers of time they could have spent in self-improvement. Some feared that reading alone at night in secret could lead to immoral behavior. Yet another complaint was that light reading weakened the intellect. Newspapers, which carried countless column inches of lightweight material and sensational coverage of crime and sex, gave "managers of virtue" plenty to disparage. As Lehuu notes, Emerson added his voice to this outcry when he encouraged readers to avoid "the spawn of the press on the gossip of the hour." In an 1858 issue of *The Atlantic Monthly*, he wrote, "If you should transfer the amount of your reading day to day in the newspaper to the standard authors,—but who dare speak of such a thing?"[10] If writers such as Emerson sometimes aligned themselves with other observers in criticizing the perils of the press, they also waged a distinctive war of their own, one in which they implicated producer, audience, and text. When it came to delivering the truth to their readers, these authors argued, newspapers failed to live up to the promise some placed in them, either because journalists and readers were flawed human beings or because the medium itself was rotten at the core, doomed by its own criteria and conventions.

ERRING HUMANS

Authors often play the role of social critic, and one could find plenty of instances in which authors have criticized the members of other professions. Ministers, for one, sometimes come up for ridicule, as in Johnson Jones Hooper's account of a camp meeting, or more serious indictment, as in *The Scarlet Letter*. The literary assault on journalism, however, belongs to an altogether different category because of the close connections between the two endeavors. Authors have relatively little in common with ministers, promoters, politicians, or ship captains. On the other hand, as we have seen in previous chapters, literature and journalism share many of the same goals and methods, as well as many of the same practitioners. Up until the nineteenth century, in fact, they were practically indistinguishable, as Franklin's career demonstrates. Between 1833 and 1861, as American authors and journalists gradually came to realize their own separate identities, authors seized every opportunity to separate themselves from their counterparts in journalism, largely by showing how their profession was better equipped to pursue and capture the truth.

Because it was managed by imperfect human beings, the chief asset of the press was also a source of peril. In the eyes of some of the era's authors, the enormous power of the press magnified the shortcomings of the humans in charge of it. If an editor or reporter was incompetent, biased, or immoral, hundreds or thousands of readers could be led astray. In *The American Democrat*, Cooper implies that more than half of the material in antebellum newspapers—not including obituaries and marriage notes—was inaccurate and adds, "This is a terrible picture to contemplate, for when the number of prints is remembered, and the avidity with which they are read is brought into account, we are made to perceive that the entire nation, in a moral sense, breathes an atmosphere of falsehoods."[11] Cooper, Poe, and others attributed the existences of such falsehood to various factors, including incompetence and bias.

In "The Mystery of Marie Roget," his fictional treatment of the murder of a real woman named Mary Rogers, Poe issued an exhaustive chronicle of journalistic incompetence, as well as one of the century's preeminent examples of literary one-upmanship. Showing characteristic relish for the task of showing off his own intellect and showing up his competitors, Poe takes shot after shot at the journalists covering the murder, using fictional papers with French names to represent specific New York publications, which he identifies in notes. *L'Etoile*, for instance, is *Brother Jonathan*, and *Le Commercial* is the *Journal of Commerce*. As we will see in Chapter 6, Poe attributed journalists' inability to discover the truth of the case to systemic problems in journalism, including a tendency to prize a story over the truth, but he also highlighted what he perceived as a number of instances of incompetence in the human journalists themselves. He notes, for instance, that *L'Etoile* has made a number of assertions that were "satisfactorily disproved" and later remarks that another one of the newspaper's assertions "shows nothing beyond its own pertinacity in error."[12] Although he praises *Le Commercial* for its "philosophical and acute" conclusions, he adds that "the premises, in two instances, at least, are founded in imperfect observation" (749). Elsewhere, he calls attention to reporters' ignorance about physics and biology. With characteristic smugness, Poe notes that, under certain conditions, a human body, "*as a general rule, would not sink at all*—a fact of which L'Etoile is evidently ignorant" (743). Similarly, he calls attention to reporting that refers to mildew and asks whether the editor of *Le Soleil* is "really unaware of the nature of this *mildew*" (759). "Is he to be told," Dupin asks, "that it is one of the many classes of *fungus*, of which the most ordinary feature is its upspringing and decadence within twenty-four hours?" (759). He also draws attention to a "gross discrepancy" that has been overlooked by numerous newspapers (768).

If incompetence kept some journalists from discovering the truth, bias kept others from reporting it. In Poe's story, this bias takes the form of prejudice among journalists unwilling to consider evidence that contradicts their theories about the murder. Dupin, for example, tells the narrator, "I wish merely to caution you against the whole tone of L'Etoile's *suggestion*, by calling your attention to its *ex parte* character at the outset" (740). Later, he accuses the same paper of "[h]aving prescribed thus a limit to suit its own preconceived notions" (740) and notes that a character, upon visiting the newspaper's editor, "offended him by venturing an opinion that the corpse, notwithstanding the theory of the editor, was, in sober fact that of Marie" (747–48). In short, in this story, one of what Poe called his "tales of ratiocination," Dupin exposes the journalists' over-reliance on deductive reasoning, which leaves them resistant to evidence that would have brought them closer to the truth.

Other authors highlighted another form of bias, the kind that results from a desire to promote or protect certain elements in the community. Cooper, for instance, attributes "untruths" to conflicts of interest and the influence of outsiders, as well as lack of time or access to the facts. As we have seen, Willis has one of the characters in her novel *Ruth Hall* complain of puffery in literary criticism and regret the "lies" he has told as a journalist. Furious at the press for its defense of or complacence about slavery, Thoreau leveled similar criticisms at journalists, noting that he had "heard the gurgling of the sewer through every column" of a Boston newspaper and using words such as "servility" and "slime" in his references to journalism.[13] In the eyes of these authors, then, journalists allowed external forces—not merely the facts or objective personal judgment—to shape their versions of the truth for their audiences.

Authors charged journalists with a subtler form of bias: the urge to conform. In an 1839 journal passage that he apparently revised for inclusion in "Self-Reliance," Emerson wrote of a minister who "is pledged to himself beforehand not to look at but one side; the permitted side; not as a man, but as a parish minister in Concord." Comparing such a minister to a "retained attorney," Emerson added that newspapers and politicians suffer from the same consequences of conformity. As a result, he concludes, "Their every truth is not quite true." Cooper made a similar accusation in a chapter on journalism in *The American Democrat*, saying, "Whenever the papers unite to commend, without qualification, it is safe to believe in either venality, or a disposition to defer to a preconceived notion of excellence, most men choosing to float with the current, rather than to resist it, when no active motive urges a contrary course, feeding falsehood, because it flatters a predilection." Such a desire for conformity leads at least one journalist away from the truth in "The Mystery of Marie Roget," where Poe accuses a writer of copying others' opinions about the murder.[14]

Cooper and others also decried the immorality of the humans charged with managing the American press. In *The American Democrat*, he laments the decline in power of moral, discreet men in America; such men, he argued, were giving way to "those who scarcely deem an affectation of the higher qualities necessary to their success." He continued, "This fearful change must, in a great measure, be ascribed to the corruption of the publick press, which, as a whole, owes its existence to the schemes of interested political adventurers." In *Home As Found*, Cooper sketches just such a journalist in Steadfast Dodge, whom he describes as hypocritical, "cowardly, envious, and malignant." Dodge's envy, Cooper explains, is the foundation of "his principles, his impulses, and his doctrines." In the hands of such a character, a newspaper is not likely to live up to its potential as an instrument of democracy or truth. In fact, Cooper mocks such ideals when he has Dodge say, "I only edit a newspaper, by way of showing an interest in mankind" and again when a different character notes that "the press is the true guardian of the public rights." Dodge's name suggests both the ideal and the reality: readers may expect him to be steadfast, but he is more likely to dodge what threatens him. Emerson seems to have known a few real journalists who resembled Dodge in their immoral natures. In his journals, he called Isaac Hill "the foulest of low libellous country newspaper editors, whose whole business was malignant lying . . . for money." Elsewhere in these journals, he says, "Nothing is so hypocritical as the abuse in all journals,—& at the South, especially,—of Mormonism & Free-Love Socialism. These men who write the paragraphs in the 'Herald' & 'Observer,' have just come from their brothel, or, in Carolina, from their Mulattoes."[15]

Of course, Poe, Thoreau, Cooper, and Emerson were themselves subject to human failings, and these failings, particularly envy of journalism's popularity and influence, may have helped to shape some of these criticisms. It is worth noting, however, that they were not alone in decrying the state of antebellum American periodicals. Parke Godwin, himself a journalist, had this to say about them:

> Few things are more to be deplored than the low tone, the unkind feeling which characterize their intercourse with each other. We do not speak merely of those flagrant violations of decency which degrade the lower class of journals. We speak of the puerility, the violence, and the want of justice, which even the most respectable journals exhibit; we speak of their proneness to distort and to exaggerate, of their recklessness of fair-dealing, of their want of candor, and of their base subservience to particular classes. Indeed, so frequent have been their offences in these respects, that their dishonesty has almost passed into a proverb.

Although he clearly believed that "the press has a worthier destiny" than to promote falsehood and to abet exploitation, indeed that it "should become a fountain of truth and moral influence," Godwin argued that government and business actually rewarded immorality and base behavior in journalists.[16]

Humans are human, and drawing attention to their foibles is common in literature. What is significant in this case is that these humans wielded control over America's press, which leading American intellectual Edward Everett called "for good or evil, the most powerful influence that acts on the public mind—the most powerful in itself and as the channel through which most other influence acts." For Thoreau and Cooper, the effect was evil, as the press had come to abuse its power. In "Slavery in Massachusetts," Thoreau argues that "probably no country was ever ruled by so mean a class of tyrants as, with a few noble exceptions, are the editors of the periodical press in *this* country." He adds that these editors "live and rule only by their servility." Cooper sounds a similar chord in *The American Democrat*, where he says, "If newspapers are useful in overthrowing tyrants, it is only to establish a tyranny of their own." Clearly stung by his own experience with the press, Cooper was not as penetrating in his analysis of the press as some of his contemporaries. Although he may have been correct in his assessment of the press's power and even in his assertion that the press was abusing this power, he did not describe in any detail the specific factors behind the abuse. Noting that journalism history "is every where the same," he argued that the press begins as "timid, distrustful, and dependant on truth for success" and then becomes a force for good, "scattering errors and repelling falsehood." Ultimately, however, "abuses rush in, confounding principles, truths, and all else that is estimable." Exactly why these "abuses rush in" is not entirely clear, although Cooper does suggest that the press operates "like an individual spoiled by success." It may be that Cooper was troubled by the power vested in the kind of journalist he sketched in *Home As Found*, where the irresponsible Steadfast Dodge, thanks to his influence over public opinion, leaves readers with a false representation of reality:

> Mr. Dodge was as good as his word, and the account appeared. The press, throughout the country, seized with avidity on anything that helped to fill its columns. No one appeared disposed to inquire into the truth of the account, or after the character of the original authority. It was in print, and that struck the great majority of the editors and their readers, as a sufficient sanction.[17]

In suggesting that most people lacked the "proper self-control" to be critical of such coverage, Cooper pointed to the role of audience in the damage he felt journalism was doing to truth.

If Cooper and other authors were concerned about the short-comings of the press's human practitioners, they were perhaps even more troubled by the weaknesses of its human readers, who helped to drive the contents of newspapers. As Schudson has noted, newspapers—once largely the instruments of political parties and business—became a commodity in the 1830s. Editors had to attract and satisfy both readers and advertisers to survive as commercial enterprises. Even Douglass, an idealistic journalist with his eye on social causes, wrote, "It is needless to say to the intelligent mind that the primary object of publishing a periodical is a matter of business—an investment of money in an enterprise that is expected to return dividends."[18] One could say the same of book publishing, but some key differences separated the two types of business. For one thing, book publishers were not dependent on advertisers for revenues; their profits came from book sales. Newspapers, on the other hand, depended more heavily on advertisers. As a result, exposing a true but embarrassing fact about a frequent advertiser could be self-destructive for a newspaper. Furthermore, book publishers could offset their losses on unpopular literary books with their sales on almanacs, Bibles, and other dependable sellers. Newspaper publishers, on the other hand, often had one source of income—the newspaper—and editors generally sought to fill much or all of the finite space with profitable material—that is, writing that would sell newspapers. Authors could help publishers remain profitable by accepting relatively small payments or royalties on their work while earning a living from other sources. In fact, only a small number of literary authors—among them Cooper, Irving, and Longfellow—made substantial incomes from their writings. Many, in fact, turned to journalism, as we saw in Chapter 2. As long as they had alternative sources of income—as Hawthorne, Emerson, Thoreau, and virtually every other author of the era did—antebellum authors could produce serious literature that did not turn a big profit or any profit at all. Dickinson, of course, did not even publish the vast majority of her poetry.

The key difference between journalism and literature, however, lies in their audiences. Whereas even published books need appeal to only a relatively small number of readers, many newspapers had to cater to mass audiences to survive. As Greeley noted, Bennett owed his success in journalism to his genius in this area. "He knew how to pick out of the events of the day the subject which engrossed the interest of the greatest number of people, and to give them about that subject all they could read," Greeley wrote. "The quality might be bad, and generally was; but it suited the multitude, and the quantity at any rate was abundant."[19]

To make money in this enterprise, of course, journalists had to produce something that readers wished to buy, and what they wanted to buy was the kind of material authors generally deplored: gossip, quirky anecdotes, and sensational coverage of crime and sex. Such "human interest" material can be found in newspapers from the eighteenth century, but it became stock-in-trade for penny papers such as Day's *Sun* and Bennett's *Herald*. Reporters of the era covered the courts and other beats promising salacious and sordid news that they could then dish out to readers. The doings of high society also made news, as the *Herald* served up news of local and distant balls, including one it called "a greater sensation in the fashionable world than anything of the kind since the creation of the world, or the fall of the beauteous woman, or the frolic of old Noah, after he left the ark and took to wine and drinking." In the 1830s and early 1840s, American newspapers featured articles on the wedding of a wealthy woman and a man who had been married five times, a duel between a woman's brothers and her suitor, a "Stone-flinger" who assassinated a "licentious" priest, a preacher who impregnated a parishioner, a man who ascended in a balloon and sent a dog to the earth with a parachute, and countless other odd and titillating stories.[20]

The most sensational of the sensational was the coverage of the murder of a prostitute named Helen Jewett and the ensuing investigation in New York in 1836. Jewett's body was found in a bed in a brothel, where she had been assaulted and killed. Suspicion fell on Richard P. Robinson, a well-to-do young man who was known to have had a relationship with Jewett. The penny press editors of New York seized on the story, no one with more gusto than Bennett, who recognized its enormous dramatic appeal. In his paper, he framed it not only as a sensational story, but also as an exposé that promised societal reform:

> Instead of relating the recent awful tragedy of Ellen Jewett as a dull police report, we made it the starting point to open up a full view upon the morals of society—the hinge of a course of mental action calculated to benefit the age—the opening scene of a great domestic drama that will, if properly conducted, bring about a reformation—a revolution—a total revolution in the present diseased state of society and morals.

The Jewett story helped Bennett in two ways, as Bennett biographer James L. Crouthamel has explained. First, it brought the *Herald*, as well as the *Sun* and the *Transcript*, huge gains in readership; according to Bennett's own figures, his circulation climbed to 15,000. Second, the experience of covering the murder developed his sense of "human interest" and helped to shape future sensational coverage of crime, sex, and death.[21]

In capitalizing on "human interest" news, Bennett and his journalistic brethren merely exploited an appetite that may be as old as language itself. Gossip, Robin Dunbar has suggested, amounts to a kind of "vocal grooming" that serves as a "bonding mechanism" in humans. As numerous contemporary and modern observers have noted, newspapers came to serve as vehicles for transmitting gossip. Quoting de Tocqueville, who attributed the popularity of newspapers to a human desire for "intercommunication and combination," Lehuu has argued, "Human-interest stories offered exposure as a substitute for human contact. . . . Thus, the rise of the penny press in the 1830s was due in part to a growing urbanization that created new social and cultural needs." The *Herald*, in fact, characterized itself as an enterprise that trafficked in gossip. An article appearing after a fire that damaged the paper's office issues this homey greeting and invitation: "On the whole . . . we bid our former kind friends and patrons a hearty, a cheerful, and pleasant good morning; and we hope that while we give them a regular call to have a little chat over their coffee and muffins, we may often see them at 202 Broadway when they have any small thing to do, cheap and good, in the advertising line, or any hint or curious piece of information to communicate to the public." Helen MacGill Hughes has noted that Bennett "was just the person his readers would have loved to have a long talk with—one who had seen everything and was ready to tell all about it."[22]

Reynolds has noted that the era's leading authors were "intimately aware of this shift toward the sensational." While Reynolds makes a compelling case for the ways that Poe, Melville, and others transformed sensational material into something of literary significance, it is also worth noting authors' attitudes toward the original coverage and the motivation behind this coverage. In one of his *Brother Jonathan* letters, Cooper snipes that half of newspapers' content amounted to gossip. One possible reason for this emphasis can be found in *Home As Found*, where he characterizes Steadfast Dodge as a slave to "public opinion." On one level, such criticisms align with some issued by the "moral stewards" Lehuu discusses. Indeed, Whitman complains, "Scurrility . . . is a sin of the American newspaper press," and Cooper worried that exciting readers meant leading them away from their powers of reason. These critiques of the press, however, go deeper to the capacity of journalists for telling the truth. In a classic case of serving two masters, Bennett and his ilk—whatever their proclamations about exposing reality and serving the public—could not always both satisfy their customers and tell the whole truth. As Tucher has explained, giving readers what they wanted sometimes involved catering to their stereotypes: "In the penny press, at this point, a true incident was one that harmonized with generally accepted and generally understood patterns, not one that forced the assimilation of extraneous and difficult variations."[23] If forced to choose between stereotypical stories and contradictory facts, editors were likely to choose the stories.

Emerson, Poe, Thoreau, and Cooper all recognized the price writers paid when serving audiences and patrons, and some explicitly accused journalists of sacrificing truth for the bottom line. In his essay on Goethe in *Representative Men*, Emerson questioned the value of a writer who finds direction outside himself—that is, one who "loses himself in the crowd," who is "no longer the lawgiver, but the sycophant, ducking to the giddy opinion of a reckless public," and who "must sustain with shameless advocacy some bad government, or must bark all the year round in opposition; or write conventional criticism; or profligate novels; or, at any rate, write without thought and without recurrence by day and by night to the sources of inspiration."[24] Although Emerson was discussing writers in general, including producers of "profligate novels," his description rings especially true for journalists, who tend to be even more susceptible to the expectations of both public and political patrons. As we will see in Chapter 6, Poe singles out journalists for catering to audiences in "The Mystery of Marie Roget."

Running a successful business in journalism depended on pleasing not only readers, but also advertisers, as Thoreau recognized. In "Slavery in Massachusetts," he accuses some of the Boston newspapers of failing to speak out for fugitive slaves, largely because they sought "to secure the approbation of their patrons." Sickened by what he perceived as their "servility," Thoreau piled on some of the most virulent invective ever aimed at journalism by an American author of the nineteenth century:

> Is there any dust which their conduct does not lick, and make fouler still with its slime? I do not know whether the Boston *Herald* is still in existence, but I remember to have seen it about the streets when

Simms was carried off. Did it not act its part well—serve its master faithfully? How could it have gone lower on its belly? . . . When I have taken up this paper with my cuffs turned up, I have heard the gurgling of the sewer through every column. I have felt that I was handling a paper picked out of the public gutters, a leaf from the gospel of the gambling-house, the groggery and the brothel, harmonizing with the gospel of the Merchants' Exchange.[25]

Through this diatribe runs a motif that clearly identifies the driving force behind these journalistic transgressions: the dependence of newspapers on profit, a dependence that makes them the servants of "patrons," not the truth.

In the eyes of Thoreau and others, the result of this subservience to audiences and patrons was a misinformed, misled public, one that was being fed stereotypes and falsehoods in place of truth. Cooper has one of his characters remark, "The people who suck in nutriment from a brain and a conscience like those of Mr. Dodge, too, commodore, must get, in time, to be surprisingly clear-sighted." Less ironically, the novel's John Effingham speaks of "a newspaper and magazine existence"—that is, a state of knowledge based only on the information found in periodicals. Effingham adds, "It is as bad as the condition of those English who form their notions of society from novels written by men and women who have no access to it, and from the records of the court journal."[26] Thoreau expresses a similar concern in "Slavery in Massachusetts," calling for an "assault on the Press," which he says "exerts a greater and more pernicious influence than the Church did in its worst period." Thoreau suggests that readers are to blame for this influence, saying, "We do not care for the Bible, but we do care for the newspaper." In placing so much faith—the word seems appropriate here, in light of Thoreau's particular analogy—in newspapers, Americans were neglecting their own access to divine truth, letting outside forces shape their thoughts. In "Self-Reliance," Emerson urges readers to look inward, but he acknowledges that many do not, noting that "the sour faces of the multitude, like their sweet faces, have no deep cause, but are put on and off as the wind blows, and a newspaper directs." For Emerson, the ideal was something altogether different: a new age in which, as he put it in his journals, "there shall not be the Atlas and the Post the Daily Advertiser & the Courier but these voices shall lose their importance in a crowd of equal & superior men."[27] Before such an age could arrive, individuals had to resist the power of newspapers and trust themselves.

Both newspapers and literary works are the instruments as well as the servants of erring humans. For Cooper and his fellow authors, however, the problem was more acute for journalism, which both wielded more influence than literature and depended more heavily on audiences and patrons, such as advertisers. These authors, however, also issued a more serious indictment of journalism, arguing that it was crippled by its very nature.

AN ERRANT GENRE

As we have seen, journalism and literature share a number of common characteristics, including a commitment to reporting some kind of truth, the use of language to convey this truth, and the employment of specific structural and linguistic elements. As journalism rose in prominence and popularity, however, it came to be known for a number of specific criteria and conventions. Remarking on several of these characteristics of newspaper journalism, one contemporary observer, writing in an 1842 issue of the *Southern Quarterly Review*, noted that "whatever is new, rare and important, is conveyed with rapidity to every reader,—is set forth in the most succinct manner, and in a style adapted to the comprehension of all."[28] Criteria and conventions such as novelty, importance, and brevity became the targets of Thoreau, Poe, Stowe, Davis, and other authors, who argued in countless critiques throughout the era that such limitations hindered or even prevented journalists in their efforts to discover and convey the truth to their readers. In short, if the shortcomings of human producers and human audiences meant that newspapers *did* not tell the truth, the very nature of journalism meant that they *could* not tell the truth.

Both authors and journalists traffic in information, but journalists deliver a particular kind, something that has come to be "news"— that is, information, usually about recent events, reported to those who have not yet learned of such events. "The primal object of the newspaper," Bowles argues in an 1851 editorial in his *Springfield Republican*, "is to give the news." Dana echoes Bowles, arguing that the "first thing which an editor must look for is news." Humans seem to have a deep thirst for news, even if the preferred type varies from person to person. Thanks to a number of factors, including the development of the printing press, newspapers became the most effective instrument for delivering news to many readers spread over a broad area, such as a town and its environs or an extensive urban area. During the antebellum era, news staffs grew, and journalists

pioneered newsgathering and transmission methods, such as the use
of expresses to outpace mail delivery and the establishment of the
Associated Press.[29]

As we have seen, most of the era's major authors read newspapers—
often, it seems, for starting points for stories or poems, but not for
news. In fact, unlike thousands of readers who thrived on the latest
intelligence about their fellow human beings, at least some of these
authors found news for the sake of news at best comical, at worst
dangerous. In *Home As Found*, Cooper has a busybody named
Mrs. Abbott send her son to eavesdrop on her neighbors at the store
and report back to her. When he says, "Suppose there is no news,"
she replies, "Then go to the nearest tavern; something must be stirring
this fine morning, and I am dying to know what it can possibly be."
This craving for news of any sort makes Mrs. Abbott a perfect counterpart of the town editor, as Cooper points out: "Mr. Dodge and
Mrs. Abbott were congenial spirits in the way of news, he living by
it, and she living on it." For Cooper, such "news" actually amounted
to gossip, as one of his characters characterizes it, saying that "people
are always ready to believe anything that will give them something
to talk about." In a hoax supposedly recounting a trans-Atlantic
balloon flight, Poe gave some New Yorkers plenty to "talk about"
and seems to have found the scene of people busying themselves
over this "news" amusing. A prefatory note that accompanied his
"Balloon Hoax" in a collection notes that the story "fully subserved
the purpose of creating indigestible aliment for the *quidnuncs*
during the few hours intervening between a couple of the Charleston
Mails." The note adds that the "rush for the 'sole paper which had
the news,' was something beyond even the prodigious." It perhaps
comes as no surprise that Poe mocked the fascination with "news."
In his poetry, personae long to leave "dull reality" and escape into
the world of dreams or other places that exist "Out of Space—out
of Time." Similarly, his tales are populated by dreamers and madmen
who block out reality, as Roderick Usher, Prince Prospero, and
C. Auguste Dupin all do by retreating to a studio or a remote palace.
What is noteworthy is that Poe, like Thoreau and others, framed his
fiction as a kind of alternative journalism, as we will see in future
chapters.[30]

The longing to escape quotidian reality may have been behind
other authors' anxieties about journalism. Especially for sailors such
as Cooper and Melville, accustomed to being detached from the
affairs of state and market for months or years on end, a newspaper
could feel like a kind of assault on the senses. Readers of *Moby-Dick*

can hear Melville's own longing for peaceful detachment in Ishmael's ruminations on life at sea:

> In the serene weather of the tropics it is exceedingly pleasant—the mast-head; nay, to a dreamy meditative man it is delightful. . . . For the most part, in this tropic whaling life, a sublime uneventfulness invests you; you hear no news; read no gazettes; extras with startling accounts of commonplaces never delude you into unnecessary excitements; you hear of no domestic afflictions; bankrupt securities; fall of stocks.[31]

On land, Melville, Cooper, and their fellow writers would have been taxed to escape such information saturation, as newspapers and newsboys met them at every turn.

For Emerson, the deluge of news was more than a source of uneasiness; it was a distraction from the truths that were to be found elsewhere, in nature and the mind. "Why covet a knowledge of new facts?" he asks in "The Poet." "Day and night, house and garden, a few books, a few actions, serve us as well as would all trades and all spectacles." He makes a similar point in "Self-Reliance," where he notes that "the whole world seems to be in conspiracy to importune you with emphatic trifles." Along with "client," "sickness," "charity," and other conspirators, he might have named newspapers, the chief vehicles for facts in many Americans' lives. For Emerson, looking outward—in newspapers, for example—for "new facts" not only was unnecessary, but also led readers away from more meaningful pursuits. In his journal, he complained: "To what base uses we put this ineffable intellect! To reading all day murders & railroad accidents."[32] Emerson may have shared his criticisms with Thoreau or been the beneficiary of his friend's own complaints: his comments about the misguided appetite for news are remarkably similar to the ones Thoreau expresses in *Walden*. As we will see in the next chapter, Thoreau's disdain for "news" was actually a disdain for the kind of news reported in newspapers and treasured by readers—that is, reports of external events. He explicitly rejected the entire endeavor of both reading and reporting "news"—at least the kind found in newspapers. "Blessed are they who never read a newspaper," he says in a letter to Parker Pillsbury, "for they shall see Nature, and through her, God." Thoreau contrasted the sort of news found in newspapers with the brand that he sought to report in *Walden*: truths extracted from the natural world.

If authors questioned readers' obsession with news, they also expressed reservations about the nature of this news. As we have seen in Chapter 1, the "information model" was taking over as the dominant pattern for journalism in the antebellum era. The press, Hazel Dicken-Garcia explains, tended to report on events rather than ideas.[33] Although they continued to publish poetry and fiction—as well as the occasional hoax—throughout the nineteenth century, newspapers were primarily conduits for facts. For authors of poetry, fiction, and even nonfiction, which itself relies largely on ideas and not only on facts, truth is a matter of more than mere information. This belief was especially strong in the antebellum era, when romanticists such as Poe, Hawthorne, and Melville were determined to penetrate surfaces in their searches for truth—or, as Ahab puts it in *Moby-Dick*, to "strike through the mask." Furthermore, authors often concerned themselves with larger principles, not mere details.

For these reasons, many of the complaints that issued from these authors' pens concerned the factual nature of journalistic reporting. In *Home As Found*, Cooper complains:

> The Americans . . . are a people of facts and practices, paying but little attention to principles, and giving themselves the very minimum of time for investigations that lie beyond the reach of the common mind; and it follows that they know little of that which does not present itself in their every-day transactions.

As we will see, Poe makes a similar observation in "The Unparalleled Adventure of One Hans Pfaall," where he notes that some people deem a story a hoax if it exceeds their power of understanding. Such people, Poe implies, understand only facts, not the kinds of higher truths that authors of literature seek to report. For these authors, reporting truth requires the use of the imagination and the intellect. Facts are merely facts; the truth is something else. Indeed, in an 1851 letter, Thoreau places facts below the products of the mind in the measure of truth. "I find that actual events, notwithstanding the singular prominence which we all allow them, are far less real than the creations of my imagination," he explains. "They are truly visionary and insignificant,—all that we commonly call life and death,—and affect me less than my dreams." He goes on to say that he tells himself, "Do not read the newspapers." These vehicles of facts, it seems, held nothing for him. As we will see, Thoreau actually expressed a deep reverence for some facts, namely those of the natural world, but valued them as signs of deeper truths. In this regard, he resembles Emerson, who stressed the importance of facts, but called for artists to translate them. In "The Poet," Emerson argues that "the highest minds of the world have never ceased to explore the double meaning, or, shall I say, the quadruple, or the centuple, or much more manifold meaning, of every sensuous fact: Orpheus, Empedocles, Heraclitus, Plato, Plutarch, Dante, Swedenborg, and the masters of sculpture, picture, and poetry."[34]

For authors, the problem with journalism was not that it reported facts, but that it treated these facts as truths in and of themselves—or, at least, readers may have been led to believe as much. Cooper, Poe, Thoreau, and Emerson may very well have agreed with the distinction suggested by media theorist Walter Lippmann. "The function of news is to signalize an event," Lippmann argues in *Public Opinion*, "the function of truth is to bring to light the hidden facts, to set them into relation with each other, and make a picture of reality on which men can act." Lippmann does not argue that journalism is, by its very nature, incapable of reporting truth, but that restrictions on such things as time and funds hinder its ability to perform this function.[35] Authors of the antebellum era pointed to other restrictions, including the criteria journalists used in determining what to report in their newspapers.

As noted in Chapter 1, journalists employ a conventional set of criteria when determining what to cover. These criteria, or "news values," include timeliness, impact, proximity, prominence, conflict, novelty, and currency. Today, students of journalism encounter these news values in textbooks and in their professors' lectures. In the nineteenth century, before the prevalence of college journalism programs, some journalists must have learned news criteria on the job. In any case, these conventions meant that some stories would make it into newspapers, while others would not—or, at least, not in a prominent place. Accounts of events that took place months or years earlier, essays about matters that seem to have little impact on readers, and descriptions of the ordinary were not "news," no matter how much "truth" they might contain. Stacked up against reports of the latest developments in a sensational murder trial, Thoreau's coverage of the natural world at Walden Pond and Dickinson's reports of emotional experiences had little chance of being a significant part of newspaper coverage.

One of the criteria that authors singled out for specific comment is timeliness. This criterion, perhaps more than any other, shaped the content of the daily newspaper in the antebellum era. In the early days of American journalism, the lack of fast transportation and communication systems meant that the information that appeared in newspapers might be months old. Some editors, furthermore, published historical accounts and other material with no obvious immediacy. By the 1830s, however, the criterion of timeliness was firmly in place. In fact, as Norma Green has noted, Benjamin Day and other editors "touted timeliness" and "attempted to build a news habit among impulse buyers with multiple daily editions that updated the front page with fresh headlines, episodic stories, and often new illustrations throughout the day." Later, the transcontinental telegraph and the trans-Atlantic cable enabled newspapers to speed the delivery of news from other parts of the country or other parts of the world. In a piece called "Annihilation of Space," one newspaper item praised the news-reporting possibilities of the telegraph, saying, "In addition to our usual facilities, we expect to be able by the agency of Prof. Morse's Magnetic Telegraph—the most wonderful and useful invention of the age—to give reports of the proceedings of the two houses up to two o'clock of each day, in our paper of the same day."[36]

The very notion that information had greater value simply because it happened yesterday instead of a year or a century or a millennium ago seems to have baffled and angered the era's authors. Poe noted that the "sole legitimate object" of newspapers was "the discussion of ephemeral matters in an ephemeral manner," implying that fires, ship arrivals, and political debates are of only passing significance, especially if the reporters of this news treat only the events themselves and not their lasting significance. In "Experience," Emerson speaks of men who ask about the news "as if the old were so bad." In *Home As Found*, Cooper locates a possible reason for the obsession with timely information. "An American 'always,' in the way of usages, extends no further back than eighteen months," he explains. "In short, everything is condensed into the present moment; and services, character, for evil as well as good unhappily, and all other things cease to have weight, except as they influence the interests of the day."[37] Whatever the cause, American newspaper readers were content to devour timely facts while authors set their eyes on timeless truths.

Another news criterion that drew fire from authors is impact, perhaps the second most important factor shaping news coverage. For at least two centuries, journalists and their readers have believed that a newspaper is responsible for reporting events that have potential consequences for many people's lives. A glance at the front page of just about any mainstream daily newspaper from the antebellum era would show that the news thought most influential was the news that dealt with politics, the law, and business. Today, serious news-paper readers are likely to complain that some newspapers do not sufficiently cover stories on these topics. In the nineteenth century, however, authors sometimes implied that newspapers provided too much coverage of them while ignoring other stories of great importance. As we will see in the next chapter, both Thoreau and Dickinson sought to fill this gap with news of their own about nature, human emotions, and spiritual matters.

Other news criteria also shaped the contents of newspapers. As noted in Chapter 1, the prominence of the people, the novelty of the incidents, or the presence of conflict in any given event increased the likelihood that journalists would cover it for their readers. All three of these criteria belong to the larger category of "human interest," which was a major driving force behind journalists' attempts to draw and satisfy their audiences. As we have seen, the predominance of human-interest criteria in the age of sensationalism left some authors concerned that journalists were more interested in producing good copy—defined as material that would delight and satisfy their readers—than in pursuing the truth. As authors would have it, given the choice between the story and the truth, journalists were choosing the story.

In the eyes of authors, then, journalists were hemmed in by their emphasis on "news" and facts, as well as criteria, such as timeliness and impact. Further complicating their communication of truth are the formal conventions that began to solidify in the nineteenth century. Brevity came to be the rule for many news items because of limits on time and space. As Hazel Dicken-Garcia explains, the exigencies of collecting news and publishing a daily newspaper left journalists little time to produce the kinds of "idea-centered" essays that had been common in earlier papers. A typical paper from the 1830s or 1840s contained only four pages, and advertising often swallowed all or much of the first and fourth pages, leaving an editor two pages for coverage of local crime, disasters, and politics, as well as news from Washington and abroad, exchanges from other American papers, and the "human interest" news that readers craved. If an event happened to be sensational, as in the case of the Jewett murder, editors lavished huge stretches of newsprint on minute details, but most events were summarized in a paragraph or even a few lines. The advent of the telegraph provided additional incentive to write concisely, as papers had to pay according to the length of their transmissions. As we will see in Chapter 6, Davis took aim at the brevity of newspaper coverage in "Life in the Iron-Mills," where a journalist has apparently told the Hugh Wolfe story—the same story that Davis tells in thousands of words—in a handful of sentence fragments. Such coverage necessarily omitted background information necessary for a full understanding of the whole truth of a story. The act of packaging events as "news" imposed additional limitations, as Cooper suggests in *Home As Found*. Steadfast Dodge, Cooper explains, "may be succinctly said to have a newspaper mind, as he reduces everything in nature or art to news, and commonly imparts to it so much of his own peculiar character, that it loses all identity with the subjects to which it originally belonged."[38]

NEWS OF THEIR OWN

Despite all of these reservations about journalists and journalism, authors frequently referred to "news" in neutral or even favorable ways. *Moby-Dick* is a case in point. Despite his pleasurable ruminations about a life free from the information found in "gazettes" and "extras," Ishmael shows a genuine interest in other kinds of news, as do other characters in the novel. They seek, welcome, and deliver, for example, "the latest news from the Feegees" and "strong news of Moby Dick." A gam, furthermore, provides seamen with an opportunity to "interchange the news." Ishmael even frames the message that some of the whalers receive from a dying whale below the sea's surface as a kind of news transmission when he describes the whale lines in a way that makes them resemble telegraph lines—a particularly timely analogy in the middle of the nineteenth century. He notes that "the three lines suddenly vibrated in the water, distinctly conducting upwards to them, as by magnetic wires, the life and death throbs of the whale, so that every oarsman felt them in his seat." The problem, then, lay not in news, but in the kind of news reported in mainstream papers and the way it was being reported. In response to these inadequacies, many of these authors offered literature as a kind of superior alternative to the brief, fact-centered coverage of timely, "important," or sensational events found in newspapers. It is, for instance, no accident that Melville's Pip—the mad artist/prophet so common in romantic literature—calls himself a "ship's-crier." He has news for Ahab, but he delivers it in the indirect fashion typical of literature. Hawthorne points to the role of literature in "covering" the world when he asserts: "A work of genius is but the newspaper of a century."[39]

Perhaps no author was more explicit and extensive in his endorsement of literature as a vehicle for truth-telling than Emerson. As we have seen, Emerson viewed America as a great poem awaiting expression and nature itself as body of truths to be read and translated. Someone, of course, would have to do the expressing, the reading, and the translating, and this someone was the writer of literature. "I find a provision in the constitution of the world for the writer or secretary, who is to report the doings of the miraculous spirit of life that everywhere throbs and works," he explains in his essay on Goethe in *Representative Men*. "His office is a reception of the facts into the mind, and then a selection of the eminent and characteristic experiences." This description of collecting facts and "editing" them for publication would seem to be exactly that of the journalist. At midcentury, when he wrote these words, Emerson could have pointed to any number of journalists, such as his acquaintance Greeley, as exemplars of the function of reporter and editor. Since they often pass along mere facts, however, journalists would seem to belong to Emerson's inferior category of reporter, one who sought mere "imitative expression," which amounts to "mere stenography." Indeed, although he does not mention journalists by name, he seems to have them, as well as their excited readers, in mind when he describes one brand of reporting:

> The ambitious and mercenary bring their last new mumbojumbo, whether tariff, Texas, railroad, Romanism, mesmerism, or California; and, by detaching the object from its relations, easily succeed in making it seen in a glare; and a multitude go mad about it, and they are not to be reproved or cured by the opposite multitude who are kept from this particular insanity by an equal frenzy on another crotchet.

Such material, the kind commonly found in the newspapers Emerson saw, contains information, but not basic principles or spiritual truths. In isolation, details of Texas, tariffs, and other newsworthy material amount to mere "mumbojumbo."[40]

Truth-telling, Emerson believed, requires not mere transcription, but translation. In the kind of reporting he espouses, "the report is something more than print of the seal" and constitutes "a new and finer form of the original." For Emerson, the writer plays an active role; he does not merely record bare facts, but "cooperates." Some humans, he adds, are equipped "with exalted powers for this second creation"; those humans are the world's poets. He explains, "There are higher degrees, and nature has more splendid endowments for those whom she elects to a superior office; for the class of scholars or writers, namely, who see connexion, where the multitude see fragments, and who are impelled to exhibit the facts in ideal order, and so to supply the axis on which the frame of things turns." Part of the problem with journalism, Emerson argues later in the essay, is that it lacks a human presence. "It makes a great difference to the force of any sentence, whether there be a man behind it, or no," he explains. "In the learned journal, in the influential newspaper, I discern no form, only some irresponsible shadow; oftener, some monied corporation, or some dangler, who hopes in the mask and robes of his paragraph, to pass for somebody." Emerson makes a similar argument for the active role of the writer in "The Poet." Here, he characterizes the poet as a "teller of news," but argues that this kind of reporter delivers not mere "color" or "form," but also "meaning." The one who best expresses America and nature, then, is not the reporter of bare facts, as the journalist might be seen to be, but the creative writer, who employs the imagination to interpret facts and produce a "second creation."[41]

Other authors issued their own, implicit arguments for the superior truth-telling capacity of literature. Indeed, both Thoreau and Dickinson seem to have enacted Emerson's theory.[42] Both "covered" nature and the self in what we might call "dispatches from the fringe," a brand of truth-telling that they framed as a form of alternative journalism. Much of Poe's work, furthermore, can be read as a kind of endorsement of the imagination, as Terence Martin has suggested, noting that Poe "leaps far beyond any social strictures by the master stroke of denying the reality of everything but the imagination."[43] In some of his tales, Poe makes a case for truth in fiction and crafts hoaxes that deliver "news of the possible" to a mass audience. Finally, Poe, Stowe, and Davis all exposed hidden truths in what we might call "investigative fiction." These authors' "news of their own" is the subject of the next three chapters.

PART II

NEWS OF THEIR OWN

CHAPTER 4

DISPATCHES FROM THE FRINGE

Readers of Henry David Thoreau's *Walden* are sometimes at a loss for what to call it. Is it an autobiography, a travel narrative, a prose poem? The book itself contains a hint, one that most readers have probably overlooked. "So many autumn, ay, and winter days, spent outside the town," Thoreau writes in the early pages of the book, "trying to hear what was in the wind, to hear and carry it express! I well-nigh sunk all my capital in it, and lost my own breath into the bargain, running in the face of it. If it had concerned either of the political parties, depend upon it, it would have appeared in the Gazette with the earliest intelligence."[1] Is *Walden*, Thoreau's lyrical and literary account of a life outside civilization, a news report?

Of all the important American writers of the antebellum era, the two whom one would be least likely to associate with journalism might be Henry David Thoreau and Emily Dickinson. Living sometimes on the outskirts of the public world, where they penned highly personal, unconventional somethings—letters? lyrics? journals?—for relatively small audiences, Thoreau and Dickinson seem more like quirky hermits than journalists, even of the literary stripe. That the private, natural worlds they represented also produced news worthy of attention, however, is exactly the point of works such as *Walden* and "This is My Letter to the World." Here and elsewhere, Thoreau and Dickinson framed their reports of nature, the self, and the divine as alternative forms of journalism.

REPORTING "WHAT WAS IN THE WIND"

John Carlos Rowe has compared *Walden* to a travel guide, writing that it is "primarily intended as a Baedeker to the order of nature, the primacy of which remains unquestioned."[2] Its numerous references to news and newspapers, however, suggest another way of reading *Walden*. Thoreau, who blasted the journalistic enterprise elsewhere in his writing, presents his book as an alternative to newspapers, one that reports the deep truths of nature instead of the superficial gossip of mankind.

Thoreau recognized the prominence that American journalism had achieved. In "Slavery in Massachusetts," he says:

> The newspaper is a Bible which we read every morning and every afternoon, standing and sitting, riding and walking. It is a Bible which every man carries in his pocket, which lies on every table and counter, and which the mail, and thousands of missionaries, are continually dispensing. It is, in short, the only book which America has printed, and which America reads. So wide is its influence.

Ubiquity, however, does not translate into reliability. Thoreau goes on to compare the newspaper editor to a preacher and asks, "But how many of these preachers preach the truth?" He compares editors to "tyrants" and adds, "And as they live and rule only by their servility, and appealing to the worst, and not the better nature of man, the people who read them are in the condition of the dog that returns to his vomit."[3]

As these words suggest, Thoreau was among the most virulent critics of journalism in the nineteenth century. In a letter to Parker Pillsbury, he says, "As for my prospective reader, I hope that he *ignores* Fort Sumpter, & Old Abe, & all that. . . . I do not so much regret the present condition of things in this country (provided I regret it at all) as I do that I ever heard of it." His position on journalism is nicely summed up in this admonition to himself: "Do not read the newspapers." Thoreau actually had some significant brushes with journalism, having published an article in a newspaper and served as an editor of the *Dial*. Furthermore, as Reynolds explains, "Thoreau knew the popular press well enough to speak of 'startling and monstrous events as fill the daily papers.'"[4] In short, Thoreau was sufficiently familiar with journalism to know what was, in his opinion, wrong with it—and to offer a substitute in the form of news of his own.

As we have seen in the previous chapter, Thoreau deplored the "servility" of some newspapers, which he felt were slaves to business interests. In *Walden*, he issues a subtler, more complex critique of the press than the one that appears in "Slavery in Massachusetts."[5] Much of what he had to say in this book reveals an overarching doubt about the very value of journalism as an endeavor. "We are a race of tit-men," he complains, "and soar but little higher in our intellectual flights than the columns of the daily paper" (107). In one of his many stabs at gossip—a major component of journalism then and now—he writes:

> My neighbors tell me of their adventures with famous gentlemen and ladies, what notabilities they met at the dinner-table; but I am no more interested in such things than in the contents of the Daily Times. The interest and the conversation are about costume and manners chiefly; but a goose is a goose still, dress it as you will. They tell me of California and Texas, of England and the Indies, of the Hon. Mr. —— of Georgia or of Massachusetts, all transient and fleeting phenomena, till I am ready to leap from their court-yard like the Mameluke bey. (329)

Thoreau clearly had journalism in mind when he referred in *Walden* to "a hundred 'modern improvements'" and the "illusion" that accompanies them, noting that "there is not always a positive advance." He explains:

> Our inventions are wont to be pretty toys, which distract our attention from serious things. They are but improved means to an unimproved end, an end which it was already but too easy to arrive at; as railroads lead to Boston or New York. We are in great haste to construct a magnetic telegraph from Maine to Texas; but Maine and Texas, it may be, have nothing important to communicate. . . . As if the main object were to talk fast and not to talk sensibly. We are eager to tunnel under the Atlantic and bring the old world some weeks nearer to the new; but perchance the first news that will leak through into the broad, flapping American ear will be that the Princess Adelaide has the whooping cough. (52)

The reference to "means" captures journalism's position as an intermediary akin to literature. Unlike literature, however, this medium was noteworthy for its speed. During Thoreau's lifetime, news was getting newer. In the 1830s and 1840s, newsboys peddled extra editions with updated developments on sensational stories. The telegraph, perfected by Samuel Morse in the 1840s, revolutionized communication, making it possible for newspapers to report on developments in faraway places hours instead of days or weeks after they occurred. Thoreau's criticism is clear: no matter how fast it can travel, some news is just not all that important, at least to him. His particular reference to a princess's illness may be taken as a dig at "human interest" news—the status of the princess would qualify her illness as "news" under the criterion of prominence—and newspapers of the nineteenth century published much of such news.

Thoreau, however, also doubted much of what his contemporaries and many modern readers would consider legitimate news content, including material that satisfies the criteria of impact and timeliness. Elsewhere in *Walden*, he writes:

> And I am sure that I never read any memorable news in a newspaper. If we read of one man robbed, or murdered, or killed by accident, or one house burned, or one vessel wrecked, or one steamboat blown up, or one cow run over on the Western Railroad, or one mad dog killed, or one lot of grasshoppers in the winter,—we never need read of another. One is enough. If you are acquainted with the principle, what do you care for a myriad instances and applications? (94)

The complaint here does not concern the tendency of newspapers to publish lightweight "human interest" news; robberies, murders, and fires all generally would qualify as "newsworthy" material on the basis of other news values, and Thoreau does not question their "impact," as he implicitly questions the value of news about a princess's illness. Rather, Thoreau finds the reporting of similar facts redundant; what really matters, he argues, is the underlying "principle," which is timeless. The word "principle," in fact, is the key to both Thoreau's dispute with journalism and his own motives in reporting the news of nature. Like the ancient philosophers mentioned in Chapter 1, Thoreau sought to understand not superficial facts, but abstract truths. He alludes to Plato's allegory of the cave when he criticizes his contemporaries' obsession with news:

> Hardly a man takes a half hour's nap after dinner, but when he wakes he holds up his head and asks, "What's the news?" as if the rest of mankind had stood his sentinels. Some give directions to be waked every half hour, doubtless for no other purpose; and then, to pay for it, they tell what they have dreamed. After a night's sleep the news is as indispensable as the breakfast. "Pray tell me any thing new that has happened to a man any where on this globe",—and he reads it over his coffee and rolls, that a man has had his eyes gouged out this morning on the Wachito River; never dreaming the while that he lives in the dark unfathomed mammoth cave of this world, and has but the rudiment of an eye himself. (93–94)

Like the chained inhabitants of the cave Socrates describes in Plato's *Republic*, this imaginary newspaper reader fails to recognize the real truth. In reporting timely facts instead of timeless truths, newspapers were at least partly to blame for the state of affairs Thoreau describes a few paragraphs later when he complains: "Shams and delusions are esteemed for soundest truths, while reality is fabulous" (95). Newspapers encouraged Americans to seek the latest news, whereas Thoreau felt that a separation from time improved perception of truth, or "reality." "When we are unhurried and wise," he says, "we perceive that only great and worthy things have any permanent and absolute existence,—that petty fears and petty pleasures are but the shadow of the reality" (95–96).

Walden is Thoreau's account of being "unhurried and wise," of seeing nature and through it the "principles" that constitute higher truth. More than that, it is an attempt to report this truth—what Dickinson would later call "the simple News that Nature told" and what Thoreau himself called simply "the meaning of Nature"—to readers who were being deluded by newspapers.[6] "Perhaps the facts most astounding and most real are never communicated by man to man," he observes in the section called "Higher Laws." "The true harvest of my daily life is somewhat as intangible and indescribable as the tints of morning or evening. It is a little star-dust caught, a segment of the rainbow which I have clutched" (216–17). Thoreau's famous explanation of the motive behind his experiment betrays his purpose:

> I went to the woods because I wished to live deliberately, to front only the essential facts of life, and see if I could not learn what it had to teach, and not, when I came to die, discover that I had not lived. . . . I wanted to live deep and suck out all the marrow of life, . . . to drive life into a corner, and reduce it to its lowest terms, and, if it proved to be mean, why then to get the whole and genuine meanness of it, and publish its meanness to the world; or if it were sublime, to know it by experience, and be able to give a true account of it in my next excursion. (90–91)

A few paragraphs later, he adds, "My instinct tells me that my head is an organ for burrowing, as some creatures use their snout and fore-paws, and with it I would mine and burrow my way through these hills. I think that the richest vein is somewhere hereabouts; so by the divining rod and thin rising vapors I judge; and here I will begin to mine" (98).[7] In these two passages, then, Thoreau points to his dual purpose—that is, to study life and to report his findings to the rest of the world. In both his intent to "mine" material from the world about him and his plan to "publish" his findings, Thoreau resembles his counterparts in journalism. While newspaper reporters were covering people and events that satisfied emerging news values such as impact and human interest, Thoreau was busy covering the natural world, which he considered a window on a deeper reality.

Much of *Walden* consists of Thoreau's descriptions of natural phenomena: bubbles in the ice, the war of the ants, the escapades of an elusive loon, the "forms which thawing sand and clay assume in flowing down the sides of a deep cut on the railroad" (304). The language in this last description is revealing: "forms," in ancient Greek philosophy, are the eternal principles that underlie surface reality. As Philip Gura has noted, Thoreau "believed that by assiduously studying nature one could arrive at the absolute ground of being."[8] In many instances, Thoreau draws parallels between the phenomena he describes and other aspects of existence, thus pointing to their universal significance. The ants he observes in battle, for instance, remind him of men, and he says, "The more you think of it, the less the difference" (230). Elsewhere, he writes:

> What I have observed of the pond is no less true in ethics. It is the law of average. Such a rule of the two diameters not only guides us toward the sun in the system and the heart in man, but draw lines through the length and breadth of the aggregate of a man's particular daily behaviors and waves of life into his coves and inlets, and where they intersect will be the height or depth of his character. Perhaps we need only to know how his shores trend and his adjacent country or circumstances, to infer his depth and concealed bottom. (291)

Similar reflections accompany the description of the effect of rain on grass and the observation on the enduring freshness of ice.[9] The most noteworthy of Thoreau's reflections on the universal significance of natural phenomena is his lengthy treatment of the "forms" found in the sandbank as winter gives way to spring. Here, as Gura and others have noted, Thoreau finds in the lobes he observes in the sand a pattern underlying creation: "Thus it seemed that this one hillside illustrated the principle of all the operations of Nature. The Maker of this earth but patented a leaf" (308). As Robert Sattelmeyer observes, "the thawing sandbank is not intended by Thoreau as a figurative equivalent of his own awakening but rather as evidence of the operation of a law that animates both nature and man."[10]

Reporting on nature, then, was Thoreau's own form of truth-telling, one that he explicitly and implicitly contrasts with journalism. Beginning with his analogy between reporting "what was in the wind" and covering "the political parties," Thoreau sets up *Walden* as an alternative to newspapers, as a kind of "news of his own." Indeed, he characterizes himself as a kind of journalist when he says, "For a long time I was reporter to a journal, of no very wide circulation, whose editor has never yet seen fit to print the bulk of my contributions, and, as is too common with writers, I got only my labor for my pains" (18). As Jeffrey Cramer has noted, this line may refer to writings that Thoreau submitted to *The Dial*, but it likely is a description of his own journals. Unlike a newspaper reporter covering events deemed newsworthy according to conventional news values, he reported on his own personal observations. Furthermore, Thoreau seems to have seen himself as a mediator akin to the journalist. He became fascinated with the work of philologist Charles Kraitsir, who had argued, "Man is a mirror of, but also a mediator between, all objects felt without and within himself, as well as between these objects and his own spirit on the one side, and between his spirit and that of his neighbors on the other." In *Walden*, Thoreau enacts a reorganization of news reporting similar to the one he advocated in "Slavery in Massachusetts," in which he had argued that Massachusetts "has few, if any organs, through which to express herself." He continues, "The editorials which she reads, like the news, come from the sea-board. . . . Let us not send to the city for aught more essential than our broadcloths and groceries, or, if we read the opinions of the city, let us entertain opinions of our own."[11] The contrasts between the mainstream news reporting that was taking shape in the antebellum era and Thoreau's own brand of journalism can be seen at various points throughout *Walden*, particularly in two mirror chapters situated near the center of the book.

In "The Village," Thoreau captures, both explicitly and implicitly, some of the basic features of conventional journalism. He notes, first, that he goes into town "to hear some of the gossip which is incessantly going on there, circulating either from mouth to mouth, or from newspaper to newspaper" (167). Thoreau's language is telling: the kind of news making the rounds of both people and newspapers is "gossip," a pejorative term for shallow, often mean-spirited information. Later in this first paragraph of the chapter, Thoreau again refers to journalism. Noting that the village resembles "a great news room" (167), he says:

> Some have such a vast appetite for the former commodity, that is, the news, and such sound digestive organs, that they can sit forever in public avenues without stirring, and let it simmer and whisper through them like the Etesian winds, or as if inhaling ether, it only producing numbness and insensibility to pain,—otherwise it would often be painful to hear,—without affecting the consciousness. (167–68)

In this paradoxical image, villagers crave news, but this news seems to have little effect on them, except to numb them to their surroundings. Perhaps the most potent parts of this "great news room" are the signs, which "were hung out on all sides to allure him [the "traveller" in the village]; some to catch him by the appetite, as the tavern and victualling cellar; some by the fancy, as the dry goods store and the jeweller's; and others by the hair or the feet or the skirts, as the barber, the shoemaker, or the tailor" (168). Such signs, of course, are advertisements, but in this context they appear specifically as newspaper ads.[12] The "standing invitation to call at every one of these houses," which the traveler also encounters, could represent various kinds of newspaper announcements, as of lyceums and revivals (168). Thoreau adds that he "escaped wonderfully from these dangers" by aiming for his destination or by concentrating "on high things, like Orpheus, who, 'loudly singing the praises of the gods to his lyre, drowned the voices of the Sirens, and kept out of danger'" (168–69). The allusion to the musician Orpheus is significant; as Theodore Dreiser would do a half-century later in *Sister Carrie*, Thoreau sets up a contrast between the low appeals of newspapers and the "high things" one can find through art.[13] When he does enter houses, he hears "the kernels and very last sieve-ful of news, what had subsided, the prospects of war and peace, and whether the world was likely to hold together much longer" (169). In this last remark, he mocks the grand conceptions that journalists had of their work—and perhaps similar conceptions held by those who read the newspapers. Finally, Thoreau describes his escape from this "great news room" and "to the woods again" (169). His escape destination is significant, not only because of the contrast between village and nature, but also because of the parallel Thoreau has drawn between conventional journalism, which covers the one, and unconventional journalism, which covers the other. Earlier in this same chapter, he notes that the gossip in the village is "as refreshing in its way as the rustle of leaves and the peeping of frogs" (167) and observes that some of the villagers, "being commonly out of doors, heard whatever was in the wind" (168). Both of these statements draw attention to the two kinds of news; the latter recalls Thoreau's characterization of his own form of newsgathering when he strove "to hear what was in the wind."

In the next chapter, "The Ponds," Thoreau describes a return to a natural setting, where he can conduct his unconventional journalism. The first sentence begins, "Sometimes, having had a surfeit of human society and gossip, and worn out all my village friends, I rambled still farther westward than I habitually dwell, into yet more unfrequented parts of the town, 'to fresh woods and pastures new'" (173). If the village was the site of gossip and numbing news, this new destination is a place of art and nature, both succinctly suggested by the allusion to John Milton's pastoral poem "Lycidas." In the village, he had encountered incessant gossip; on the pond, he sits with a deaf fisherman: "Our intercourse was thus altogether one of unbroken harmony, far more pleasing to remember than if it had been carried on by speech" (174). As Thoreau's subsequent descriptions reveal, he manages a different sort of colloquy here. As if interviewing the principles in the world he is covering, he hits his boat with his paddle, and animals around him respond. He plays a flute, and a perch lingers near him. Later in the chapter, he launches a lengthy description of Walden Pond. As Thoreau has it in "The Ponds," nature reports itself to the careful observer—one who is, like him, "determined to know beans" (161). Situated atop a hill, Thoreau can read the news of the pond, as when a fish breaks the surface of the water to eat an insect. He concludes, "It is wonderful with what elaborateness this simple fact is advertised,—this piscine murder will out,—and from my distant perch I distinguish circling undulations when they are half a dozen rods in diameter" (187). Furthermore, one needs only the simplest technology to gather this news. In what may be a subtle joke on the telegraph, introduced only a few years before Thoreau's move to Walden, the author depicts himself gathering the news of nature by a different kind of line when he describes fishing in the pond. He launches his account with an account of leaving civilization and retreating to "the woods" (174). He proceeds to describe "communicating" by means of a line with a world hidden in the depths of Walden Pond:

> These experiences were very memorable and valuable to me,—anchored in forty feet of water, and twenty or thirty rods from the shore, surrounded sometimes by thousands of small perch and shiners . . . and communicating by a long flaxen line with mysterious nocturnal fishes which had their dwelling forty feet below, or sometimes dragging sixty feet of line about the pond as I drifted in the gentle night breeze, now and then feeling a slight vibration along it, indicative of some life prowling about its extremity, of dull uncertain blundering purpose there, and slow to make up its mind. . . . It was very queer, especially in dark nights, when your thoughts had wandered to vast and cosmogonal themes in other spheres, to feel this faint jerk, which came to interrupt your dreams and link you to Nature again. (175)

Like Morse's telegraph line, Thoreau's fishing line transmits news from another place. Whereas Maine and Texas may "have nothing important to communicate," however, this natural world holds, for Thoreau, elemental and timeless truths. As a dutiful reporter covering the beat of the natural world, Thoreau passes on this news of nature to the readers of his dispatches.

In doing so, he employs a form of expression different from the straightforward language of journalism. Later in *Walden*, he complains, "It is a ridiculous demand which England and America make, that you shall speak so that they can understand you," and adds, "I fear chiefly lest my expression may not be *extra-vagant* enough, may not wander far enough beyond the narrow limits of my daily experience, so as to be adequate to the truth of which I have been convinced" (324). The abstract truth he seeks to report requires a literary language. As we saw in Chapter 1, authors such as Emerson and Melville appreciated the limits of language and employed the indirect, suggestive tools of literary expression to capture the truth.

For all of his differences with journalism, however, Thoreau maintained a crucial link with his newspaper counterparts. Knowing that the imagination could carry a person away from the truth, whether of the physical or the spiritual world, he anchored his reporting in fact. He called on humans to penetrate "the mud and slush of opinion, and prejudice, and tradition" until they arrive at "a hard bottom and rocks in place, which we can call *reality*, and say, This is, and no mistake; and then begin, having a *point d'appui*" (97–98). In a passage particularly important for truth-tellers of all sorts, Thoreau observes, "It is remarkable how long men will believe in the bottomlessness of a pond without taking the trouble to sound it" and notes that he determined Walden's depth—"exactly one hundred and two feet"—by engaging with its physical reality. "I fathomed it easily with a cod-line and a stone weighing about a pound and a half," he explains, "and could tell accurately when the stone left the bottom, by having to pull so much harder before the water got underneath to help me" (285–87). In saying that he "fathomed" Walden, Thoreau is of course speaking literally, but the word also refers to the intellectual process by which humans attempt to understand, to reach the depths, of reality in general. If they are not careful to remain close to the facts—whether those facts relate to loons and ponds or to humans and societies—their conclusions may stray from the truth. Although "the imagination, give it the least license, dives deeper and soars higher than Nature goes" (288), the truth has limits: "There is a solid bottom every where" (330). Thoreau made a similar point in a letter he wrote to H. G. O. Blake. Evoking a mathematician's practice of simplifying problems by removing "incumbrances," Thoreau explained the he "would stand upon facts."[14] Both journalistic and literary truth-tellers would be wise to heed Thoreau's advice in *Walden*: "In sane moments we regard only the facts, the case that is. Say what you have to say, not what you ought. Any truth is better than make-believe" (327).

"THE SIMPLE NEWS THAT NATURE TOLD"

If there is any major American writer more peripheral that Thoreau, it is Emily Dickinson, who, as Thomas Johnson has noted, "did not live in history and held no view of it, past or current."[15] Unlike Whitman, with whom she is often compared, she never worked for a newspaper; only seldom, in fact, did she venture into the society on which newspapers report. News, however, interested, even preoccupied Dickinson. The evidence is right there in her poems, where dozens of references to "News," "News-Boys," "Bulletins," and reporters betray an appetite for, even an awful respect for, the information that passes from human to human and from nature to human. The news that most interested Dickinson, however, was not the news that made up much of the contemporary papers of the era. Like Thoreau, Dickinson openly doubted the value of the kind of news found in these papers, but framed her literature as a kind of alternative journalism in which she reported the news that really mattered.

References to "News-Boys" and "Bulletins" might seem uncharacteristic of a poet seemingly so remote from society, but we should remember that even Dickinson was not immune to the pervasive presence and influence of the press in the decades before the Civil War, nor did she wish to be. As we have seen, she regularly read the *Springfield Republican* and other periodicals and even seems to have clipped and stored items she found in the press. The editor of the *Republican*, Samuel Bowles, was a friend of the family, perhaps even the mysterious "Master" Dickinson revered in several of her letters.

Furthermore, if Dickinson never wrote for a newspaper, she nevertheless played the role of a reporter for much of her life. Serving in a capacity familiar to many women of the era, she regularly exchanged news with friends and family members through personal correspondence. Cristanne Miller notes that she was "the letter writer of the Dickinson family, taking over her mother's function of keeping her brother Austin informed about the doings at home and passing on her parents' and sister's messages." Like her friend Bowles, she was a kind of intermediary, in her case linking the family at home with an outside audience.[16] This function can be seen in a letter she wrote to Austin in October 1851. The first several paragraphs contain what we might call "personal" communication: a description of the reception of Austin's letter ("I received what you wrote, at about 2 ½ oclock yesterday."), a response to its content ("You say we must'nt trouble to send you any fruit, also your clothes must give us no uneasiness. I dont ever want to have you say any more such things."), and regards from a mutual acquaintance ("Martha wants to see you very much indeed, and sends her love to you."). Midway through the paragraph in which she mentions Martha, Dickinson turns explicitly to the business of reporting the "news":

> Vinnie tells me *she* has detailed the *news*—she reserved the *deaths* for me, thinking I might fall short of my usual letter somewhere. In accordance with her wishes, I acquaint you with the decease of your aged friend—Dea Kingsbury. He had no disease that we know of, but gradually went out. Martha Kingman has been very sick, and is not yet out of danger. Jane Grout is slowly improving, tho' very feeble yet.

Here, Dickinson acknowledges her regular role as family reporter—the writer of the "usual letter"—and provides what was then and still is common newspaper content, an obituary, along with news of the health of various individuals. She goes on to report on the plans and doings of other individuals ("Father has written to Monson to have them all come up here and make us a family visit. . . . Howland has gone to Conway—will probably be here again in the course of two or three weeks.") and to describe a striking event in town:

> There was quite an excitement in the village Monday evening. We were all startled by a violent church bell ringing, and thinking of nothing but fire, rushed out in the street to see. The sky was a beautiful red, bordering on a crimson, and rays of a gold pink color were constantly shooting off from a kind of sun in the centre. People were alarmed at this beautiful Phenomenon, supposing that fires somewhere were *coloring the sky*. The exhibition lasted for nearly 15. minutes, and the streets were full of people wondering and admiring.

Here and in other letters, Dickinson frames the content of her reports as "news." The exchange of news was an important part of correspondence in the nineteenth century, as indeed it is today. In some of her letters to Annie Fields, wife of her publisher James T. Fields, Rebecca Harding Davis practically demanded such reports. In one such letter, she says, "<u>Do</u> write—[tell?] me every thing you have done or thought or said—all the news—new ideas—spirits—books—people—scandal— who and what will be in the next Atlantic?" In a later letter, she writes that she wishes for "a <u>long</u> letter . . . full of home news." Correspondents such as Davis and Dickinson, then, conceived of letters in journalistic terms—specifically, as means of reporting "home news."[17]

If Dickinson established herself as a family reporter, she also showed signs that she was not always a reliable—or, at least, a traditional—one. As she noted in the passage above, her sister apparently had reason to think that she might "fall short" of her "usual letter." In fact, Dickinson sometimes betrays an interest in other kinds of material, which she reports as a kind of alternative to the traditional "home news" of correspondence. In an 1852 letter to Austin, she writes, "Vinnie will tell you all the news, so I will take a little place to describe a thunder shower which occurred yesterday afternoon—the very first of the season." She goes on to describe the imagery of the storm, as well as the responses of both animals and humans: "The air was really scorching, the sun red and hot, and you know just how the birds sing before a thunder storm, a sort of hurried, and agitated song—pretty soon it began to thunder, and the great 'cream colored heads' peeped out of their windows—then came the wind and rain and I hurried around the house to shut all the doors and windows."[18] This letter provides a glimpse of Dickinson's poetic project. Leaving "all the news"—that is, the traditional kind—to another reporter, she turns to a literary description of a natural phenomenon.

On one level, the word "News," which appears in more than 30 of Dickinson's poems, is a kind of stand-in for broader terms, such as "message" and "information," which may have not fit neatly into certain poetic lines. Nevertheless, a close analysis of these and other poems shows Dickinson investigating and challenging some key journalistic principles. Although she continually emphasizes the importance of news, showing both the need for it and its capacity for dramatic impact, Dickinson, like Thoreau, questions conventional news judgment and implicitly endorses a kind of reporting that will illuminate the natural and spiritual realms. She resembles Thoreau, too, in her concern that news will not reach an audience, perhaps because both its content and its reporters do not fit conventional molds. Furthermore, Robert Weisbuch and Martin Orzeck have noted that "the Dickinson of the poems, 'not myself,' she told Higginson with a professional's confidence, but 'the Representative of the Verse' (L 268), does not initiate outer action but responds, like a reader herself, to an unnamed something-out-there."[19] This characterization resembles that of a reporter, someone who covers a story without becoming part of it. Finally, although Dickinson is the most private of America's major poets, she did, at least on some occasions,

conceive of an audience of more than one, since she is known to have
sent some of her poems to multiple recipients.[20] Such details suggest
that Dickinson—in her poetry, as she had in her letters—played roles
similar to that of the journalist, reporting on events or impressions,
sometimes for multiple readers.

News, defined broadly, often carries enormous import in Dickinson's
poetry. In 1319, "How News Must Feel when Travelling," she notes
that news enters a home "like a Dart" and says:

> What News must think when pondering
> If News have any Thought
> Concerning the stupendousness
> Of its perceiveless freight!

In other poems, Dickinson demonstrates the impact that this "freight"
can have on those who come in contact with it. In 645, "Bereavement
in Their Death to Feel," news of death has the ability to "paralyze"
those who encounter it. Poem 1290, "The Most Pathetic Thing I Do,"
shows news breaking through a more pleasant fiction, leaving the
speaker sorry that she has broken this news to herself. A certain kind
of news, Dickinson writes in 1665, "I Know of People in the Grave,"
could bring joy to the dead.[21]

The importance of news can be seen, too, in the need that some
of Dickinson's potential recipients have for it. The speaker of 570,
"I Could Die—to Know," craves information about another person,
perhaps a loved one, who is absent. Although "News-Boys salute the
Door," this speaker is left without the news that she really desires, so
that all she can do is imagine where he might be:

> Coals—from a Rolling Load—rattle—how—near—
> To the very Square—His foot is passing—
> Possibly, this moment—
> While I—dream—Here—

Similarly, the speaker of 1633, "Still Own Thee—Still Thou Art," so
desires information from a dying person that she considers turning
journalist herself and interviewing this person before he or she goes
to a "reportless Grave":

> Which question shall I clutch—
> What answer wrest from thee
> Before thou dost exude away
> In the recallless sea?

In 622, "To Know Just How He Suffered—Would Be Dear—,"
Dickinson portrays a craving for this same kind of news, the kind
that links the emotional experiences of two individuals, be they two
humans or a human and Christ. Her persona begins, "To know just
how He suffered—would be dear—." This poem, however, adds a
dimension to the transmission of news, suggesting that the figure
making the news—that is, the dying one—also may be seeking a connection with those who hear the news, for the speaker asks:

> What was his furthest mind—Of Home—or God—
> Or what the Distant say—
> At news that He ceased Human Nature
> Such a Day –

Dickinson suggests that the newsmaker may be aching for some
knowledge of how those who hear the news will react to it.

If Dickinson appreciated the import of some kinds of news, this
news does not seem to have been of the conventional variety. In
1089, "Myself Can Read the Telegrams," she contrasts conventional
news with a different sort:

> Myself can read the Telegrams
> A Letter chief to me
> The Stock's advance and Retrograde
> And what the Markets say
>
> The Weather—how the Rains
> In Counties have begun.
> 'Tis News as null as nothing,
> But sweeter so—than none.

In the first stanza, she acknowledges the kind of business news that
appears in various media—telegrams, letters, and, one may assume,
newspapers. As a regular reader of the *Republican* and a friend of its
editor, she surely was familiar with reports of markets and the like.
In the second stanza, however, she turns to a different form of news.
Her suggestion that this information, which concerns nature, is "as
null as nothing" may reflect conventional news judgment; as Thoreau
suggests, reporters and editors are more interested in politics than
nature.

Contemporary journalism, then, left a gap that Dickinson, like
Thoreau, sought to fill. Throughout her poems, she issued a number
of dispatches from nature, referring to the news of the sun's arrival

in 318, "news of Dews" in 513, and "the News of Night" in 638. In her most famous statement on the subject, 441, she situates her persona as a kind of reporter serving as the link between nature and her audience:

> This is my letter to the World
> That never wrote to Me—
> The simple News that Nature told—
> With tender Majesty

It is not difficult, of course, to see a link between this persona and Dickinson, who reported nature's "simple News" in numerous poems on birds, flowers, and other elements of the natural world. Like the news she describes in 1319, such news could constitute a stupendous freight, as she suggests in 327, "Before I Got My Eye Put Out," in which the speaker expresses a kind of gratitude for blindness because it limits the impact of the potent news from nature. If she could possess—through sight—meadows, mountains, forests, stars, "Motions of the Dipping Birds," "Morning's Amber Road," she could not withstand it. "The News," she says, "would strike me dead—."

A second, related form of news carries similar potency. Just as Dickinson took on the persona of a nature reporter in "This Is My Letter to the World," her persona in 827, "The Only News I Know," covers the spiritual realm. She writes, "The Only News I know / Is Bulletins all Day / From Immortality." Again willfully ignoring more conventional news about business and politics, she concludes, "If Other News there be— / . . . / I'll tell it You," subtly suggesting that news of anything other than spiritual matters may not constitute news at all—at least by her criteria, which clearly differ from those that journalists were using to select material for newspapers. In poem after poem, she refers to news of salvation (901), "Good News" that "A Soul had gone to Heaven" (947), and news of death and immortality, as well as such decidedly otherworldly matters as "The largest Fire ever known," which mysteriously "Occurs each Afternoon" and yet elicits "no report to men" (1114). This latter detail may be interpreted as a critique of conventional journalism, which, in its obsession with worldly concerns, is missing the real story. A similar critique can be seen in 594:

> The Battle fought between the Soul
> And No Man—is the One
> Of all the Battles prevalent—
> By far the Greater One—

No News of it is had abroad—
Its Bodiless Campaign
Establishes, and terminates—
Invisible—Unknown—

No History—record it—
As Legions of a Night
The Sunrise scatters—These endure—
Enact—and terminate—

As in "The Largest Fire Ever Known," a great event is not being reported. Perhaps because it has no tangible component—it is a "Bodiless Campaign"—it does not satisfy the conventional criteria of news judgment and thus remains "Invisible—Unknown." Dickinson seems to have feared that her important news from the fringe was eluding not only those charged with transmitting information, but also its potential audience. In 630, "Lightning Playeth—all the While—" the recipients of "News" remain oblivious, neglecting even to stop their talking or to make the sign of the cross.

This failure of both transmitters and recipients to recognize the real news may explain why so many of Dickinson's poems about communication feature images of distance and detachment. In 513, "Like Flowers, that Heard the News of Dews," news is but a "rumor" and a "Hint" that barely touches its recipients. Flowers, for example, "heard the news of Dews, / But never deemed the dripping prize / Awaited their—low Brows," and "Arctic Creatures" are only "dimly stirred— / By Tropic Hint." Similarly, some important spiritual news apparently has not resonated with humans, for the poem concludes, "The Heaven—unexpected come, / To Lives that thought the Worshipping / A too presumptuous Psalm—." In other poems, those who might be making or sending news are separated from those who might receive it. In 441, "This is My Letter to the World," the persona sends her message to hands she "cannot see." The speaker in 622 merely longs, without satisfaction, for news of "just how He suffered," and the suffering one is far from those who might hear the news of his demise.

Dickinson was hardly alone in creating images of messages in danger of not reaching or moving an audience. One need only think of Bartleby at work in the Dead Letter Office, Poe's "MS. Found in a Bottle," or other similar images to realize that American writers of the nineteenth century were anxious about the communication process. Still, communication must continue for the sheer act of connecting has value, as Dickinson notes in 1089, "Myself Can Read the Telegrams," when she says that news of natural phenomena is "as null

as nothing, / But sweeter so—than none." A message of any sort
arouses a positive emotional response, perhaps because it reminds the
speaker of other people and of the possibility of connecting with them
through information. The message is the medium. Ultimately, in fact,
this connection matters more than the news that forms it. Such is the
conclusion of 743, "The Birds Reported from the South—," in which
the speaker resists the "News express" coming from birds, as well as
other attempts at contact by flowers, seemingly intent on isolating
herself from all news from nature, perhaps all news of any sort. At
last, however, she connects with "a Mourner"; despite an apparent
lack of formal communication—the speaker "offered Her no word"
and "never questioned Her"—they unite on the basis of "A Wiser
Sympathy." The reference to sympathy, of course, reflects a fascination that pervaded the era, but it also mirrors a concern that Dickinson
expresses in her letters, where she writes of awaiting and desiring letters
from correspondents such as Austin and Susan Gilbert.[22]

Reporting Dickinson's own brand of news, however, requires a
language different from the kind found in conventional journalism.
As Cristanne Miller has suggested, Dickinson's grammar, including
her use of pronouns and uninflected verbs, gives her poetry "a quality
of timelessness and unspecifiable event," exactly the opposite of what
one would find in newspapers, which provided timely coverage of specific events. Her use of symbolism and metaphor, furthermore, puts
her in the position of capturing the truth in indirect language. In her
own words, she was telling the "Truth," but telling it "slant" (1129).
Here, her relationship and correspondence with Bowles is instructive.
In Bowles, Dickinson had a connection to one of the leading journalists in the country—a man who breathed journalism. In his biography
of Dickinson, Sewall notes that Bowles viewed the information he
gathered from personal contacts as material for a newspaper. George
Merriam's nineteenth-century biography of Bowles, furthermore, suggests that he lacked "leisure for exploring excursions into the infinite."[23]
Here, then, was an embodiment of news and newspapers—the perfect
foil for Dickinson's own poetic "excursions into the infinite." In a letter
she wrote to Bowles when he was seriously ill in early 1861, Dickinson
offered a peek into her own method of reporting on the world. The
letter, one guesses, would have perplexed the journalist, for it is every bit
as indirect and suggestive as one of her enigmatic poems. After referring
to a "little 'Meeting'" regarding him some time in the past, she says:

> We voted to remember you—so long as both should live—including
> Immortality. To count you as ourselves—except sometimes more

tenderly—as now—when you are ill—and we—the haler of the two—and so I bring the Bond—we sign so many times—for you to read, when Chaos comes—or Treason—or Decay—still witnessing for Morning.

In a later paragraph, the letter's prose—if it can be called that—gives way to poetry, like a bird taking flight:

We offer you our cups—stintless—as to the Bee—the Lily, her new Liquors—

Would you like Summer? Taste of our's—
Spices? Buy, here!
Ill! We have Berries, for the parching!
Weary, Furloughs of Down!
Perplexed! Estates of Violet—Trouble ne'er looked on!
Captive! We bring Reprieve of Roses!
Fainting! Flasks of Air!
Even for Death—a Fairy Medicine—
But, which is it—Sir?

Sewall argues that the letter constitutes a kind of defense of poesy, at least in regards to its potential for his recuperation. "Indeed," Sewall writes, "she seems to be showering him with metaphors to convince him of the value of metaphors (and of her poems) and of their specific value, right now, to help him get well."[24] With this tour de force of poetic language, Dickinson shows the journalist an alternative form of communication. One can only speculate on what Bowles made of it. What we do know is that his *Springfield Republican* did not publish many of her poems, leaving her to ponder the different sorts of news that it and she were reporting—and the audiences these two forms of news were or were not reaching.

Reporting her own brand of news in letter-poems that she sent to him, Dickinson was Bowles's correspondent in both senses of the word; indeed, she played exactly the role that had given birth to the term in an earlier age—that of recording events in a letter and sending that letter to a newspaper. The "World" to whom she addressed her letters, however, rarely saw them. "Bulletins . . . / From Immortality" and the "simple News that Nature told," especially when delivered in Dickinson's strange idiom, were not the type of conventional news that Bowles and his fellow editors were accustomed to publishing. Like Thoreau, Dickinson could have said—with more regret, even heartbreak—that she was "reporter to a journal . . . whose editor has never yet seen fit to print the bulk" of her contributions. Partly because they were reporting a brand of news that was timeless, however, their dispatches from the fringe today are read by millions of people who have never heard of Benjamin Day or James Gordon Bennett. If they were alive today, both Dickinson and Thoreau could say of their literature, as Thoreau wrote of the ice collected from Walden, that people from afar were drinking at their wells.[25]

CHAPTER 5

TRUTHFUL HOAXES

Fiction is, of course, a lie. It presents readers with false worlds, in which people who never existed do things that never happened. To resonate with these readers, however, fiction must have some air of reality: characters, in terms of their motivations and emotions, must resemble real people, and, in most cases, events must have some plausibility. When a writer takes the extra step of suggesting that his or her story not only could have happened, but also really did happen—that, in fact, this story exists not in a false world of the author's creation, but in the actual, physical world—then fiction becomes something else: a hoax.

Thanks to the efforts of literary giants and lesser-known journalists, the hoax has a long history in American letters. Over the last three centuries, it has assumed a diversity of forms and served a variety of purposes, ranging from the light diversions popular in April 1 editions of modern news publications and programs to the fabrications of ambitious or desperate reporters to artful dodges aspiring to something more creative or meaningful.[1] In the midst of the sibling rivalry that grew out of America's antebellum media revolution, the hoax became, in the hands of one of its most skillful practitioners, a sophisticated argument for the truth of the lie.

THE HOAX IN AMERICAN JOURNALISM

Because it carries factual coverage of the world's events, the newspaper has long been a favorite vehicle for America's hoaxers. In the company of articles about real crimes, ship arrivals, and political debates, an account of, say, a balloon trip across the Atlantic Ocean can masquerade as one more story about the real world. In the eighteenth century, newspapers carried a number of Benjamin Franklin's hoaxes, including an account of a witch trial and a single mother's defense of giving birth to children out of wedlock.[2] Franklin, the era's leading author and leading journalist, worked at a time when journalism and literature were still intimate acquaintances. His own *Pennsylvania Gazette* published not only accounts of the colonial assemblies and criminal trials, but also poems and satirical essays. Even after journalists began focusing on "news," however, newspapers continued to publish the occasional hoax. In 1848, Horace Greeley's *New York Tribune* published an article about a fictional battle between the Irish and the British, one in which 6,000 British soldiers died.[3] During the Civil War, the *Brooklyn Eagle* city editor Joseph Howard, Jr., created a fake presidential proclamation calling for 400,000 men to be drafted, and the proclamation appeared in both the *New York World* and the *Journal of Commerce*.[4] Other hoaxes described the escape of animals from a zoo, a theatre fire, and a wild man loose in the rural Northeast.[5] Many less elaborate hoaxes probably went undetected. Theodore Dreiser confessed to fabricating material when he worked for Joseph Pulitzer's *New York World* in the 1890s. In his memoir *Newspaper Days*, he explains, "I knew now that what my city editors wanted was not merely 'accuracy, accuracy, accuracy,' but a kind of flair for the ridiculous or remarkable even though it had to be invented, so that the pages of the paper and life itself might not seem so dull."[6]

In the twentieth century, journalism evolved into a quasi-profession, complete with university degree programs and professional organizations such as the American Society of News Editors, and hoaxing became less common—or did it?[7] In fact, a number of commentators on journalism have suggested that slack fact-checking and newsroom pressures enable or even encourage fabrication by modern journalists.[8] Because many hoaxes probably still go undetected, we do not know how much of what we read in modern newspapers is absolutely accurate. What we do know is that the consequences of perpetrating a serious hoax in journalism have become much greater. Indeed, the revelation of a hoax is itself a major news story. When Janet Cooke's 1980 article on "Jimmy," a boy addicted to heroin, turned out to contain fabricated material, her newspaper, the *Washington Post*, returned her Pulitzer Prize and printed a front-page apology. *The New York Times* printed an even longer mea culpa in 2003 after it determined that Jayson Blair had been filing fabricated stories in the paper. These repercussions for hoaxers point to a basic premise about modern journalism. As we have seen, truth is supposed to be at the heart of the journalistic enterprise.

Expectations were somewhat different in the nineteenth century, as evident in a case study of the era's most sensational hoax. In a series of six articles he published in the *New York Sun* in the summer of 1835, Richard Adams Locke described winged moon creatures, which astronomer John Herschel supposedly had discovered with the use of a powerful telescope. Coming as it did during the revolution of the penny press, the *Sun*'s Moon Hoax, as it has come to be called, electrified the New York public. It apparently even inspired a 2,000-foot canvas, billed in the *Sun* as "*Harrington's Great Lunar Panorama*," which depicted "man-bats, woman-bats, and golden pheasants; the volcanoes; the cataracts; the crystal scenery." This chapter in the history of the American journalistic hoax points to one possible motivation behind the fictional news story. Whereas many hoaxers may have fabricated details or entire stories to advance their careers or save the effort of digging up facts, others may have had less personal reasons for duping the public. In her study of crime reporting in the era of the penny press, Andie Tucher has argued that newspapers engaged in a form of entertainment known as "humbug." Tucher explains that America's greatest practitioner of humbug, P. T. Barnum, differentiated between a humbug and a swindle. "A successful humbug is not a power play by one side only; it involves the participation, the consent, and even the pleasure of *both* parties," Tucher says. "Where a swindle deprives one of choice, a humbug demands it." Tucher goes on to argue that journalistic humbug fit neatly into the democratic zeitgeist, since readers could sort through the details and form their own judgments. A quotation from the *Philadelphia Inquirer* in the *New York Sun* during the sensation surrounding the Moon Hoax makes the same case, saying, "It is not worth while for us to express an opinion as to the truth or falsity of the narrative, as our readers after an attentive perusal of the whole story, decide for themselves."[9]

MORE THAN A JOKE: POE'S DEFENSE OF FICTION

If the hoax could be a source of amusement or an early form of participatory journalism, it could also—in the right hands—serve other purposes. The experiences of one author from the nineteenth century show an attempt to produce something we might call the "truthful hoax," a hybrid genre that allowed writers to report their own versions of the truth—news, for example, of the possible and the ideal—by disguising them as news. With the possible exception of Franklin, no major American author was more engaged in the hoax genre than Edgar Allan Poe. The author of the "Balloon Hoax," one of the classics in the genre, he also dabbled in other forms of deception, inventing narratives about his life, enlisting in the Army under a false name, and, if some modern scholars are correct, passing off satire as horror fiction. G. R. Thompson went so far as to argue, "Almost everything that Poe wrote is qualified by, indeed controlled by, a prevailing duplicity or irony in which the artist presents us with slyly insinuated mockery of both ourselves as readers and himself as writer." The hoax would seem an ideal genre for Poe, who reveled in the world of imagination, yet lived in a culture that prized "useful information," who considered himself above the masses, but could not convince them of his superiority. As Daniel Hoffman has noted, literature allowed Poe to escape the real world, where poverty and abandonment were his lot. It also allowed him to get the better of this world. "His ultimate joke on the world," observes Terence Martin, "would have been to make it his own in and by means of the imagination."[10] A hoax doubled the joke: Poe could not only craft his own reality, but also package it as journalism and pass it off to an unsuspecting audience of "quidnuncs" in search of news. Poe dramatized this literary method in a tale that itself has been characterized as a hoax.[11]

One of Poe's longer and lesser-known stories, "Hans Phaall—A Tale" first appeared in the *Southern Literary Messenger* in 1835. It later appeared in collections of Poe's works under different titles, eventually with "Pfaall" as the spelling of the main character's last name. The bulk of the story consists of a letter in which Pfaall describes a voyage to the moon in a hot-air balloon. The letter comes back to his village of Rotterdam not in the hands of Pfaall, who supposedly has been living on the moon for the past five years, but apparently through the aid of one of the lunar inhabitants Pfaall has discovered. Poe's tale resembles a hoax; however, unlike the Moon Hoax, which appeared in the *New York Sun* shortly after Poe's tale appeared, "Hans Pfaall" appeared not in a newspaper, but in a literary publication. Furthermore, as Burton Pollin noted, Poe seemed content to have the story read as a fictional work until 1839.[12] That year Poe called it a hoax, perhaps trying to lend it some of the luster that had accrued around Locke's hoax. In fact, "Hans Pfaall" is not a hoax, but the story of a hoax, as well as a commentary on journalism, literature, and truth. In it, Poe shows how a writer of fiction, by disguising his musings as factual truth, makes his material marketable while simultaneously conveying and even enacting other forms of truth. In short, "Hans Pfaall" is a kind of argument for the truth value of fiction.

By 1835, Poe had made a number of attempts to enter the literary marketplace. Neither his first three books of poetry nor his early efforts at writing fiction could have given him any reason to believe that he could make a living as an author. In fact, very few American authors, unless their names were Washington Irving or James Fenimore Cooper, could expect as much. What paid in the antebellum American marketplace was journalism. Indeed, as we have seen, many writers without other sources of income turned to journalism to make a living. Poe did the same when he accepted a position as editor of the *Southern Literary Messenger* in 1835. The *Messenger* was not a newspaper, but it was a form of journalism; it provided Poe with a steady, if meager, income churning out reading material, mainly reviews, for regular consumption by subscribers.

In a number of ways, "Hans Pfaall" sets up an opposition between imaginative literature and factual journalism. In one corner we find Hans Pfaall, a dreamer whom his own wife considers "an idle body—a mere make-weight—good for nothing but building castles in the air" (395). A literary descendant of Rip Van Winkle, Pfaall longs to escape the world, especially as creditors are hounding him. Explaining the purpose of his flight, he says, "I determined to depart, yet live—to leave the world, yet continue to exist—in short, to drop enigmas, I resolved, let what would ensue, to force a passage, if I could, *to the moon*" (399). To some extent, his plan works. Eventually, his former environs disappear, and he says, "Of individual edifices not a trace could be discovered, and the proudest cities of mankind had utterly faded away from the face of the earth" (407). The moon, furthermore, proves to be a dreamland akin to the settings of many of Poe's own dreams and tales. Pfaall explains, "Fancy revelled in the wild and dreamy regions of the moon. Imagination, feeling herself for once unshackled, roamed at will among the ever-changing wonders of a shadowy and unstable land" (412). Pfaall was not alone in conceiving of the moon as a place to avoid earthly concerns. During the craze over the Moon Hoax, an article in the *New York Sun* suggested speculation in real estate on the moon, where speculators and residents would be free from many annoyances, including the "hideous howlings" of dogs, "law suits about disputed boundaries or partition fences," or taxes "for the support of an expensive municipal government."[13]

Like so many of Poe's narrators, Hans Pfaall may be seen as a stand-in for Poe himself: a dreamy writer who longed to escape into the realm of imagination, but who feels burdened by the weight of reality. What separates Pfaall from, say, Arthur Gordon Pym, however, is the means of his escape. He apparently has managed to leave the earth in a balloon "manufactured entirely of dirty newspapers" (388). Furthermore, journalism is a rival that has threatened his ability to make a living. Pfaall is a bellows-mender, and he explains, "People who were formerly the very best customers in the world, had now not a moment of time to think of us at all. They had as much as they could do to read about the revolutions, and keep up with the march of intellect and the spirit of the age. If a fire wanted fanning, it could readily be fanned with a newspaper" (391). Pfaall's former customers no longer need a bellows because they can use their newspapers to fan fires—not only literally, but also figuratively. Threatened by this business competitor, Pfaall "soon grew poor as a rat," in no position to support his family (391).

In light of these key details, Pfaall's plan takes on new significance. His story is no mere flight of fancy, but an artfully constructed plan for succeeding in the literary marketplace. It is, in a word, a hoax. In his frame narrative, Poe presents several hints that Pfaall's letter—indeed, the entire story of his disappearance and the charade involving the dwarfish figure bearing the letter—is a hoax. In his initial description of the balloon, for instance, the narrator compares it to a "fool's-cap" (388). Near the end of the tale, he says, "Some of the over-wise even made themselves ridiculous by decrying the whole business as nothing better than a hoax" (427). He then goes on to list some of their objections to the story. He notes, for instance, that Pfaall, who claims in his letter to have been on the moon for five years, has been seen recently in a tavern with his supposed creditors and that an earless dwarf has gone missing from a nearby town.

The term "hoax" might be applied to any form of fraud in which the author attempts to pass off one thing as something else. In this case, however, Poe characterizes Pfaall's ploy as a specific brand of fraud—that is, the newspaper hoax. It is, after all, a balloon made of "dirty newspapers" that Pfaall uses to get his hoax off the ground— literally. Furthermore, as Marcy Dinius has noted, Pfaall sees the commercial value of his writings.[14] In his letter, he offers more details in exchange for a "reward." After describing his voyage in great detail, he hints at juicy tidbits of the moon's climate, landscape, and inhabitants. "All this, and more—much more—would I most willingly detail," he says. "But, to be brief, I must have my reward. I am pining for a return to my family and to my home: and as the price of any farther communications on my part . . . I must solicit . . . a pardon for the crime of which I have been guilty in the death of the creditors upon my departure from Rotterdam" (426). In short, Pfaall has dreamt up a work of fanciful fiction, dressed it up as a true account—complete with newsprint—and then tried to barter with it. As fiction, his story stands little chance of earning him a living in the American literary marketplace; however, because it masquerades as something true, carried aloft by newspapers, he thinks it may find a market.

In hoaxing the public, however, Pfaall is not merely selling out. At the same time that he is trying to trick readers into buying a work of fiction, he is actually delivering a different form of truth—that is, a truthful hoax. The tale's narrator points to this fact when he responds to some people's charges that Pfaall's story is a hoax, noting that "hoax, with these sort of people, is, I believe, a general term for all matters above their comprehension" (427). In other words, Pfaall's attempt to exchange a bogus story for his freedom might seem to be a scam—but only to those who do not appreciate the value of fiction. The story indeed is not factual, but that is not to say that it lacks value—or even that it is not, on some level, true. In dismissing it as fiction, readers reveal their own ignorance, for fiction provides its own form of truth. Only readers who have a low capacity for comprehension, who believe only the kind of "real" news they read in newspapers, and who cannot appreciate higher truths—that is, those above their comprehension—would dismiss something *because* it is fiction. Pfaall, in fact, makes a case for the truthful nature of literature when he alludes to the connection between his story and life on earth. He says he has "much to say" of the lunar inhabitants, "of their manners, customs, and political institutions," and "of the incomprehensible connection between each particular individual in the moon, with some particular individual on the earth—a connection analogous with, and depending upon that of the orbs of the planet and the satellite, and by means of which the lives and destin[i]es of the inhabitants of the one are interwoven with the lives and destinies of the inhabitants of the other" (425–26). His fictional account of lunar inhabitants, in other words, has a connection—though incomprehensible—to the lives of real human beings on earth. This argument for the truth in a hoax might be read as a defense of the literary enterprise. Speaking for all authors of fiction, Pfaall argues that imaginative stories—even ones about moon beings—can convey truth.

There is yet another dimension to the truthful hoax, however. Poe's statement about "matters beyond their comprehension" bears a striking similarity to a statement published in the *New York Sun* after the initial installment of the Moon Hoax: "Consummate ignorance is always incredulous to the higher order of scientific discoveries, because it cannot possibly comprehend them." In his study of Poe's tale, David Ketterer argues, "The account of Pfaal's trip to the moon is part of the reality that man is normally unaware of." He adds, "Much of the information that Pfaal divulges concerning the infinite rarefaction of air . . . anticipates aspects of *Eureka* and would surely have been endorsed by Poe."[15] Poe's fiction, in other words, points toward what he believed constituted a scientific truth, or at least a scientific hypothesis. Indeed, when we read Pfaall's story in this light, many of its details come into focus. At the outset of the story, the narrator of the frame concedes the bizarre nature of Pfaall's account, but characterizes it not as incredible, but as revolutionary. He says, "Indeed, phenomena have there occurred of a nature so completely unexpected—so entirely novel—so utterly at variance with preconceived opinions—as to leave no doubt on my mind that long ere this all Europe is in an uproar, all physics in a ferment, all reason and astronomy together by the ears" (387). Much of Pfaall's narrative, furthermore, consists of detailed, even laborious, explanations of his calculations and equipment, as if he is arguing for the feasibility of such a voyage. For example, he challenges the notion that there is a limit to earth's atmosphere and describes a method for converting rarefied air into something a human could breathe. He even suggests that the unexpected birth of his cat's kittens during the flight will provide him with the opportunity to "test" a hypothesis concerning the impact of atmospheric pressure on organisms, as if fiction could be a locale for the study of natural phenomena. A note that Poe attached in a later version of the story also points to his intentions. Here, he exposes the weaknesses in various moon stories and complains, "In none, is there any effort at *plausibility* in the details of the voyage itself" (433). Contrasting his own story with these others, he concludes, "In 'Hans Pfaall' the design is original, inasmuch as regards an attempt at *verisimilitude*, in the application of scientific principles (so far as the whimsical nature of the subject would permit,) to the actual passage between the earth and the moon" (433). This final statement might seem to be merely an endorsement of his own realistic technique, but this attempt at realism goes beyond helping readers to suspend their disbelief. Poe was hoping to show the promise of the science he described in hopes of making it real. Indeed, we can see in Hans Pfaall's actions a model for how we as readers might respond to his text. It is, after all, the act of reading "a small treatise on Speculative Astronomy" (392) that fires Pfaall's imagination and leads to his innovations. Readers of his hoax may follow his example and create innovations of their own. Poe would return to this particular brand of "truth in a hoax" nearly a decade later in his most famous contribution to the genre.

NEWS OF THE POSSIBLE

In another account of a fabulous balloon trip, we see an example of Poe's own work as a hoaxer. "The Balloon Hoax," as this story has come to be known, originally appeared in the *New York Sun* in 1844. Unlike the story of Hans Pfaall, this account clearly has the trappings of a news article: a headline over it announces the fabulous news that men have crossed the Atlantic Ocean in a balloon and indicates that the story has come "BY EXPRESS VIA NORFOLK." Like Pfaall's letter, "The Balloon Hoax" provides scientific details of the flight. The clue to this hoax's value as a bearer of truth appears in a prefatory note that accompanied a version of the story published later:

> The subjoined *jeu d'esprit* with the preceding heading in magnificent capitals, well interspersed with notes of admiration, was originally published, as matter of fact, in the "New-York Sun," a daily newspaper, and therein fully subserved the purpose of creating indigestible aliment for the *quidnuncs* during the few hours intervening between a couple of the Charleston mails. The rush for the "sole paper which had the news," was something beyond even the prodigious; and, in fact, if (as some assert) the "Victoria" *did* not absolutely accomplish the voyage recorded, it will be difficult to assign a reason why she *should* not have accomplished it.[16]

The remarks indicating that the story satisfied some news-junkies' craving for information, especially a scoop, constitutes a mild satire aimed at journalism and its readers, especially since this "news" is a hoax. The most interesting portion of the note, however, is the final part, in which Poe alludes to two forms of news: the actual and the possible. The dependent clause at the beginning of the statement—"if (as some assert) the 'Victoria' *did* not absolutely accomplish the voyage recorded"—hints at the nature of this report, almost conceding that the journey did not actually take place. The independent—and thus, syntactically, weightier—clause that follows this concession, however, virtually negates the concession: "It will be difficult to assign a reason why she *should* not have accomplished it." The idea that the events Poe describes could have happened—even if they actually did not—is precisely the point of this hoax, as it was part of the message in Hans Pfaall's story. In publishing this form of alternative journalism, he was reporting what we might call the "news of the possible."[17] If such a form of journalism seems outlandish, it may simply be because Poe presented it in the form of a hoax instead of being forthright about its speculative nature. In fact, Poe stressed the verisimilitude of his hoax in a series that has come to be known as *Doings of Gotham*, published in the *Columbia Spy* the following month. Without letting on that he is himself the author of the hoax, Poe, after gushing over the "intense sensation" the story created, notes that "the more intelligent believed, while the rabble, for the most part, rejected the whole with disdain." He goes on to explain that the story contained no "internal evidence of falsehood," unlike Locke's Moon Hoax, which "would not bear even momentary examination by the scientific," and even argues that the story could inspire a real flight, saying:

> There is nothing put forth in the Balloon-Story which is not in full keeping with the known facts of aeronautic experience—which might not really have occurred. An expedition of the kind has been long contemplated, and this *jeu d'esprit* will, beyond doubt give the intention a new impulse. For my own part, I shall not be in the least surprised to learn, in the course of next month, or the next, that a balloon has made the actual voyage so elaborately described by the hoaxer. The trip might be made in even less time than seventy-five hours—which give only about forty miles to the hour.[18]

His hoax, Poe might have argued, *was* true; it just wasn't true *yet*.

The notion of a kind of journalism that reports possibilities instead of realities was alive in the nineteenth century, as we can see in a speech that journalist John Bigelow gave in honor of his late partner, William Cullen Bryant. Bigelow noted that Bryant, himself a poet as well as a longtime editor of the *New York Post*, subscribed to a school of journalism that "aims to control and direct society; to teach it and to lead it; to tell not so much what it has been doing as what it ought to do or to have done." The modern journalism scholar Julie Hedgepeth Williams has made a similar observation, noting that American journalists have pursued both factual reality and change that would lead to a better reality. "The press had a purpose of publishing the truth," Williams explains. "Should that truth be what was literally there? Or should it construct a reality that Americans presumably needed to achieve?" Bryant's school of the "ideal" largely addressed political questions, but Poe's hoax plays a similar role for science, directing society toward what could be done in the realm of invention and aviation. It is for this reason that the story emphasizes the details of the balloon—its exact length and weight, for instance—instead of the narrative of the voyage. If Poe's hoax fits under this heading of "ideal" journalism, it also belongs to the realm of literature as defined by Aristotle, who argued that "it is not the function of the poet to relate what has happened, but what may happen—what is possible according to the law of probability or necessity." Some, in fact, recognize Poe as a pioneer in a specific genre of literature—that is, science fiction. Whether one labels it as "ideal" journalism, literature, or science fiction, "The Balloon Hoax" delivers a special form of truth, the truth of the possible.[19] Speculative purposes can be seen in Poe's other hoaxes, as well. In "Von Kempelen and His Discovery," published in the Boston periodical *Flag of Our Union* on April 14, 1849, Poe reacts to news of the Gold Rush by reporting some news of his own. After recounting the arrest of Von Kempelen and the discovery of metal under his bed, Poe ends with this startling conclusion: "All that as yet can fairly be said to be known, is, that *pure gold can be made at will, and very readily, from lead, in connection with certain other substances, in kind and in proportions, unknown.*" Again, the point is speculation, as Poe reveals early in the story, saying, "My object is simply, in the first place, to say a few words of Von Kempelen himself . . . ; and, in the second place, to look in a general way, and speculatively, at the *results* of the discovery."[20] Inexplicably, the hoax ends before Poe achieves this second purpose, but his intention is clear. In yet another hoax, "The Facts in the Case of M. Valdemar," published in the *American Review* in 1845, Poe states his speculative purpose early, having his narrator explain that he sought to determine whether a dying person could be hypnotized, whether the onset of death affected mesmeric influence, and whether mesmerism could postpone death.[21] Thanks once again to the power of fiction—this time presented brazenly under the heading of "Facts"—Poe comes to some speculative conclusions, which he relates in his account of M. Valdemar's speech while under mesmeric influence and his ultimate—and literal—dissolution. Journalism—at least any kind that stayed true to its purpose of reporting on actual reality—could not take readers into such worlds. Readers of "straight news," however informed they might have been of the actual, ran the danger of being uninformed about the possible. Paradoxically, as Poe's truthful hoaxes demonstrate, fiction could be a vehicle for conveying one form of truth.

Poe's hoaxes could have inspired or edified readers even if they failed to fool them. Poe surely took some additional satisfaction, however, in knowing that he did dupe some readers. By his own report, his "Balloon Hoax" produced "a far more intense sensation than anything of that character since the 'Moon-Story' of Locke." Describing the scene around the office of the *New York Sun*, which published the hoax, Poe says:

> On the morning (Saturday) of its announcement, the whole square surrounding the "Sun" building was literally besieged, blocked up—ingress and egress being alike impossible, from a period soon after sunrise until about two o'clock P. M. In Saturday's regular issue, it was stated that the news had been just received, and that an "Extra" was then in preparation, which would be ready at ten. It was not delivered, however, until nearly noon. In the meantime I never witnessed more intense excitement to get possession of a newspaper. As soon as the few first copies made their way into the streets, they were bought up, at almost any price, from the news-boys, who made a profitable speculation beyond doubt. I saw a half-dollar given, in one instance, for a single paper, and a shilling was a frequent price. I tried, in vain, during the whole day, to get possession of a copy.

Poe may have embellished or even fabricated this account of a craze for this story, but accounts by others suggest that another one of his hoaxes did create a stir and dupe some readers. "The article in the American Review of this month entitled '*The Facts of M. Valdemar's Case*, by EDGAR A. POE,' is of course a romance—who could have supposed it otherwise?" Horace Greeley asked in his *New York Tribune*. "Those who have read Mr. Poe's Visit to the Maelstrom, South Pole, &c. have not been puzzled by it, yet we learn that several good matter-of-fact citizens have been, sorely." Greeley added that "whoever thought it a veracious recital must have the bump of Faith large, very large indeed." Mesmerist Robert Collyer noted that the story of Valdemar caused "a very great sensation" in Boston, and Poe quoted the poet Elizabeth Barrett as saying the story was "going the rounds of the newspapers" and putting people "into 'most admired disorder', or dreadful doubts as to 'whether it can be true.'"[22]

Sensation is one measure of a hoax's success as a practical joke, and there can be little doubt that Poe enjoyed putting one over on readers. Indeed, Burton Pollin notes that the author "had always shown a leaning toward 'diddling' or fooling the public." Poe's responses to Greeley and Collyer, however, point again to a larger purpose. He quoted Greeley's comments in his own *Broadway Journal* and added:

> For our parts we find it difficult to understand how any dispassionate transcendentalist can doubt the facts as we state them; they are by no means so incredible as the marvels which are hourly narrated, and

believed, on the topic of Mesmerism. *Why* cannot a man's death be postponed indefinitely by Mesmerism? *Why* cannot a man talk after he is dead? *Why?*—*Why?*—that is the question; and as soon as the Tribune has answered it to our satisfaction we will talk to it farther.

In a separate note published a week later, Poe noted that "there are a certain class of people who pride themselves upon Doubt, as a profession." In response to Collyer, who had asked Poe for a defense he could use "to put at rest the growing impression that your account is merely a *splendid creation* of your own brain, not having any truth in fact," Poe conceded that "there was a very small modicum of truth in the case of M. Valdemar," but also said, "If the story was not true, however, it should have been—and perhaps 'The Zoist' [a spiritualist publication] may discover that it *is* true after all."[23] These comments may have been Poe's attempts to evade the question of his story's authenticity or to make a joke of the entire thing; however, the thread that runs through these remarks is worth noting. In the face of doubts, Poe pleads possibility or, at least, desirability. Perhaps he was thinking of journalists when he mocked those "who pride themselves upon Doubt, as a profession." It was, after all, Greeley, the most famous journalist in America, who wrote the item to which he was responding, and Poe mentions Greeley's paper, the *New York Tribune*, explicitly in his response. The responses to the journalist and the mesmerist are, like the hoaxes themselves, arguments for the news of the possible or desirable.

For a writer—or, indeed, a reader—with Poe's appreciation of and capacity for imagination, a hoax could be truthful in yet one more sense. Stuart Levine quotes a passage from "The Balloon Hoax" showing a balloonist's "emotional response" to the journey and says, "The excitement seems genuine, and, significantly, one cause of the exhilaration is a vision of natural beauty consistent with Poe's taste and aesthetics. . . . Poe is going farther than the mere credibility of his hoax demands; one suspects that the enthusiasm is his own." In fact, in an essay on Richard Adams Locke, Poe described his own reaction upon reading Sir John Herschel's "Treatise on Astronomy." Noting that he "had been much interested in what is there said respecting the possibility of future lunar investigations," he says, "The theme excited my fancy, and I longed to give free rein to it in depicting my day-dreams about the scenery of the moon—in short, I longed to write a story embodying those dreams." The hoax, then, was a means by which Poe could realize the truth of lunar exploration in another sense—by simply putting it into words and making it real for his imagination. In a later work called "The Power of Words," as Allen Tate noted, Poe alludes to "creative power through verbal magic."[24] His hoaxes allowed him to exercise this power.

In the midst of a journalistic tidal wave that threatened to inundate literary efforts at truth-telling, Edgar Allan Poe—purveyor of puzzles and master of the dodge—responded exactly as one would have expected. In crafting fanciful fiction and passing it off as faithful fact, he and his alter ego Hans Pfaall could thrill their imaginative sensibilities and, by reporting "news of the possible," set the world on a course toward the advances they imagined—all while enjoying a colossal joke on their earthbound contemporaries.

CHAPTER 6

INVESTIGATIVE FICTION

If *Chicago Times* editor Wilbur Storey was right that one purpose of a newspaper is to "raise hell," then investigative reporters might be called its chief hell-raisers. In an extension of their profession's role as a reporter of reality, investigative journalists seek to expose readers to hidden realities, often those involving corruption, injustice, and societal wrongs. Known by various names—"crusade," "exposé," "muckraking"—their form of journalism is as old as American journalism itself. Indeed, exposure and reform have long been integral components of the journalistic endeavor.

In its role as a "watchdog" or the "Fourth Estate," however, the press attracted criticism from a number of American authors, some of whom sought to replace investigative journalism with a particular brand of news of their own, something we might call "investigative fiction."[1] Exploring the deeper realities of the human experience, of course, has long been a hallmark of literature, but what sets these antebellum American writers apart is their explicit reaction to the phenomenon of journalism. As we will see in this chapter, Poe, Stowe, and Davis all set up their own forms of truth-telling in opposition to a press that, in their eyes, was failing in its role as reporter and reformer. Both Poe and Davis, in fact, issued pointed critiques of journalism—critiques akin to those we saw in Chapter 3—at the same time that they crafted arguments for the superiority of literature in investigating and exposing hidden realities. In what amount to some of the most striking examples of one-upmanship in the competition between journalism and literature in the nineteenth century, "The Mystery of Marie Roget," *Uncle Tom's Cabin*, and "Life in the Iron-Mills" all argue that literature—not journalism—provides readers with a window on the truth.

CRUSADERS AND MUCKRAKERS

Although even basic reporting involves some kind of investigation, the field of investigative journalism is a distinct endeavor, one that involves more initiative and depth of treatment. Traditional news gathering, as Walter Lippmann and Paul Williams have noted, relies heavily on information that has been filtered through official channels—police headquarters and public records offices, for instance—and often consists largely of relaying information about the events described in these channels. As Lippmann explains, a traditional reporter may report on a business owner only after his official declaration of bankruptcy makes his story visible. Investigative journalists, however, actively seek information outside these channels or scour them more carefully. Often this information is worth reporting because it involves a wrong that needs to be righted. Another common attribute in investigative journalism, then, is a reform agenda. Such reform is made more likely by the depth of investigative reporting, which exposes the miscellaneous forces behind a phenomenon. Referring to both the reformist motivation and the depth of treatment, Williams explains that an investigative journalist looks for "trouble" and asks "the essential question: 'Why?'"[2]

Early American newspapers had plenty of hell-raisers. Indeed, what would have been the first American newspaper, Benjamin Harris's *Publick Occurrences: Both Foreign and Domestick*, never achieved the criterion of regular publication precisely because its only issue, dated September 25, 1690, upset local authorities, who promptly shut down Harris's operation. Over the next three centuries and more, as James Aucoin has shown in his history of the genre, James Franklin and others engaged in investigative journalism. Noting that Franklin printed one of "*Cato's Letters*," one calling for "the exposing . . . of publick Wickedness," Aucoin argues that Harris and Franklin launched the exposé in American journalism. Investigative journalism experienced something of a renaissance in the antebellum era, when penny papers and the reformist press both embraced it. Hazel Dicken-Garcia notes that the rise of the "information model" coincided with a greater stress on the "watchdog" role of the press, adding that "the public had a right to know about such abuses in order to be able to correct them and protect individuals from powerful institutions." The British philosopher James Mill, as J. Herbert Altschull notes, "perceived the press as the *main* instrument to force the government into making social change."[3] For penny-press editors such as Benjamin Day and James Gordon Bennett, furthermore, exposures and crusades made for good reading—and, thus, good sales by newsboys, who could call out the latest sensational developments as they sold papers on the streets. As Aucoin explains, Day and Bennett, like the modern investigative reporters Williams describes, fleshed out their coverage of the sensational murder of prostitute Helen Jewett with material gathered outside official channels, and activist organs seized on this genre of journalism, as well. "Even more than the penny papers," Aucoin adds, "reform publications adopted the exposé as an instrument for promoting social change, thereby extending the reach of exposure journalism to incorporate the strategy of outraging the public so it will demand improvements."[4]

If investigation and reform were considered legitimate aims of newspapers and magazines in the nineteenth century, they were not always successful. This particularly ambitious form of journalism was hampered not only by the human failings and news conventions described in Chapter 3, but also by logistical constraints. As any modern editor will admit, investigative journalism is the most expensive form of journalism. Digging beneath the regular police reports, political speeches, and other information transmitted through official channels takes time, energy, ingenuity, and guts. Noting the limitations of time and money, as well as space, Edward Jay Epstein argues:

> Under these conditions, it would be unreasonable to expect even the most resourceful journalist to produce anything more than a truncated version of reality. Beyond this, however, even if such restraints were somehow suspended, and journalists had unlimited time, space, and financial resources at their disposal, they would still lack the forensic means and authority to establish the truth about a matter in serious dispute.

The journalists of the nineteenth century often operated under constraints even tighter than those affecting the journalists of the modern era. In the early days of the *New York Herald*, Bennett sometimes produced all of the newspaper's copy single-handedly. Even with the four journalists on his staff in 1839 or the 15 who worked for the *Herald* in the 1850s, Bennett would have been hard pressed to cover all the news of New York and still spare staff to dig up and write investigative reports. As William Huntzicker has explained, Bennett could get around such limitations by merely dropping hints. On one occasion, for example, he published a piece in which the author, identified as "Uncle Sam," suggested corruption in the customs office. "With this approach," Huntzicker argues, "Bennett could raise questions without investing heavily in staff, and he could pose an independent, anti-establishment stance and create a feeling of investigation and exposure."[5] Such scaled-back "exposé," however, hardly deserves the title of "investigative journalism" and was not likely to satisfy any serious seekers after truth.

The constraints on journalism in general and investigative journalism in particular left a gap that a number of literary authors sought to fill with investigative fiction. In works that predated similar efforts by Upton Sinclair and Truman Capote by decades, Poe, Stowe, and Davis sought to replace faulty journalistic coverage of important stories with literary treatments of the same subjects. In their attempts to outdo their journalistic counterparts, these authors provided more background material, employed the tools of fiction—particularly characterization—and simply outthought reporters. The results were fictional accounts that, at least in the authors' eyes, came closer to the truth than the ostensibly factual coverage provided by newspapers.

POE'S COVERAGE OF THE ROGERS MURDER

With the publication of "The Murders in the Rue Morgue" in 1841, Poe launched a new genre, the detective story. His brilliant C. Auguste Dupin was the first in a long line of fictional sleuths, from Sherlock Holmes to Jack Bauer and beyond. Before there was Dupin, however, there was James Gordon Bennett, along with countless other journalists who combed through the evidence from real crimes and issued their own conclusions.[6] Indeed, it surely is no accident that Dupin, in the first of Poe's "tales of rationation," outwits not only the police, but also the journalists. Like those who are covering the crime for the newspapers, Dupin seeks to deliver the truth behind the mysterious murders of Madame L'Espanaye and her daughter in their home in Paris. "My ultimate object," he explains, "is only the truth." Before they can tell the truth, however, both brands of investigators must uncover the truth—something they do with very different degrees of success. The *Gazette des Tribunaux* reports, "To this horrible mystery there is not as yet, we believe, the slightest clew." A later edition says, "There is not . . . the shadow of a clew apparent." Dupin, on the other hand, gathers several clues, not merely at the scene of the crime, but even in the newspapers' own accounts, effectively out-reasoning his journalistic counterparts. As their nearly identical titles suggest, "The Murders in the Rue Morgue"—the title Poe gave his own story—and "The Tragedy in the Rue Morgue"—the title he gave one of the newspaper accounts—are parallel versions of truth-telling. The difference is that, while the newspaper cannot find or even recognize a clue, the imaginative Dupin solves the mystery, scooping the journalists and beating them at their own game.[7] When Poe put Dupin on the trail of the killer of Marie Roget, he entered new territory. This time, the mystery Poe sought to solve and the journalists he sought to outwit were real. As Poe explains in a note accompanying the 1845 republication of "The Mystery of Marie Roget," the title character is a stand-in for Mary Rogers, a cigar girl who turned up missing in New York in 1841. Once again, Poe presents parallel investigations, and once again Dupin emerges supreme—at least in Poe's version of events, if not in reality. Along the way, Poe presents a far more elaborate critique of journalism, showing how his brand of investigative fiction is the preferable form of truth-telling.

Like Helen Jewett's murder, which had electrified the New York public five years earlier, the death of Mary Rogers was an ideal subject for sensational coverage by Bennett and his journalistic brethren. She was young and apparently pretty, known to a number of New Yorkers, including several newspapermen. Her death, moreover, was mysterious, tinged with shades of sex and violence. On July 25, 1841, she left her home in New York, apparently to visit her aunt. On July 28, her body was discovered on the surface of the Hudson River near Hoboken. A month later, an innkeeper named Frederica Loss claimed to have discovered women's clothes in some woods near the river. In early October, the body of Mary's fiancé, Daniel Payne, was discovered near these same woods.[8]

Police, press, and public alike joined the investigation. While police interrogated suspects, journalists printed salacious details and commentary, and ordinary people visited Hoboken. All told, more than a dozen newspapers, including Bennett's *Herald* and Bryant's *Evening Post* in New York, as well as Philadelphia's *Saturday Evening Post* and Newark's *Daily Advertiser*, covered the story. Suspects and speculation abounded. It was thought that Mary had been raped and murdered by members of a gang, that she had been killed by a single man—if not Payne, then a spurned lover named Alfred Crommelin, a sailor named William Kiekuck, or another acquaintance or stranger—that she had died as a result of an abortion attempt, even that she had not died at all but had in fact returned home. By October, no one had been tried, much less convicted, for the murder, and the story fizzled. More than a year later, however, Justice Gilbert Merritt, who had visited the innkeeper Frederica Loss on her deathbed, swore to a statement in which he claimed that Loss and her sons "kept one of the most depraved and debauched houses in New Jersey, and that all of them had a knowledge of and were accessory to, and became participants in the murder of said Mary C. Rogers, and the concealment of her body." Four days later, the *New York Tribune* claimed Loss had told Merritt that Rogers died at the inn as a result of an abortion, that her sons had disposed of the body in the river, and that later her clothes were planted in the woods.[9]

Before this last development, Poe, perhaps at the request of Rogers's employer, had decided to write his own account of the investigation, eventually publishing it in three installments in *Ladies' Companion* between November 1842 and February 1843. Having distinguished himself as the author of ingenious detective fiction, Poe tried to use his reasoning powers to penetrate the mystery. He changed the name of the deceased to Marie Roget and set the story in Paris, where Dupin had solved the fictional murders of Madame L'Espanaye and her daughter in "The Murders in the Rue Morgue." In a note he later attached to the story, he explains, "Herein, under pretence of relating the fate of a Parisian *grisette*, the author has followed, in minute detail, the essential, while merely paralleling the inessential facts of the real murder of Mary Rogers."[10] In early installments of the story, Dupin suggests the involvement of an anonymous naval officer who was a "secret lover" of Rogers; however, he may have learned of Merritt's statement and revised the final installment, as well as the version that appears in his 1845 *Tales*, as John Walsh has argued.[11]

In the note accompanying the 1845 version, he claimed that "the confessions of *two* persons . . . made, at different periods, long subsequent to the publication, confirmed, in full, not only the general conclusion, but absolutely *all* the chief hypothetical details by which that conclusion was attained" (723). Poe indeed may have been right in his solution—and he may have been wrong. His boast of external confirmation notwithstanding, the truth is that no one—not the police, not the newspapers, not even the various later commentators—has definitively identified the cause of Mary Rogers's death. Dupin may have solved the mystery of Marie Roget, but the mystery of Mary Rogers persists.

"The Mystery of Marie Roget" is not, however, merely an attempt to solve a real crime. Because of the way Poe chose to tell his story, it is also one of the most significant critiques of journalism from the antebellum era. As Davis and other writers would do later, Poe juxtaposes his fictional narrative with journalistic accounts, asking readers to contrast the two approaches to truth-telling. In trying to one-up his journalistic counterparts, Poe sought to prove the superiority of literature in the reporting of truth.

In the story, as he had in his comments on magazines and in his hoaxes, Poe acknowledges the power of the press. Using exactly the same phrase he would later use in "Von Kempelen and His Discovery," he notes that newspapers have created a "general impression" (734); in other words, thanks to their large circulations and the faith that readers put in them, newspapers have shaped citizens' understanding of events.[12] Indeed, since journalism is the only source of information for most people—excepting police investigators and anyone directly involved with the incident—it has a virtual lock on these people's understanding of the murder. The problem, however, is that journalists, in Poe's view, are plagued by a number of shortcomings—sensationalism, inaccuracy, ignorance, "pack journalism," and faulty reasoning—that draw them away from this truth. In "The Mystery of Marie Roget," as he does in the hoaxes we examined in Chapter 5, Poe issues a critique—this time more explicit and more scathing—of journalism and suggests reasons why fiction, such as the kind he has produced in this short story, provides more insight into the truth. He makes his purpose explicit in a note, explaining that "all argument founded upon the fiction is applicable to the truth: and the investigation of the truth was the object" (723). Through the medium of fiction, then, Poe sets out to arrive at the truth behind actual events.

In his tale about Hans Pfaall, Poe likened journalism to both balloon and bellows, capable of giving rise to hoaxes and fanning fires. In "The Mystery of Marie Roget," he goes a step further, suggesting that the quest for a novel story actually leads journalists away from the truth. "We should bear in mind that, in general, it is the object of our newspapers rather to create a sensation—to make a point—than to further the cause of truth," Dupin explains. "The latter end is only pursued when it seems coincident with the former" (738). A newspaper cannot distinguish itself by simply adopting "ordinary opinion," Dupin goes on to say. "The mass of the people regard as profound only him who suggests *pungent contradictions* of the general idea" (738). Poe had made a similar observation in a note accompanying "The Balloon Hoax," subtly ridiculing readers' hunger for exclusive stories in this remark: "The rush for the 'sole paper which had the news,' was something beyond even the prodigious."[13] Poe accuses one newspaper, *Brother Jonathan*—*L'Etoile* in the story—of making the extraordinary suggestion that Mary Rogers was still alive simply to attract attention. Dupin says, "What I mean to say is, that it is the mingled epigram and melodrame of the idea, that Marie Roget still lives, rather than any true plausibility in this idea, which have suggested it to L'Etoile, and secured it a favorable reception with the public" (738). In short, since readers appreciate the novelty of "*pungent contradictions,*" even preferring the *outré* to the plausible, newspapers are going to give it to them.

Poe takes the journalists to task for a number of other shortcomings, as well. As noted in Chapter 3, he frequently accuses journalists of incompetence, calling attention to, among other things, their ignorance of physics and biology (743, 759). Errors, furthermore, are likely to survive and multiply in an environment where journalists liberally borrow from each other instead of doing their own reporting and thinking. Having already accused journalists of favoring extraordinary opinions over common ones, Poe turns around and criticizes some papers for what modern journalism scholars would call "pack journalism"—the tendency to follow the lead of other media instead of operating independently. Dupin remarks that statements made in one paper "have been tacitly received by every paper in Paris, with the exception of *Le Moniteur*" (740). Elsewhere in the story, he singles out one imitative journalist, noting that "it is a pity its inditer was not born a parrot—in which case he would have been the most illustrious parrot of his race. He has merely repeated the individual items of the already published opinion; collecting them, with a laudable industry, from this paper and from that" (750–51).

Poe's most telling criticism is his indictment of the reasoning he has found in the newspapers. A particular paragraph Dupin reads, Poe writes, amounts to "a tissue of inconsequence and incoherence" (743). Later, Dupin notes another fault in reasoning. "I presume you smile at the *sequitur,*" he says to his friend. "You cannot be made to see how the mere *duration* of the corpse on the shore could operate to *multiply traces* of the assassins. Nor can I" (744). He notes, too, that a writer for one of the papers, on more than one occasion, "unwittingly reasons against himself" (745). Crippled by excesses of deductive reasoning, one newspaper has "prescribed . . . a limit to suit its own preconceived notions" (740), and the editor of *L'Etoile* has taken offense at someone who suggested a conclusion contrary to his own (747–48).

The foil for the bumbling, irrational reporters and editors is the extraordinary Dupin, who rises above the problems that lure journalists away from truth because he takes what might be called a more "literary" approach to solving the mystery of Mary/Marie's death. Like so many of Poe's artist figures, from Hans Pfaall to Roderick Usher to Prince Prospero, Dupin resides in a world remote from quotidian reality. In the weeks following the murder, the narrator explains, he and his friend "gave the Future to the winds, and slumbered tranquilly in the Present, weaving the dull world around us into dreams" (724).

Later, he explicitly notes their separation from journalism, saying, "Engaged in researches which had absorbed our whole attention, it had been nearly a month since either of us had gone abroad, or received a visiter, or more than glanced at the leading political articles in one of the daily papers" (728). Such detachment serves them well, enabling them to think on another level, as Dupin suggests when he says, "I have before observed that it is by prominences above the plane of the ordinary, that reason feels her way, if at all, in her search for the true, and that the proper question in cases such as this, is not so much 'what has occurred?' as 'what has occurred that has never occurred before?'" (736–37). Occupying a plane above the ordinary world covered by journalism and freed from the daily exigencies of reporting on "what has occurred," Dupin and the narrator can contemplate other matters, including what makes an event extraordinary. In short, they are more likely to see the big picture and not simply the particulars. Similarly, as one might expect of an artist, Dupin examines the case from a broad angle, one that takes into account evidence outside the immediate event.[14] He argues that "the *larger* portion of all truth has sprung from the collateral; and it is but in accordance with the spirit of the principle involved in this fact, that I would divert inquiry, in the present case, from the trodden and hitherto unfruitful ground of the event itself, to the cotemporary circumstances which surround it" (752).

Elsewhere in the story, furthermore, Dupin introduces what might be called "literary thinking" into his analysis, showing an understanding that, as he would have it, might have escaped journalists. Drawing on his understanding of human psychology, for instance, he remarks: "Those who would hesitate at such a wager, have either never been boys themselves, or have forgotten the boyish nature" (761). Similarly, in speculating on the killer's actions, he enters the world of the mind:

An individual has committed the murder. He is alone with the ghost of the departed. He is appalled by what lies motionless before him. The fury of his passion is over, and there is abundant room in his heart for the natural awe of the deed. His is none of that confidence which the presence of numbers inevitably inspires. He is *alone* with the dead. He trembles and is bewildered. Yet there is a necessity for disposing of the corpse. He bears it to the river, but leaves behind him the other evidences of guilt; for it is difficult, if not impossible to carry all the burthen at once, and it will be easy to return for what is left. But in his toilsome journey to the water his fears redouble within him. The sounds of life encompass his path. A dozen times he hears or fancies the step of an observer. Even the very lights from the city bewilder

him. Yet, in time, and by long and frequent pauses of deep agony, he
reaches the river's brink, and disposes of his ghastly charge—perhaps
through the medium of a boat. But *now* what treasure does the world
hold—what threat of vengeance could it hold out—which would have
power to urge the return of that lonely murderer over that toilsome
and perilous path, to the thicket and its blood-chilling recollections?
(764–65)

This exploratory venture into the mysteries of the human mind is
perhaps less common—some would say inappropriate—in journalism,
but forms a major part of the literary endeavor, especially for an author
such as Poe, who plumbed these depths in "The Tell-Tale Heart,"
"The Imp of the Perverse," and other tales.[15] In "The Mystery of
Marie Roget," Dupin operates on a separate, higher plane of reason
and uses literary means in his attempt to penetrate a mystery that has
baffled those supposedly shackled by the shortcomings of journalism.

STOWE'S ABOLITIONIST EXPOSÉ[16]

When the Fugitive Slave Law was passed in September 1850, it made
news—a lot of news. With predictably diverse opinions, newspapers
across the country reacted to both the new law and its aftermath.
The *Constitution* in Middletown, Connecticut, called on readers to
support the rule of law, while the *New Hampshire Sentinel, Farmer's
Cabinet,* and *New York Independent* strongly opposed it, using words
such as "abnoxious," "odious," and "iniquitous." Reporting on the
transfer of the captured fugitive Henry Long's case to a district court,
the *New York Evangelist* encouraged the "friends of freedom" to
"contribute the means of carrying the case up to the Supreme Court,
in case of Long's conviction."[17]

One newspaper reader, however, was not content to let the press
wage war on the Fugitive Slave Law or on slavery in general. "You
dont know how my heart burns within me at the blindness and
obtuseness of good people on so very simple a point of morality as
this," Harriet Beecher Stowe wrote in a letter to her brother Henry
Ward Beecher in February 1851. She continued,

Must we forever keep calm and smile and smile when every sentiment
of manliness and humanity is kicked and rolled in the dust and lies
trampled and bleeding and make it a merit to be exceedingly cool—
I feel as if my heart would burn itself out in grief and shame that such
things are—I wish I had your chance—but next best to that it is to have
you have it—so fire away—give them no rest day nor night.[18]

Stowe, of course, would get her chance. A little more than four months after she wrote this letter, the first installment of *Uncle Tom's Cabin* appeared in the *National Era*. When it came out in book form the following year, it quickly became the greatest literary sensation of the century, selling 300,000 copies inside of a year and leaving contemporaries and modern scholars ranging from Charles Dudley Warner to Ann Douglas to remark on its extraordinary impact on the American reading public.[19] The most famous of these commentators, Abraham Lincoln, supposedly said to Stowe, upon meeting her in the White House in 1862, "So you're the little lady who started the great war."[20]

A number of journalists—notably William Lloyd Garrison, Frederick Douglass, and Horace Greeley—might have made similar claims for their own roles in building consensus for a war fought largely over the institution of slavery. Journalism historian Rodger Streitmatter has argued that "the abolitionist press—black as well as white—succeeded in articulating and broadcasting throughout the nation the moral indictment of slavery that precipitated the Civil War."[21] Nevertheless, Stowe, like Poe and other fellow authors of the period, was not satisfied with the job that journalists as a whole were doing in their self-proclaimed role as truth-tellers. In *Uncle Tom's Cabin*, she issues a subtle but clear critique of journalism, implicating not only its producers, but also its readers: passive men who, like Senator Bird and Augustine St. Clare, treat their newspaper not as an entry into the world but as a refuge from it. At the same time, she substitutes her own investigative fiction. Using the tools of literature—fictional characters and incidents, dialogue, imagery, and other devices—Stowe replaces the often shallow treatment of slavery in contemporary newspapers with a broader, deeper exposé of an institution that destroyed both individuals and families.

Stowe knew journalism as both an insider and an outsider. She was a reader of the *Philanthropist* and *Western Monthly Magazine*, as we saw in Chapter 2, but she also contributed to the magazine and other publications. When her brother Henry Ward Beecher took over as temporary editor of the *Cincinnati Journal and Western Luminary* in 1836, she helped him fill his columns. In a letter to her husband from this time, she wrote, "Yesterday evening I spent scribbling for Henry's newspaper in this wise; 'Birney's printing-press has been mobbed, and many of the respectable citizens are moving in the line of their prejudices.'" She noted that their "family *newspaper*" brought them "not a little diversion." Between March 1833 and January 1851, furthermore, she placed a number of items in the *Western Monthly Magazine*, the *New York Evangelist*, and the *National Era*.[22]

In her biography, *Harriet Beecher Stowe: A Life*, Joan D. Hedrick has suggested that what Stowe saw in the American press left her feeling dissatisfied, even livid. Hedrick explains, "The mealy-mouthed postures of editorialists and clergymen who hemmed and hawed and attempted 'to hush up and salve over such an outrage on common humanity' infuriated her."[23] In the letters in which she leveled her criticisms, she usually implicated complacent Christians in general without singling out journalists. For example, she complained to Henry in early 1851,

> Is it possible that Henry Long is hopelessly sold and that in all this nation of freemen there is not one deliverer brave enough and strong enough to recover him . . . and are there Christians that can find nothing better to do than cry peace when such things are done. How I detest that cool way of lumping together all the woes and crimes, the heart-breaks, the bitter untold agonies of thousand poor bleeding helpless hearts, many creatures with the bland expression its very sad to be sure—very dreadful—but we mustn't allow our feelings to run away with us, we must consider &c., &c, &c.[24]

It may be that Stowe, writing to her brother, was reluctant to attack journalists directly, since he was one of them. In another part of this letter, however, she may be singling out one writer for the *New York Observer*. "To day I read over Storrs article in answer to the N York observer," she explains. "You dont know how my heart burns within me at the blindness and obtuseness of good people on so very simple a point of morality as this."[25] Whether her target was the press or its readers, Stowe was clearly exasperated with what she regarded as some Christians' complacency, which left her feeling, as she stated to her sister Catharine Beecher, "almost choked sometimes with pent up wrath that does no good."[26] Hedrick suggests that Stowe felt stifled because of limitations that prevented women from acting in the public spheres of academia, church, and politics.[27] Ultimately, of course, she found her voice. As Hedrick records, Isabella Beecher wrote to Stowe, saying, "Now, Hattie, if I could use a pen as you can, I would write something that would make this whole nation feel what an accursed thing slavery is." Stowe responded by standing and announcing, "I will write something. I will if I live." By the middle of March, she had begun writing *Uncle Tom's Cabin*.[28]

The novel that emerged out of Stowe's exasperation with the current responses to slavery reveals even more about her attitude toward journalism than her letters do. Far more nuanced than Poe's sarcastic digs in "The Mystery of Marie Roget" or Thoreau's explicit attacks on newspapers, *Uncle Tom's Cabin* nevertheless participates in the widespread denunciation of journalism coming from the pens of American authors in the nineteenth century. In her critique, Stowe indicts both the impotence of newspapers and the complacency of their mostly male readers, neither of which is taking abolition seriously enough. Indeed, instead of doing the reform work that she expected of journalism, newspapers in her novel provide a form of escape or, worse, act as an agent abetting slavery.

A brief examination of literary and journalistic theories may help illuminate the nature of Stowe's argument with the press. As James Baldwin famously noted, *Uncle Tom's Cabin* belongs to the genre of the protest novel.[29] More recently, George Goodin has included it in a long tradition of "victim-of-society novels." Whatever the label, Stowe's work is an obvious attempt to expose—and to right—a wrong. There is, of course, nothing unique in such an attempt. As Goodin notes, examples of novels of social protest go back at least to the late eighteenth century.[30] What makes *Uncle Tom's Cabin* and similar works notable is the explicit critique of a competing genre.

Stowe's frustration with the impotence of journalism on the slavery question can be seen in the role that newspapers play in *Uncle Tom's Cabin*. Not once does a character find any inspiration in a newspaper, even though Senator Bird, Augustine St. Clare, and, in a flashback, St. Clare's father continually read them. Although she never divulges exactly what Bird and the St. Clares are reading in their papers, other parts of the novel point to particular journalistic failings. The press, Stowe suggests, is insensitive to the situation of American slavery and is not recognizing its gravity:

> When despairing Hungarian fugitives make their way, against all the search-warrants and authorities of their lawful government, to America, press and political cabinet ring with applause and welcome. When despairing African fugitives do the same thing,—it is—what *is* it?[31]

As Stowe sees it, when the press does cover fugitive slaves, it reveals only a small part of the story; indeed, she attributes Senator Bird's insensitivity to the plight of fugitive slaves at least partly to the failure of the press to cover the whole story (125).

Journalism's sins, in Stowe's eyes, were not entirely those of omission. Newspapers were also supporting slavery in a variety of ways. In addition to publishing the kinds of advertisements that Senator Bird reads, which help slave owners to recover fugitive slaves, papers often announced impending slave auctions like the ad that Mr. Haley sees (161). Some newspapers, furthermore, openly promoted the cause of slavery, as St. Clare notes when he responds to his wife, who has mentioned a church sermon defending slavery, "I can learn what does me as much good as that from the Picayune, any time, and smoke a cigar besides; which I can't do, you know, in a church" (241).

In suggesting that the press was not adequately addressing the slavery question, Stowe was only partially correct. In fact, a number of newspapers—including abolitionist papers such as Garrison's *Liberator* and Douglass's *North Star*, and mainstream papers such as Greeley's *New York Tribune*—regularly reported on issues surrounding slavery. In her brother Henry's *Independent*, furthermore, Stowe could have found a number of such articles. For example, "A Voice from New England," which appeared in the January 2, 1851, issue, promises opposition to the Fugitive Slave Law:

> We shall lift no hand of violence against the sovereign law of the land. *Nor shall we lift a hand against him who flees from unrighteous bondage.* Nor shall we shut our mouths and promise to be dumb henceforth in regard to the iniquity of the system of Slavery. We shall bear the penalty which the law may inflict upon us. We shall dare to speak the truth, however unpalatable it may be.

The front page of the same issue features a lengthy disquisition, "The Civil Law: Man's Obligation to Obey It," in which the author, quoting scripture, argues that Christians must obey God's law instead of human law, including the Fugitive Slave Law.

Such responses to slavery, however, could hardly have satisfied Stowe, for her feelings on the subject went well beyond logical analysis. Hedrick argues that "the namby-pamby postures of 'good people'—so disproportionately reasonable and scripture-quoting and full of lengthy, dull, and tedious explanations that lost their audience and left them wondering what all the fuss was about—made Harriet feel as though she would explode."[32] Stowe's exasperation was not unwarranted. Even in a relatively passionate article appearing in Greeley's *Tribune*, known for its anti-slavery position, a curiously complacent undertone is evident. Noting that some Americans would like to see the slave trade abolished in Baltimore, as it had been in the District of Columbia, the correspondent goes on to editorialize on the horrors of slavery:

> If there is any sight more harrowing to the feelings of a *man* than another, that sight is a gang of Slaves, chained together, being marched to a vessel to be transported to the Southern States. I have seen those

who have been torn from parents and friends, thus marched off to a separation for life, from all that they held dear, or could desire to live for.

The reporter concludes these remarks, however, in a noncommittal manner: "But enough, the day is not so very far distant when this disgrace will be seen, or heard no more, in Maryland."[33] Such insufficient coverage must have appalled Stowe. With or without the slave trade in Maryland, she was aware that southern slavery continued to crush men, women, and children, and northerners were bound by the Fugitive Slave Law to return escapees to its horrors.

In Stowe's eyes, a problem greater than newspapers' inept coverage of slavery may have been the complacency of newspaper readers. For some, Stowe suggests, journalism was merely a form of refuge from uncomfortable realities. That newspapers could serve as a form of escape might have come as a surprise to Poe, whose characters are more likely to escape *from* them into realms of fancy or contemplation.[34] For Stowe, however, newspapers were failing readers precisely because they were not presenting enough of reality. As such, they could serve as an acceptable form of retreat for men in particular, especially when they were confronted by their wives with prickly questions about the "peculiar institution."

Like his father, who "betook himself to a nap, or the newspaper" after dismissing his wife's "pathetic appeals" (297), Augustine St. Clare regularly retreats into his newspaper when challenged. After watching his wife, daughter, and cousin leave for church, he acknowledges his daughter Evangeline's role in bringing him to God. Nevertheless, "he smoked a cigar, and read the Picayune, and forgot his little gospel" (240). Later, when Ophelia demands some official word that she has control of Topsy, he promises to provide it but instead "sat down, and unfolded a newspaper to read" (400). In the most telling of these episodes, two forms of news compete for St. Clare's attention when Ophelia tells her cousin, who has been reclining with his paper, that Prue has been whipped to death. Although he hears Ophelia "going on, with great strength of detail, into the story, and enlarging on its most shocking particulars" (288), St. Clare is nonplussed, responding only that he "thought it would come to that, some time." When Ophelia urges him to action, he merely concludes, "The best we can do is to shut our eyes and ears, and let it alone" (289). He returns to his newspaper, preferring the apparently unchallenging "news" he finds there over the shocking dose of reality that his cousin has just delivered to him.

Source: The York Family at Home, Joseph H. Davis, New Hampshire, 1837, Watercolor, pencil, and ink on wove paper, courtesy of Abby Aldrich Rockefeller Folk Art Museum, The Colonial Williamsburg Foundation, Williamsburg, VA; Gift of the Museum of Modern Art.

Although St. Clare notes that newspapers occasionally report on the "horrid cruelties and outrages" of slavery (322), it is not surprising, of course, that antebellum southern journalists did not tell the whole story. In her scenes featuring Senator Bird, however, Stowe suggests that the same could be said of northern newspapers. After Mrs. Bird challenges his support of the fugitive slave legislation, the Ohio senator experiences some "vexation"; nevertheless, "seating himself in the arm-chair," he "began to read the papers" (115). As in the case of St. Clare's retreats, we never learn exactly what Bird finds in his journalistic refuge on this occasion. The subject of the articles or advertisements, it seems, is not significant, but what is clear is that Senator Bird's newspaper reading, like that of St. Clare, provides him with an opportunity for escape and relaxation.

Stowe's depiction of men reading their newspapers for relaxation was not unique at the time. Indeed, as Thomas Leonard has shown, contemporary artistic renderings of newspaper readers presented similar images. For instance, in Nicolino Calyo's 1840 painting *Reading Room, Astor House*, an 1860 sketch by Lefevre J. Cranstone, and an 1857 *Harper's Weekly* illustration entitled "How We Sit in Our Hotel Rooms," men read newspapers while reclining in chairs and resting their feet on tables. Other paintings, Leonard notes, show newspapers serving as barriers between men and family members:

> Eastman Johnson gave patriarchs newspapers to hold like shields as they sat in family portraits. These are formidable readers of the parlor. In *The Brown Family* (1869) the gentleman near the hearth is planted like an oak and only tips his paper slightly to acknowledge the child who has reached out to interrupt reading. The father in *The Hatch Family* (1871) sinks behind his newspaper and is oblivious to his fourteen relatives in the drawing room. Evidently the men who commissioned these paintings were pleased to be walled off by the news.[35]

Leonard's characterization of men "walled off by the news" perfectly captures the attitudes of Augustine St. Clare and Senator Bird, both of whom find refuge in their newspapers from both family members and the day's most pressing issues.

Reality, however, can sometimes penetrate a man's wall. Senator Bird puts down his paper when his wife calls him to the kitchen, where he sees Eliza and her son Harry. While the previous scene is then reenacted, this time the arrival of the two escaped slaves has abruptly introduced a human element into the couple's debate. After

Eliza and Harry go to sleep, Bird again turns to his paper, but, unlike the mother and child, he now finds no repose:

> Mr. and Mrs. Bird had gone back to the parlor, where, strange as it may appear, no reference was made, on either side, to the preceding conversation; but Mrs. Bird busied herself with her knitting-work, and Mr. Bird pretended to be reading the paper.
>
> "I wonder who and what she is!" said Mr. Bird, at last, as he laid it down.
>
> "When she wakes up and feels a little rested, we will see," said Mrs. Bird.
>
> "I say, wife!" said Mr. Bird, after musing in silence over his newspaper. "Well, dear!"
>
> "She couldn't wear one of your gowns, could she, by any letting down, or such matter? She seems to be rather larger than you are." (117)

As if roused from his sleep by an encounter with slavery in all of its ugly reality, Senator Bird now only "pretends" to peruse his paper. Ultimately, he contradicts his own position on fugitive slaves and decides to help Eliza and Harry continue their journey. The confrontation with the reality of slavery has overcome the incomplete version of the truth he had found in newspapers, as Stowe explains:

> [H]is idea of a fugitive was only an idea of the letters that spell the word,—or, at the most, the image of a little newspaper picture of a man with a stick and bundle, with "Ran away from the subscriber" under it. The magic of the real presence of distress,—the imploring human eye, the frail, trembling human hand, the despairing appeal of helpless agony,—these he had never tried. (125)

Unlike St. Clare, Senator Bird eventually takes action, not because of anything he has seen in the shallow, apparently soporific newspapers he reads, but because of the "news" that comes right into his kitchen.

As a number of scholars have suggested, Stowe's rhetorical arguments against slavery may be viewed on several levels. S. Bradley Shaw has focused on her use of "domestic rhetoric"; Mason I. Lowance has shown how Stowe borrowed from biblical rhetoric to set up a typological relationship between Eva and Uncle Tom; and Catharine E. O'Connell has made a compelling case for Stowe's rejection of religious and republican rhetoric in favor of sentimental rhetoric.[36] One might go further and say that Stowe also rejected the rhetoric of journalism—both the logical, sermonic approach often seen in religious publications and the sometimes shallow, factual treatment of slavery found in mainstream newspapers—and made her own case against slavery in the form of investigative fiction. In "The Freeman's Dream: A Parable," which appeared in the *National Era* in August 1850, she first used fiction to fight the fugitive-slave legislation, presenting readers with the story of a man who fails to help runaway slaves and then encounters an angry God.[37] In *Uncle Tom's Cabin*, she again turned to literature to make an impact on readers.

In her novel's preface, Stowe makes a case for the power of fiction to bring about reform: "The poet, the painter, and the artist, now seek out and embellish the common and gentler humanities of life, and, under the allurements of fiction, breathe a humanizing and subduing influence, favorable to the development of the great principles of Christian brotherhood" (3). Lest anyone think that fiction, by its very nature, cannot tell the truth, Stowe explains that her story has roots in reality. "In the northern states," she writes, "these representations may, perhaps, be thought caricatures; in the southern states are witnesses who know their fidelity. What personal knowledge the author has had, of the truth of incidents such as here are related, will appear in its time."[38] Later in the novel, she defends her portrayal of one of its central characters with a similar argument: "Eliza, such as we have described her, is not a fancy sketch, but taken from remembrance, as we saw her, years ago, in Kentucky" (26). Eventually, Stowe would publish an entire book, *A Key to Uncle Tom's Cabin*, furthering the case for the "fidelity" of her fiction. In the opening sentences of Chapter 1 of this book, Stowe says:

> At different times, doubt has been expressed whether the representations of "Uncle Tom's Cabin" are a fair representation of slavery as it at present exists. This work, more, perhaps, than any other work of fiction that ever was written, has been a collection and arrangement of real incidents,—of actions really performed, of words and expressions really uttered,—grouped together with reference to a general result, in the same manner that the mosaic artist groups his fragments of various stones into one general picture. His is a mosaic of *gems*,—this is a mosaic of facts.[39]

For Stowe, investigative fiction—like good investigative journalism—was grounded in reality.

Stowe's method in reporting her news is exactly what one would expect of a fiction writer. Using dialogue, imagery, and description, she fleshes out her characters, allowing readers to see them as human beings deserving of sympathy. Where readers of newspapers might see only "a man with a stick and bundle," readers of Stowe's novel

see a black slave with a name, George Harris, who as a child had no
family and knew "nothing but whipping, scolding, starving," and
who as an adult knows no country (154). They see a slave mother
who is willing to brave the woods and an ice-filled Ohio River to
avoid being separated from her son; a slave girl whose sensibilities are
so warped by constant brutality that she asks to be whipped; and a
host of other characters and scenes that capture the truths of slavery
in its hideous detail. As Stowe puts it in her preface, "The object of
these sketches is to awaken sympathy and feeling for the African race,
as they exist among us; to show their wrongs and sorrows, under a
system so necessarily cruel and unjust as to defeat and do away the
good effects of all that can be attempted for them, by their best friends,
under it" (4). Several times Stowe presents scenes in which characters
arrive at epiphanies only after they are confronted with real people
and situations: as already noted, Senator Bird changes his mind about
helping runaway slaves after he meets Eliza and Harry, and, similarly,
her encounters with Rosa help Ophelia understand the reality of "the
universal custom to send women and young girls to whipping-houses,
to the hands of the lowest of men . . . there to be subjected to brutal
exposure and shameful correction. She had *known* it before; but hitherto
she had never realized it, till she saw the slender form of Rosa almost
convulsed with distress" (415). Through fiction, Stowe is able to provide rounded, more human portraits even of southern slave owners,
capturing, for example, the complex motivation that drives St. Clare's
actions—or more precisely, his lack of action.

In Stowe's eyes, however, the most important news of the novel
comes not through newspapers or fictional portraits but through the
Bible, itself a form of literature. Stowe suggests this emphasis when
she describes Eva's response to the scriptures:

> The parts that pleased her most were the Revelations and the Prophecies,—
> parts whose dim and wondrous imagery, and fervent language, impressed
> her the more, that she questioned vainly of their meaning;—and
> she and her simple friend, the old child and the young one, felt just
> alike about it. All that they knew was, that they spoke of a glory to
> be revealed,—a wondrous something yet to come, wherein their soul
> rejoiced, yet knew not why; and though it be not so in the physical,
> yet in moral science that which cannot be understood is not always
> profitless. For the soul awakes, a trembling stranger, between two dim
> eternities,—the eternal past, the eternal future. . . . Its mystic imagery
> are so many talismans and gems inscribed with unknown hieroglyphics;
> she folds them in her bosom, and expects to read them when she passes
> beyond the veil. (338)

Through "mystic imagery" and evocative language, the Bible, like other forms of literature, presents readers with "hieroglyphics," conveying meaning that is both enigmatic and powerful. This is not the quotidian "news" that Senator Bird and St. Clare are likely to find in their papers, but something far more profound, something that requires the language of literature.

Eva, of course, soon has her opportunity to "read" this message in full when she moves to the next world. What is more interesting, however, is the manner in which this same opportunity comes to her father. One evening after his daughter's death, St. Clare leaves the house in search of "the news" (408). At a cafe where he has begun to read a newspaper, he becomes entangled in a brawl in which he is fatally stabbed. On his deathbed, his face shows that he has found peace. Let down by the newspapers of this world, St. Clare, in death, finally receives the Good News—that which his daughter, rightly named Evangeline, tried to convey to him. To Stowe, this is the most important news of all.

In Stowe's view, such good news, as well as the dismal news of slavery, is best delivered through the medium of literature. *Uncle Tom's Cabin* makes this case not only through its critique of journalism and endorsement of fiction but also through its own phenomenal success, which testifies to the impact that literature can exert on readers. "No woman before or since Stowe has so successfully written a novel designed to stir up the nation in the cause of the major issue of the day," states Ann Douglas. Douglas notes that Stowe "helped to make what had been the protest of only a small minority of abolitionists the concern, even the preoccupation, of hundreds of thousands of Americans."[40] In proposing literature as an alternative to journalism, furthermore, Stowe added her powerful voice to that of other nineteenth-century American writers who were reacting to the shallow, sensationalistic, and otherwise flawed depictions of reality that they encountered in contemporary journalism by composing news of their own.

DAVIS'S REVELATIONS OF REALITY

In the vein of *Uncle Tom's Cabin*, Rebecca Harding Davis's most famous story, "Life in the Iron-Mills," offers readers a brand of investigative fiction designed to tell the story that journalism has missed. Davis's corrective mission can be seen in the story's opening, in which she announces the presence of a "secret" and tells her reader, "I want to make it a real thing to you."[41] "Life in the Iron-Mills" has been rightly analyzed as an early form of realism.[42] As such, it belongs to the wide-scale rejection of romanticism that came from the pens of

Davis and her contemporaries. The story, however, is just as much a rejection of—and substitute for—contemporary journalism.

Among the authors of the era, Davis was one of the most ambivalent when it came to journalism. Much that was associated with the enterprise appealed to her. In her correspondence with Annie Fields, wife of *Atlantic* editor James T. Fields, she begged her friend to report "all the news," or, as she put it in one letter, "home news."[43] As Sharon Harris has noted, she particularly appreciated the "new" in *news*. In her correspondence with James Fields about her first novel— titled, significantly, "The Story of To-Day," when it appeared serially in the *Atlantic*—she expressed her desire to see it in print "soon." She added, "Forgive me, but I am afraid if it was kept long it would be as stale as uncorked champagne." In a later letter about another work, she wrote, "I forgot to say—won't you publish John Lamar as soon as you can? I have a fancy for writing of *today* you see."[44] Harris explains that Davis's fiction explored topics "while they were at the forefront of American thought rather than from hindsight" and adds, "The 'story of to-day' remained central to her literary voice throughout her life."[45] Facts, too, were important to Davis, as can be seen in her reminiscence about the Transcendentalists in her memoir *Bits of Gossip*:

> Whether Alcott, Emerson, and their disciples discussed pears or the war, their views gave you the same sense of unreality, of having been taken, as Hawthorne said, at too long a range. You heard much sound philosophy and many sublime guesses at the eternal verities; in fact, never were the eternal verities so dissected and pawed over and turned inside out as they were about that time, in Boston, by Margaret Fuller and her successors. But the discussion left you with a vague, uneasy sense that something was lacking, some back-bone of fact.

Other works, including "Two Methods with the Negro" and "The House on the Beach," express a faith in facts, as well.[46] Finally, as Whitney A. Womack has noted, Davis's early career coincided with numerous reform movements in the United States.[47] In *Bits of Gossip*, Davis recalls her early encounters with reformers, especially one named Francis LeMoyne.[48] Tillie Olsen has argued that this "troubling, radical figure" had a profound effect on Davis, providing "her first awareness of the gulf of pain and wrong outside herself."[49] Years after her encounter with LeMoyne, Davis used her fiction to expose readers to hidden truths. In Harris's words, "Her purpose in developing a fiction of the commonplace was to expose the harsh realities of life and to demand change: change that would require hard work and confrontation with those realities."[50]

As a discipline that prized timeliness, facts, and exposure, journalism would seem to have been a natural choice for Davis. For much of her adult life, in fact, she would write extensively for newspapers, as we have seen in Chapter 2. Before publishing "Life in the Iron-Mills" in 1861, she worked as a correspondent for the *Intelligencer* in her hometown of Wheeling, Virginia, publishing editorials and reviews, as well as literary material. Later, she wrote for Greeley's *New York Tribune* and the *Independent*.[51] She also defended journalism as a "respectable" career for women.[52] In her view, however, readers could not rely on journalism for a complete account of reality. The reasons for her dissatisfaction can be found in her most famous story.

"To the readers of that April 1861 *Atlantic*," Tillie Olsen has written, "*Life in the Iron Mills* came as absolute News, with the shock of unprepared-for revelation."[53] Although she does not follow up this observation with any discussion of journalism, Olsen's statement nicely captures the project on which Davis embarked in her first major short story. Through the medium of fiction, she sought to report "News" that could bring about a "revelation" for her readers. This news, furthermore, was relevant to her contemporaries. Although the story is set some three decades earlier, the narrator notes that the people mentioned in it have "duplicates swarming the streets to-day."[54] Both a critique of and a substitute for contemporary journalism, "Life in the Iron-Mills" is Davis's first major work of investigative fiction.

Through her characterization of reporters and newspapers in the story, Davis suggests that journalism provides only an incomplete, distorted version of reality, leaving a gap that literature must fill. The actions of the reporter who interviews the mill overseer in the middle of the story, for instance, are revealing. Like Davis herself, this reporter is pulling a story out of the iron mills. Whereas the author seeks to unearth the "secret" of working-class life (4), however, this reporter is merely "getting up a series of reviews of the leading manu-factories" (12). At a moment when he easily could have recorded the scene before him of men working in infernal conditions, he is busy interviewing the overseer, who is "talking of net profits just then,—giving, in fact, a schedule of the annual business of the firm" (12). His remarks to the overseer confirm the true subject matter of his story:

> "Pig-metal," mumbled the reporter,—"um!—coal facilities,—um!—hands employed, twelve hundred,—bitumen,—um!—all right, I believe, Mr. Clarke;—sinking-fund,—what did you say was your sinking-fund?" (13)

The news value of impact perhaps in the back of his mind, this reporter records the financial details of the mill. It may be, too, that Davis is criticizing the press's bias in favor of business. In any case, this journalist is clearly ignoring another story, one that apparently does not satisfy his criteria for news.

When it comes time to report on the laborers themselves, journalism tells only part of the story, leaving readers with an incomplete understanding of reality. At this point in the story, Hugh Wolfe has been found with stolen money. Readers of Davis's version of events know that he did not take the money, that he accepted it from Deborah, that he intended to return it, and that he started to succumb to temptations, including the vision of "himself as he might be" (23). In short, thanks to Davis's literary rendering of the behind-the-scenes events and the characters' psychological states, readers of her story know not just what Wolfe has done, but why he has done it. The newspaper version of the story, on the other hand, is barely a sketch: "Circuit Court. Judge Day. Hugh Wolfe, operative in Kirby & John's Loudon Mills. Charge, grand larceny. Sentence, nineteen years hard labor in penitentiary" (25–26).[55] Furthermore, it appears in a part of the paper that women apparently do not usually see; the narrator notes that Doctor May's reading of the story to his wife is "an unusual thing;—these police-reports not being, in general, choice reading for ladies" (25). The account provides only the bare bones—court, names, charge, sentence—delivered, literally, in fragments. Davis accentuates the effect of such incomplete coverage by presenting a reader's reaction. After reading this item, Doctor May cries, "Scoundrel! Serves him right! After all our kindness that night! Picking Mitchell's pocket at the very time!" (26). Thanks to the flawed journalistic version of the story, this reader not only lacks the necessary information to come to an appropriate judgment, but also comes away with an inaccurate impression: he assumes—logically, on the basis of this news story—that Wolfe has himself stolen the money. Of course, journalism has not exactly made the mistake in accuracy—it was merely reporting on a trial that itself involved a mistake—but, unlike the author of the short story, it has failed to investigate the full story and thus has left readers with an incomplete version of reality. Elsewhere in the story, the narrator alludes to the nature of this kind of coverage, saying:

> Do you want to hear the end of it? You wish me to make a tragic story out of it? Why, in the police-reports of the morning paper you can find a dozen such tragedies: hints of ship-wrecks unlike any that ever befell on the high seas; hints that here a power was lost to heaven,—that there a soul went down where no tide can ebb or flow.

Commonplace enough the hints are,—jocose sometimes, done up in rhyme. (25)

The "morning paper," then, provides only "hints," leaving it up to an author, such as Davis, to provide "the end of it." These hints, furthermore, come from journalists who sometimes do not even take these tragedies seriously, giving them "jocose" treatment or turning them into doggerel.

Journalists do finally come around—in their fashion. After the despondent Wolfe has committed suicide in his cell, the "local editors" are among the horde that flocks to the scene of the tragedy. Now that he is dead, a sensational suicide, Wolfe is finally news. Davis provides no other details of the journalists' actions, but their appearance at this late moment is an indictment in itself. Journalism is too late to help this laborer. If its treatment of the working class in the past is any indication, furthermore, it will do nothing to prevent another such tragedy.

"Life in the Iron-Mills" is more than a critique of journalism, however; it is also a substitute for it. In "covering" the story of the working class in her own, literary way, Davis sought to report some news of her own. From the story's very beginning, she frames her material as a kind of investigative report, or exposé. The opening sentence presents an image and a question: "A cloudy day: do you know what that is in a town of iron-works?" (3). The image of clouds suggests that something is being hidden; the follow-up question, furthermore, confronts the reader with a question about meaning. The rhetorical question in this opening sentence sets up the rest of the story by preparing the reader for an explanation of "what that is." In subsequent paragraphs, the narrator announces an intention to expose some information about this obscure segment of American reality. Employing more images of things that obscure, she invites the reader to join her, in "the thickest of the fog and mud and foul effluvia," and "hear this story." She continues, "There is a secret down here, in this nightmare fog, that has lain dumb for centuries: I want to make it a real thing to you" (4). The narrator's purpose, then, is clear: she seeks to uncover a hidden reality, just as an investigative journalist is supposed to do. Indeed, as David Reynolds has noted, newspaper exposés of the antebellum era often employed the metaphor of "lifting the veil that covers hidden corruption."[56] As her criticisms of journalism throughout the story show, however, Davis believed that newspapers were, for various reasons, failing to expose hidden realities. Hampered by their news values or a bias toward moneyed interests, as well as their packaging constraints, these supposed reporters of truth have left readers with an incomplete view of reality.

The narrator's announced intention "to make it a real thing" suggests that she is going to expose the reality that others have failed to expose; however, in a paradoxical turn, she admits that her own account will itself not be perfectly transparent. "I dare make my meaning no clearer," she says, "but will only tell my story" (4–5). In more ways than one, this sentence identifies the literary nature of Davis's exposé. Literature, by its very nature, suggests rather than states; thus, Davis might seem to make its meaning less clear than the explicit language of journalism. Still, the second half of this sentence suggests that literature can stand on its own. By simply telling a "story," an author can make a "real thing" of a "secret." Davis makes a similar case for literature later in the story, again initially conceding the imperfection of her approach but then hinting at its value:

> A reality of soul-starvation, of living death, that meets you every day under the besotted faces on the street,—I can paint nothing of this, only give you the outside outlines of a night, a crisis in the life of one man: whatever muddy depth of soul-history lies beneath you can read according to the eyes God has given you. (10)

Even Davis's own investigative fiction, then, is not perfect; it cannot penetrate all that obscures the workers' tragedy. Still, it provides "the outside outlines" and, perhaps most importantly, it encourages more investigation. As a straightforward account of facts, journalism is ostensibly a self-evident genre; literature, on the other hand, is by its very nature an indirect approach to the truth, one that calls on readers to tease out the deeper meaning. By using their own eyes, Davis says, these readers can decipher "whatever muddy depth of soul-history lies beneath" the "outlines" that she provides in her story.

The reasons that literature can succeed in such an endeavor are apparent in the story, which serves as a countertext to the incomplete, inaccurate coverage of Hugh Wolfe in the newspaper. Whereas the newspaper has summed up a crucial event in Wolfe's life in a sparse court report, Davis's story uncovers the surrounding events that culminated in his conviction and sentence: the brutalizing working and living conditions, Deborah's desire to do something for Wolfe, Wolfe's own rationalization about retaining possession of stolen money. Literature, in short, can provide a more thorough investigation of a human life or event. Lisa Long has argued that Davis and her contemporary Elizabeth Stuart Phelps were "engaged in finding out what their characters are 'made of,' of mapping the internal unseen."[57] Echoing the invitation in her introduction, Davis's narrator calls on the reader to take a close look at the world surrounding Wolfe.

> I want you to come down and look at this Wolfe, standing there among the lowest of his kind, and see him just as he is, that you may judge him justly when you hear the story of this night. I want you to look back, as he does every day, at his birth in vice, his starved infancy; to remember the heavy years he has groped through as boy and man,—the slow, heavy years of constant, hot work. (11)

Similarly, the narrator calls attention to the deeper story behind the story's other major character, Deborah:

> Deeper yet if one could look, was there nothing worth reading in this wet, faded thing, half-covered with ashes? no story of a soul filled with groping passionate love, heroic unselfishness, fierce jealousy? of years of weary trying to please the one human being whom she loved, to gain one look of real heart-kindness from him? (9)

In both of these passages we find the language of exposure: "look" appears four times, and "see" and "reading" each appear once. Davis goes on to suggest this "story" has remained hidden because it has been ignored: "If anything like this were hidden beneath the pale, bleared eyes, and dull, washed-out-looking face, no one had ever taken the trouble to read its faint signs: not the half-clothed furnace tender, Wolfe, certainly" (9). Although Davis explicitly accuses Wolfe of ignoring Deborah's deeper story, it is worth noting that "no one" has tried to decipher the meaning in her face; as already noted, journalists are clearly among those who have missed the story that Davis's literature is telling. This investigative fiction allows readers not only to see the larger story behind a person's actions, but also to react accordingly, as Davis suggests when she implores, "Be just,—not like man's law, which seizes on one isolated fact, but like God's judging angel, whose clear, sad eye saw all the countless cankering days of this man's life, all the countless nights, when, sick with starving, his soul fainted in him, before it judged him for this night, the saddest of all" (11). Whereas journalism "seizes on one isolated fact"—that is, Wolfe's supposed crime—Davis's account traces at least a portion of "the countless cankering days of this man's life."

In the years after she published "Life in the Iron-Mills," Davis returned repeatedly to the genre of investigative fiction. In *Put Out of the Way*, a fictional counterpart to a work of nonfiction by her husband, Clarke Davis, she addressed the treatment of the insane in the United States. The novel was every bit as successful as some investigative journalism in that it helped bring about legal reform. In another novel, *John Andross*, Davis presented a fictional treatment of the Tweed Ring, a subject covered in the *New York Tribune*, for which she was working at the time. Even outside of such obvious examples, Davis used her investigative fiction to expose hidden realities around her. In an essay called "The Middle-Aged Woman," which appeared in *Scribner's Monthly Magazine* in 1875, she called attention to "the great, decent, religious, unknown majority, never to be interviewed, or published in any shape, out of whose daily lives grow the modesties, the strength, the virtue of American homes, the safety of our future."[58] If the middle-aged woman escaped the notice of journalists—that is, was "never to be interviewed"—she and other women did not escape the notice of Davis, who reported on their lives in such stories as "Anne," "The Wife's Story," and "In the Market." As "Life in the Iron-Mills" had, these later forms of investigative fiction exposed the hidden and made it a "real thing" for readers.

More than an answer to journalism, Davis's stories of "to-day" were, like "The Mystery of Marie Roget" and *Uncle Tom's Cabin*, a sign of things to come. In the 1890s and early 1900s, in the midst of careers in journalism, Stephen Crane exposed the lifestyles and motivations of the poor in *Maggie: A Girl of the Streets*, and Frank Norris examined the story behind the wheat market in *The Pit*. In the first decade of the twentieth century, during the age of the muckrakers, Upton Sinclair published one of America's most famous and influential fictional exposés, *The Jungle*, which blew the lid off the meat-packing industry. Decades later, Truman Capote looked behind the superficial details of a newspaper story about a murder and produced a "nonfiction novel," *In Cold Blood*, exploring the lives of both the victims and the killers. In the tradition of Poe, Stowe, and Davis, these later authors of investigative fiction employed the tools of literature to report news of their own.

EPILOGUE

In one respect, the sibling rivalry in American letters produced no clear victor. In 1861, despite its meteoric rise, journalists had not displaced authors as the nation's designated truth-tellers. At the same time, the nation's literary class had not turned readers away from journalism; indeed, the appetite for war news would drive interest in newspapers even higher over the next four years. Although they enjoyed numerous triumphs of their own, authors of the postbellum era bristled at the powerful presence of journalism, just as Poe and Thoreau had. In the decades that followed the Civil War, a new group of authors took up the question of how best to tell the truth in language. In novels and stories ranging from *A Modern Instance* to *Sister Carrie*, Henry James, William Dean Howells, Mark Twain, and Theodore Dreiser explored the role of commercial pressures, audience expectations, and other factors in shaping journalistic versions of reality.[1] Meanwhile, journalists ridiculed the attempts of authors such as Stephen Crane to do a reporter's work. The rivalry raged on.

If neither journalists nor authors emerged as clear victors, this sibling rivalry did reward one group of Americans. As readers of the critiques and hybrid genres that emerged from this war, we stand to gain a deeper understanding of various approaches to truth-telling—an understanding that can help light the way for the future of American stories. At the threshold of a new information age, we confront a dizzying array of media and genres: blogs, wikis, YouTube, social-networking media, reality television, mockumentaries, "fake news," creative nonfiction, literary journalism, and untold numbers of forms yet to be invented. The craze over texting and tweeting shows how far we have come since the revolutionary advent of the telegraph, yet Thoreau's response to this earlier invention remains timely. Then and now, Americans have tingled over giving and absorbing the latest news—"As if," Thoreau says in *Walden*, "the main object were to talk fast and not to talk sensibly" (52). The Internet revolution invites all of us to be storytellers and story readers. Which stories should we choose to tell, and how should we choose to tell them? Which ones should we choose to believe?

If the long, rich tradition of journalism and literature is any evidence, there is room in the big tent of American letters for all kinds of truth-telling—from straight news to truthful hoaxes and more. After Thoreau, Stowe, Davis, and others showed that authors could report some news of their own, a number of American writers produced hybrid works ranging from new investigative fiction, such as Upton Sinclair's muckraking novel *The Jungle*, to works of "New Journalism," such as Tom Wolfe's *The Right Stuff*. Today, hybrid genres such as creative nonfiction and literary journalism are among the most popular forms of writing among both readers and scholars. Furthermore, as Shelley Fisher Fishkin has noted, writers such as Ernest Hemingway have demonstrated the value of applying journalistic principles to the writing of fiction.[2]

This tent, however, has its dark corners. Whatever lessons reporters and editors learned from the examples of Janet Cooke and Stephen Glass, journalistic fabrication has not gone away. In 2003, the *New York Times* had to admit that one of its reporters, Jayson Blair, had made up source material and had pretended to be reporting from various places when he was actually in New York. In another high-profile case the following year, Jack Kelley of *USA Today* was accused of fabrication. In 2005, fabrications turned up in the *Boston Globe*, *Tampa Tribune*, and other newspapers. Outside the world of journalism, memoirs by James Frey and former baseball player Matt McCarthy have raised questions about authenticity. Even amateurs have gotten into the act. In 2009, two couples, perhaps inspired by the boom of reality television and YouTube, set out to secure their 15 minutes of fame by staging a balloon disaster and crashing a presidential dinner.[3] Journalists and scholars have cited various factors behind journalistic transgressions: the "pressure to produce," competition among reporters, "the desire to please," poor "quality control" in newsrooms, and the difficulty of verifying all of the material in a reporter's story.[4] Yet another culprit—one that underlies many of these others—is a central, powerful, and troubling principle that we have seen in this study: the conflict between a story and the truth.

In his memoir *A Good Life*, Ben Bradlee recounted his involvement with the fiasco surrounding Janet Cooke. "To me, the story reeked of the sights and sounds and smells that editors love to give their readers," Bradlee wrote. "The possibility that the story was not true never entered my head." Similar statements have turned up as observers have sought to explain similar transgressions by Glass and others. "These days," Margaret Wolf Freivogel argues, "the successful reporter must not only get the facts right and the right facts, but also unearth those delicious details and heart-wrenching scenes that will make the news sing." In his account of his own time in the dark part of the tent, Glass explained, "I remember thinking, 'If I just had the exact quote that I wanted to make it work, it would be perfect.' And I wrote something on my computer, and then I looked at it, and I let it stand." Great material may be a red flag, as columnist Jack Shafer suggests. "I shouldn't have believed his story about the alleged sex orgy staged by . . . a bunch of pot-smoking young Republicans at a D.C. convention," Shafer says. "It's just too good to be true."[5]

All of this talk about supposedly factual material that is "too good to be true" points to the powerful, yet dangerous role of story in truth-telling. On the one hand, storytelling can bring the facts to life. Recalling the legitimate coverage of the Iraq war by correspondent Anthony Shadid, Philip Bennett noted that such coverage "put human voices, real narratives, daily quotidian details in the context of this giant event." He added, "And in some ways those stories turned out to be truer, in a way, than the broad sort of narrative of those events." In other cases, however, writers' notions of what makes a good story may lead them to invent the ingredients that don't happen to be at hand. In a penetrating essay on Scott Thomas Beauchamp's controversial "Baghdad Diaries," published in *The New Republic* in 2007, journalist Peggy Noonan suggests that Beauchamp's stories may have rung true with at least one kind of reader because they resembled Hollywood treatments of the Vietnam War. "If that's what you absorbed during the past 20 or 30 years, it just might make sense to you, it would actually seem believable, if a fellow in Iraq wrote for you about taunting scarred women, shooting dogs, and wearing skulls as helmets," Noonan says. "*This is the offhand brutality of war. You know. You saw it in a movie.*" Mark Twain, who wrote his share of both journalism and fiction—as well as a few hoaxes that straddled the line between the two—put his finger on this point when he issued this pledge to the readers of his *Buffalo Express*: "I shall always confine myself strictly to the truth, except when it is attended with inconvenience." Facts can be really handy or really inconvenient, depending on how neatly they align with the writer's conception of a good story.[6]

The fault, it turns out, lies not entirely in Stephen Glass or any of the other fallen stars, but also in ourselves.[7] If they are to report the authentic truth, whether that is objective reality or some higher principles, both journalists and authors must resist the temptations to mold the ingredients to fit our appetites for irony, stereotypes, myth, and imagery. The choices that writers make in selecting and packaging this material will continue to betray their own subjectivity, of course, but they must always make these choices based on their own honest impressions, and they must anchor these impressions in facts—people, dates, events, and tangible objects that can be seen, heard, and documented. The approach Thoreau took in reporting on the news of nature in *Walden* might serve as a model for truth-tellers everywhere: fathom first and then reflect. Journalists, authors, bloggers, and other would-be reporters must be willing to look at reality and say, "It is what it is." Furthermore, they must keep in mind that readers deserve accurate labels. Authors of literature may freely employ their poetic license, but journalists and others who claim to be writing nonfiction should abide by those conventions of the discipline, including faithfulness to facts. To do otherwise is not only to mislead readers, but also to cash in, illegitimately, on the appeal of truth. Great journalists and great authors, after all, agree on two things: stories are alluring, but the truth is hard.

NOTES

INTRODUCTION

1. Ann Reilly Dowd, "The Great Pretender," *Columbia Journalism Review* 37 (July/August 1998): 14–15.
2. "Times Reporter Who Resigned Leaves Long Trail of Deception," *New York Times*, May 11, 2003, http://www.nytimes.com/2003/05/11/national/11PAPE.html; Ivor Shapiro, "Why They Lie: Probing the Explanations for Journalistic Cheating," *Canadian Journal of Communication* 31 (2006): 261–66; Ron F. Smith, *Groping for Ethics in Journalism* (Ames: Iowa State Press, 2003), 135; Benjamin Hill and Alan Schwarz, "Errors Cast Doubt on a Baseball Memoir," *New York Times*, March 2, 2009, http://www.nytimes.com/2009/03/03/sports/baseball/03book.html; Motoko Rich, "Pondering Good Faith in Publishing," *New York Times*, March 8, 2010, http://www.nytimes.com/2010/03/09/books/09publishers.html?emc=eta1; Cynthia Miller, "Introduction: At Play in the Fields of the Truth," *Post Script* 28 (Summer 2009): 3–8.
3. Ronald Zboray provides an extensive discussion of these and other factors in *A Fictive People: Antebellum Economic Development and the American Reading Public* (New York: Oxford University Press, 1993). I explore developments such as these in greater depth in chapters 1 and 2.
4. Edwin Emery and Michael Emery, *The Press and America: An Interpretive History of the Mass Media* (Englewood Cliffs, NJ: Prentice-Hall, 1984), 135, 140–46; Frank Luther Mott, *American Journalism: A History: 1690–1960* (New York: Macmillan, 1962), 304. See also Alfred McClung Lee, *The Daily Newspaper in America: The Evolution of a Social Instrument* (New York: Macmillan, 1947), 63–64.
5. Oliver Wendell Holmes, *Ralph Waldo Emerson* (Boston: Houghton, Mifflin, 1885), 115.
6. In *Narrating the News: New Journalism and Literary Genre in Late Nineteenth-Century American Newspapers and Fiction* Karen Roggenkamp has argued that journalism and literature "grew increasingly divergent in the early twentieth century" (119). As I will show, an earlier divergence occurred in the antebellum era.
7. Throughout the book, I use the term "author" for a writer known primarily for poetry, fiction, and other forms of literature and "journalist"

for someone writing for a newspaper or magazine. As I discuss in Chapter 2, a number of American authors also worked as journalists at one time or another; however, as their critiques of journalism show, these writers primarily identified themselves with literature.

8. Doug Underwood, *Journalism and the Novel: Truth and Fiction, 1700–2000* (Cambridge: Cambridge University Press, 2008), 3–14; Shelley Fisher Fishkin, *From Fact to Fiction: Journalism & Imaginative Writing in America* (Baltimore: Johns Hopkins University Press, 1985), 55; Edgar M. Branch, introduction to *Early Tales & Sketches* (Berkeley: University of California Press, 1979), 26; David S. Reynolds, *Beneath the American Renaissance* (Cambridge: Harvard University Press, 1988); Michael Robertson, *Stephen Crane, Journalism, and the Making of Modern American Literature* (New York: Columbia University Press, 1997); Fred Fedler, *Media Hoaxes* (Ames, IA: Iowa State University Press, 1989); Roggenkamp, *Narrating the News*.

9. Jerome McGann, "Rethinking the Center, Remapping the Culture: Poe and the American Renaissance" (panel discussion at the Edgar A. Poe Bicentennial Symposium, Charlottesville, VA, April 3–4, 2009).

10. Philip Bennett, interview with Frank Stasio, *The State of Things*, North Carolina Public Radio, 12 October 2009, http://wunc.org/tsot/archive/search_media?review_state=published&start.query: record:list:date=2009-10-12%2023%3A59%3A59&start.range: record=max&end.query:record:list:date=2009-10-12%2000% 3A00%3A00&end.range:record=min&path=/websites/wuncplone_ webslingerz_com/tsot/archive&month:int=10&year:int=2009. Bennett was responding to Stasio, who, alluding to the failure of investigative journalism to resonate with audiences, asked, "Do we have to find a different way to tell stories, or do we give up?" After answering in the affirmative, Bennett added, "I don't know what that way is. I think we need to feel our way towards it. I think we're sort of stuck in a rhythm that was established a generation ago with New Journalism and devices that were used for long-form narrative writing that have scarcely received an update, even though the world of communications and technology has changed so dramatically."

Chapter 1

1. David Folkenflik, "'The Wire' to Focus on Baltimore Newspaper," National Public Radio, December 28, 2007, www.npr.org/templates/story/story.php?storyId=17668964&sc=emaf.

2. A few modern critics have commented on this rivalry. Robert Scholnick has noted that editors Horace Greeley and Charles Gordon Greene "understood that the competition for readers and for political and cultural influence would be played out in the arts and features sections of the papers as well as in the editorial and news columns" (165). In a study of the relationship between journalism and literature in the

postbellum era, David Kramer argues that a comparison of works by Henry James and Charles A. Dana "reveals a rivalry for similar terrain, a competition for audience, for readers" (140). Michael Robertson has noted the hostility of both James and William Dean Howells toward journalism. No scholar, however, has fully explored the basis and the consequences of this rivalry as it emerged in antebellum America. As I will show in other chapters of this book, America's authors issued a detailed, often caustic critique of their journalistic counterparts, criticizing both their transgressions and their very conventions, and often responded to the phenomenon of journalism with what I call "news of their own." See Robert Scholnick, "'The Ultraism of the Day': Greene's *Boston Post*, Hawthorne, Fuller, Melville, Stowe, and Literary Journalism in Antebellum America," *American Periodicals* 18 (2008): 163–91; David Kramer, "Masculine Rivalry in *The Bostonians*: Henry James and the Rhetoric of 'Newspaper Making'," *The Henry James Review* 19 (1998): 139–47; Michael Robertson, *Stephen Crane, Journalism, and the Making of Modern American Literature* (New York: Columbia University Press, 1997), 11–54.

3. Edwin Emery and Michael Emery, *The Press and America: An Interpretive History of the Mass Media* (Englewood Cliffs, NJ: Prentice-Hall, 1984), 3, 12, 24, 85n; Frank Luther Mott, *American Journalism: A History: 1960–1960* (New York: Macmillan, 1962), 11–12; Elizabeth Christine Cook, *Literary Influences in Colonial Newspapers* (Port Washington, NY: Kennikat Press, 1966); Lennard Davis, *Factual Fictions: The Origins of the English Novel* (New York: Columbia University Press, 1983); Doug Underwood, *Journalism and the Novel* (Cambridge: Cambridge University Press, 2008), 34. Underwood explains, "In looking back to the eighteenth century as the birthplace of both the modern novel and modern journalism, one has to imagine a time when the line between the real and the imagined was very much blurred and when notions of 'objectivity' and 'factuality' were in a fluid and largely undefined state. . . . The explosive growth of periodicals in the early eighteenth century that contained news, essays, criticism, political commentary, gossip, polemics, humor, satire, burlesque, parody, poetry, invented and imagined tales—often appearing in mixed and varied formats—was the 'primordial soup' from which today's fiction and literary journalism emerged, as Jenny Uglow has put it."

4. Edward J. Epstein, "The American Press: Some Truth About Truths," in *Ethics and the Press*, ed. John C. Merrill and Ralph D. Barney (New York: Hastings House, 1975), 60; Society of Professional Journalists, "SPJ Code of Ethics," http://www.spj.org/ethicscode.asp; Fred Brown, "Asking right questions a key to minimizing harm," "Reading Room," Society of Professional Journalists, http://www.spj.org/rrr.asp?ref=3&t=ethics. A note accompanying SPJ's Code of Ethics explains, "The SPJ Code of Ethics is voluntarily embraced by thousands of journalists, regardless of place or platform, and is widely used

in newsrooms and classrooms as a guide for ethical behavior. The code is intended not as a set of 'rules' but as a resource for ethical decision-making. It is not—nor can it be under the First Amendment—legally enforceable."

5. Bennett is quoted in William E. Huntzicker, *The Popular Press, 1833–1865* (Westport, CT: Greenwood Press, 1999), 30–31; Samuel Bowles, article in February 3, 1855, issue of *Springfield Republican*, reprinted in *Interpretations of Journalism: A Book of Readings*, ed. Frank Luther Mott and Ralph D. Casey (New York: F. S. Crofts, 1937), 116; "The Newspaper and Periodical Press," *Southern Quarterly Review* 1 (January 1842): 21.

6. Ralph Waldo Emerson, "The Poet," in *The Collected Works of Ralph Waldo Emerson*, Vol. III, ed. Alfred R. Ferguson and Jean Ferguson Carr (Cambridge: Belknap Press of Harvard University Press, 1983), 4; Emerson, "Goethe, or the Writer," in *Collected Works*, Vol. IV, 162; Herman Melville, *Pierre* (New York: Russell & Russell, 1963), 90; Davis is quoted in Sharon Harris, *Rebecca Harding Davis and American Realism* (Philadelphia: University of Pennsylvania Press, 1991), 125.

7. "Truth," in *The Oxford English Dictionary*, 2nd ed., 1989. A related sense of the first definition provided here is "agreement with the thing represented, in art or literature; accuracy of delineation or representation; the quality of being 'true to life.'"

8. Plato, *Republic*, in *The Collected Dialogues of Plato*, ed. Edith Hamilton and Huntington Cairns (Princeton, NJ: Princeton University Press, 1961), 747–50; Aristotle, *Poetics*, in *Criticism: The Major Texts*, ed. Walter Jackson Bate (New York: Harcourt, Brace, 1952), 25.

9. David Paul Nord, *Communities of Journalism: A History of American Newspapers and Their Readers* (Urbana: University of Illinois Press, 2001), 98; Andie Tucher, *Froth and Scum: Truth, Beauty, Goodness, and the Ax Murder in America's First Mass Medium* (Chapel Hill: University of North Carolina Press, 1994), 62–75; Bennett is quoted in Michael Schudson, *Discovering the News: A Social History of American Newspapers* (New York: Basic Books, 1978), 54.

10. *The Oxford English Dictionary* contains eight senses for "fact." Here and throughout this book, I use the word in the sense of 4a: "Something that has really occurred or is actually the case; something certainly known to be of this character; hence, a particular truth known by actual observation or authentic testimony, as opposed to what is merely inferred, or to a conjecture or fiction; a datum of experience, as distinguished from the conclusions that may be based upon it" or the related 6a: "That which is of the nature of a fact; what has actually happened or is the case; truth attested by direct observation or authentic testimony; reality." These definitions generally underlie the use of the word by journalists, as the quotations in this chapter show.

11. Philip Patterson and Lee Wilkins, *Media Ethics: Issues and Cases* (New York: McGraw-Hill, 2008), 20; David Weir and Dan Noyes, *Raising*

Hell: How the Center for Investigative Reporting Gets the Story (Reading, MA: Addison-Wesley, 1983), 1. For other modern discussions of the centrality of factual accuracy, see Jerry Schwartz, *Associated Press Reporting Handbook* (New York: McGraw-Hill, 2002), 22, 24; Melvin Mencher, *News Reporting and Writing* (Madison, WI: Brown & Benchmark, 1994), 23.

12. Schudson, *Discovering the News*, 77; Dicken-Garcia, *Journalistic Standards in Nineteenth-Century America*, 82; Eric Sundquist, introduction to *Frederick Douglass: New Literary and Historical Essays* (Cambridge: Cambridge University Press, 1990), 3; Frank Luther Mott, *American Journalism*, 37; Emery and Emery, *The Press and America*, 84; Alexander Hamilton is quoted in Emery and Emery, *The Press and America*, 112. For antebellum journalists' references to facts, see James Crouthamel, *Bennett's New York Herald and the Rise of the Popular Press* (Syracuse, NY: Syracuse University Press, 1989), 21, and the March 4, 1837, issue of *The Colored American*. See also Dan Schiller, *Objectivity and the News* (Philadelphia: University of Pennsylvania Press, 1981), 83–85, and Andie Tucher, *Froth and Scum*, 155.

13. Rebecca Harding Davis, "Life in the Iron-Mills," in *A Rebecca Harding Davis Reader*, ed. Jean Pfaelzer (Pittsburgh: University of Pittsburgh Press, 1995), 4; Sharon Harris, *Rebecca Harding Davis and American Realism*, 6; Nathaniel Hawthorne, *The House of the Seven Gables*, in *Complete Novels* (New York: Literary Classics of the United States, 1983), 351; Herman Melville, *The Confidence-Man* (New York: Russell & Russell, 1963), 243–44; John Irwin, *American Hieroglyphics* (New Haven: Yale University Press, 1980), 13–14; Ralph Waldo Emerson, "Experience," in *The Collected Works of Ralph Waldo Emerson*, Vol. III, ed. Alfred R. Ferguson and Jean Ferguson Carr (Cambridge: Harvard University Press, 1983), 39; William Shakespeare, *Hamlet*, 1.5.166, in *The Riverside Shakespeare* (Boston: Houghton Mifflin, 1974), 1151.

14. WFAE-Charlotte, March 28, 2009.

15. Herman Melville, *Moby-Dick* (New York: W. W. Norton, 2002), 349; Epstein, "The American Press: Some Truth About Truths," 61; Woodward is quoted in Brian Brooks et al., *News Reporting and Writing* (Boston: Bedford/St. Martin's, 1999), 13.

16. Edgar Allan Poe, "The Fall of the House of Usher," in *Collected Works of Edgar Allan Poe*, ed. Thomas Ollive Mabbott (Cambridge: Belknap Press of Harvard University Press, 1978), 405; Edgar Allan Poe, "Ligeia," in *Collected Works*, 313.

17. In *Republic*, Plato suggests that poets are mere imitators who are "three removes from . . . the truth" because they, like painters, imitate the physical world, failing to capture the truths that lie behind this world (823).

18. In his lengthy discussion of language in Book 3 of *Essay Concerning Human Understanding* (New York: Dover, 1959), Locke writes,

"Words, by long and familiar use, as has been said, come to excite in men certain ideas so constantly and readily, that they are apt to suppose a natural connexion between them. But that they signify only men's peculiar ideas, and that *by a perfect arbitrary imposition*, is evident, in that they often fail to excite in others (even that use the same language) the same ideas we take them to be signs of." (2:12). In Chapter 9 of this book, "Of the Imperfection of Words," Locke identifies a number of specific reasons why language is ambiguous.

19. Philip F. Gura, *The Wisdom of Words: Language, Theology, and Literature in the New England Renaissance* (Middletown, CT: Wesleyan University Press, 1981), 62.

20. Ibid., 66.

21. Ibid., 82–83, 129–31.

22. "Story," *The Oxford English Dictionary*; Brooks, *News Reporting and Writing*, 6. In the OED, the earliest citation in which *story* refers to a newspaper article is dated 1892, but the word is used this way in an item quoted in an article called "Herschel's Great Discoveries" in the September 1, 1835, issue of the *New York Sun*. It reads, in part: "It is not worth while for us to express an opinion as to the truth or falsity of the narrative, as our readers after an attentive perusal of the whole story, decide for themselves. Whether true or false, the article is written with consumate ability, and possesses intense interest." The passage, presented as a quotation from the *Philadelphia Inquirer*, treats "story" and "article" as synonyms. The use of *story* for an entertaining work of fiction goes back at least to the sixteenth century.

23. Norma Green, "Concepts of News," in *American Journalism*, ed. W. David Sloan and Lisa Mullikin Parcell (Jefferson, NC: McFarland, 2002), 39; "GALVANISM EXPELLING DEVILS," *Baltimore Sun*, August 15, 1846; "VERY REMARKABLE," *New York Herald*, August 31, 1835; "SARATOGA SPRINGS, 25th August 1835," *New York Herald*, August 31, 1835; Isabelle Lehuu, *Carnival on the Page: Popular Print Media in Antebellum America* (Chapel Hill: University of North Carolina Press, 2000), 69; Edgar Allan Poe, "The Philosophy of Composition," in *Essays and Reviews* (New York: Literary Classics of the United States, 1984), 13.

24. Michael Schudson, "Why News Is the Way It Is," *Raritan* 2 (1983): 122–23.

25. "Terrible Story—Seduction, Insanity, and Death," *Brooklyn Daily Eagle*, March 1, 1843, 2; Jack Lule, *Daily News, Eternal Stories: The Mythological Role of Journalism* (New York: Guilford, 2001), 3; Schudson, "Why News Is the Way It Is," 122–23; Andie Tucher, *Froth and Scum: Truth, Beauty, Goodness, and the Ax Murder in America's First Mass Medium* (Chapel Hill: University of North Carolina Press, 1994), 70–71, 62–63; "The Swallow's Cave, at Nahant. A ROMANCE IN REAL LIFE," *New York Herald*, July 10, 1837, 1; "Ups and Downs," *Berkshire County Whig*, May 15, 1845, p. 1.

For a discussion of human-interest material in penny newspapers, see Helen MacGill Hughes, *News and the Human Interest Story* (New York: Greenwood Press, 1940), 8. Day and Bennett were not the first to publish such stories. Benjamin Franklin included them in his *Pennsylvania Gazette* in the previous century. In the era of the penny press, however, human-interest journalism was pervasive and, apparently, extremely popular.

26. Emery and Emery, *The Press and America*, 205; Huntzicker, *The Popular Press, 1833–1865*, 6; article on a riot, in the *New York Herald*, August 30, 1852; article on Daniel Webster's death, in the *New York Herald*, February 26, 1852; article on congressional deliberations, in *New York Mercury*, February 27, 1834, p. 1; Huntzicker, *The Popular Press, 1833–1865*, 20; Lehuu, *Carnival on the Page*, 50; Schiller, *Objectivity and the News*, 70.

27. Edgar Allan Poe, "Dream-Land," in *Collected Works*, 344; Edgar Allan Poe, "The Unparalleled Adventure of One Hans Pfaall," in *The Imaginary Voyages*, ed. Burton R. Pollin (Boston: Twayne, 1981), 391, hereafter cited in text.

28. Don Henley, "Dirty Laundry," *I Can't Stand Still* (Warner Brothers, 1982).

29. Emerson, "The Poet," in *The Collected Works of Ralph Waldo Emerson*, Vol. III, ed. Alfred R. Ferguson and Jean Ferguson Carr (Cambridge: Harvard University Press, 1983), 22; Walt Whitman, *Leaves of Grass*, in *Complete Poetry and Collected Prose* (New York: Literary Classics of the United States, 1982), 5, 33, 35–37, 67–69; "POLICE OFFICE," *New York Herald*, August 31, 1835.

30. Walt Whitman, "Once I Pass'd through a Populous City," in *Complete Poetry and Collected Prose*, 266; Shelley Fisher Fishkin, *From Fact to Fiction: Journalism and Imaginative Writing in America* (Baltimore: Johns Hopkins University Press, 1985), 15, 25; Poe, "Marginalia," in *Essays and Reviews*, 1384. Poe described the process in this way: "I have proceeded so far, secondly, as to prevent the lapse from *the point* of which I speak—the point of blending between wakefulness and sleep—as to prevent at will, I say, the lapse from this border-ground into the dominion of sleep. Not that I can *continue* the condition—not that I can render the point more than a point—but that I can startle myself from the point into wakefulness—*and thus transfer the point itself into the realm of Memory*—convey its impressions, or more properly their recollections, to a situation where (although still for a very brief period) I can survey them with the eye of analysis." See also Mark Canada, "The Right Brain in Poe's Creative Process," *The Southern Quarterly* 36 (Summer 1998): 96–105.

31. Stephen Railton, *Fenimore Cooper: A Study of His Life and Imagination* (Princeton: Princeton University Press, 1978), 167–68.

32. William E. Huntzicker, *The Popular Press, 1833–1865*, 167, 165; Crouthamel, *Bennett's New York Herald and the Rise of the Popular*

Press, 43; Ronald Zboray, *A Fictive People: Antebellum Economic Development and the American Reading Public* (New York: Oxford University Press, 1993), 90–109, 58, 72–75.

33. Zboray, *A Fictive People*, 15. Zboray writes, "Despite glowing accounts of book readership in the antebellum United States, innovations in printing technology by no means caused such a drop in the price of books as to make them widely available. Prices for hardcover books during the antebellum years commonly ranged between 75 cents and $1.25, about half that of the late eighteenth century. However, economically secure, skilled white male workers made only about $1 a day; women often made only a quarter of that" (11). Some paperbacks could be purchased for 12 ½ cents, Zboray explains, but prices for these books more often were between 38 and 63 cents (11–12).

34. Ibid., 108–. Elsewhere, Zboray argues, "Within the chaos of industrial economic development, readers clung to facts to guide them. This popular positivism shone through numeracy, newspapers, and the self-culture movement and ultimately discouraged the reading of fiction" (131). See also Schiller, *Objectivity and the News*, 86. For a discussion of gift-books, jumbo papers, and other publications that appealed to Americans' appetites for spectacle, see Lehuu, *Carnival on the Page.*

35. Quoted in Zboray, *A Fictive People*, 128. Zboray adds, "The superabundance and easy availability of news-bearing papers gave readers little incentive to venture into reading fiction in book form. Their leisure hours could be filled entirely with newsprint, and the taste for news might compete with that for fiction" (129).

36. Fuller is quoted in Scholnick, "'The Ultraism of the Day,'" 164; Lehuu, *Carnival on the Page*, 9; Zboray, *A Fictive People*, 32–33, 73–74. Stephen Railton has noted that Thoreau and Cooper were on different sides of the divide over the value of the past in antebellum America. In light of this vast difference in outlook, it is worth noting that these two writers agreed on at least one thing: both issued vicious attacks on the press. See Railton, *Fenimore Cooper*, 188.

37. Lehuu, *Carnival on the Page*, 29; Bennett is quoted in Schudson, *Discovering the News*, 53; Thoreau, *Walden*, ed. J. Lyndon Shanley (Princeton: Princeton University Press, 1971), 6–7, hereafter cited in text; Reynolds, *Beneath the American Renaissance*, 255; Terence Whalen, *Edgar Allan Poe and the Masses* (Princeton: Princeton University Press, 1999), 86.

Chapter 2

1. David Nord, *Communities of Journalism: A History of American Newspapers and Their Readers* (Urbana: University of Illinois Press, 2001), 94.

2. Sandor Farkas, *Journey in North America, 1831,* trans. Arpad Kadarkay (Santa Barbara: American Bibliographic Center—Clio Press, 1978), 165.

3. For discussions of images in antebellum newspapers, see James L. Crouthamel, *Bennett's New York Herald and the Rise of the Popular Press* (Syracuse, NY: Syracuse University Press, 1989), 34, and William E. Huntzicker, *The Popular Press, 1833–1865 (The History of American Journalism)* (Westport, CT: Greenwood Press, 1999), 54.

4. Frank Luther Mott, *American Journalism: A History: 1690–1960* (New York: Macmillan, 1962), 203; colophon from *Independent Chronicle and Boston Patriot,* August 30, 1820; colophon from *New York Columbian,* November 22, 1809, 1; Thomas C. Leonard, *News for All: America's Coming-of-Age with the Press* (New York: Oxford University Press, 1995), 6–12; Ronald Zboray, *A Fictive People: Antebellum Economic Development and the American Reading Public* (New York: Oxford University Press, 1993), 14.

5. Edgar Allan Poe, "The Literati of New York City," in *Essays and Reviews,* ed. G. R. Thompson (New York: Literary Classics of the United States, 1984), 1214. In his profile of Richard Adams Locke, where this remark appears, Poe goes on to call the advent of the penny press "one of the most important steps ever yet taken in the pathway of human progress" (1221). One must wonder how sincere Poe was in this encomium on the penny press. As we will see, he mocked the mass media elsewhere.

6. Edwin Emery and Michael Emery, *The Press and America: An Interpretive History of the Mass Media* (Englewood Cliffs, NJ: Prentice-Hall, 1984), 140, 144, 114; Crouthamel, *Bennett's New York Herald and the Rise of the Popular Press,* 37; Mott, *American Journalism,* 303.

7. Bennett is quoted in Michael Schudson, *Discovering the News: A Social History of American Newspapers* (New York: Basic Books, 1978), 53; Dan Schiller, *Objectivity and the News* (Philadelphia: University of Pennsylvania Press, 1981), 16; "The Newspaper and Periodical Press," *Southern Quarterly Review* 1 (January 1842): 8–9. See also Leonard, *News for All,* 19.

8. Zboray, *A Fictive People,* 14, 32–33, 73–74. Zboray explains that periodical depots, at first places where periodicals were stored, eventually were major venues for the sale of both periodicals and books. Newspaper offices served similar purposes in communities not as large as Boston. A number of factors made newspapers and books popular on trains; Zboray explains, "The American railway journey encouraged reading in many ways. Most obviously, trains provided a smoother ride than stagecoaches. . . . Also, the noisiness of rail cars put a damper on conversation. The long distances between destinations meant that the traveler faced long stretches of time with little else to do but read" (74).

9. Leonard, *News for All,* xi, 13, 117–20; Mackay is quoted in Zboray, *A Fictive People,* 128–29; Samuel Bowles, February 3, 1855 article, in *Interpretations of Journalism,* ed. Frank Luther Mott and Ralph D. Casey

(New York: F. S. Crofts, 1937), 115; Ralph Waldo Emerson, *The Journals and Miscellaneous Notebooks of Ralph Waldo Emerson*, Vol. 10, 1847–1848, ed. Merton M. Sealts, Jr. (Cambridge, MA: Belknap Press of Harvard University Press, 1973), 353.

10. Nord, *Communities of Journalism*, 2–3; Isabelle Lehuu, *Carnival on the Page: Popular Print Media in Antebellum America* (Chapel Hill: University of North Carolina Press, 2000), 48–57; Schiller, *Objectivity and the News*, 76.

11. Nathaniel Hawthorne, "Old News," in *Tales and Sketches* (New York: Literary Classics of the United States, 1982), 251; Stowe is quoted in E. Bruce Kirkham, *The Building of Uncle Tom's Cabin* (Knoxville: University of Tennessee Press, 1977), 36.

12. David S. Reynolds, *Beneath the American Renaissance* (Cambridge: Harvard University Press, 1988), 255, 171; Julian Hawthorne is quoted in ibid., 254–55; Robert J. Scholnick, "'The Ultraism of the Day': Greene's *Boston Post*, Hawthorne, Fuller, Melville, Stowe, and Literary Journalism in Antebellum America," *American Periodicals* 18 (2008): 166; Nathaniel Hawthorne, "Wakefield," in *Tales and Sketches*, 290–91, 298.

13. Reynolds, *Beneath the American Renaissance*, 276, 171, 310, 231; Edgar Allan Poe, *The Letters of Edgar Allan Poe*, ed. John Ward Ostrom (New York: Gordian Press, 1966), 65, 125, 361.

14. Jack L. Capps, *Emily Dickinson's Reading* (Cambridge, MA: Harvard University Press, 1966), 128, 134, 140; Dickinson, L 133, autumn 1853, in *The Letters of Emily Dickinson*, ed. Thomas H. Johnson (Cambridge: Belknap Press of Harvard University, 1986), 264; George Frisbie Whicher, *This Was a Poet* (Philadelphia: Dufour, 1952), 170; Karen Dandurand, "Dickinson and the Public," in *Dickinson and Audience*, ed. Martin Orzeck and Robert Weisbuch (Ann Arbor: University of Michigan Press, 1996), 256–57. See also *The Poems of Emily Dickinson*, Vol. 3, ed. Thomas H. Johnson (Cambridge, MA: Belknap Press of Harvard University Press, 1955), 965–66, and Dickinson's L908, in which she writes, "I wish I could find the Warrington Words, but during my weeks of faintness, my Treasures were misplaced, and I cannot find them . . ." (828). In a note accompanying Poem 1396 ("She Laid Her Docile Crescent Down"), Johnson writes, "In the upper corners of this copy ED pasted two cuttings from newspapers: at the left a star and crescent, and at the right tombstones slanting against another. The tombstone illustration is a clipping from the *Hampshire and Franklin Express* of 12 December 1856. . . . The disparity in the date of the clipping and the poem leads one to conjecture that she kept a scrapbook or a file of items which to her were meaningful."

15. Joan Kirkby, "Dickinson Reading," *Emily Dickinson Journal* 5 (Fall 1996): 253; Capps, *Emily Dickinson's Reading*, 130, 138.

16. Richard Sewall, *The Life of Emily Dickinson* (New York: Farrar, Straus and Giroux, 1974), 2:466, 473.

17. Leonard, *News for All*, 93–100. See, for example, the letters dated April 3, 1848, and April 17, 1848, in *The Correspondence of Henry David Thoreau*, ed. Walter Harding and Carl Bode (New York: New York University Press, 1958), 217–19.

18. Ralph Waldo Emerson, *The Journals and Miscellaneous Notebooks of Ralph Waldo Emerson*. Vol. 11, 1848–1851, ed. A. W. Plumstead and William H. Gilman (Cambridge, MA: Belknap Press of Harvard University Press, 1975), 268; Vol. 14, 1854–1861, ed. Susan Sutton Smith and Harrison Hayford (Cambridge, MA: Belknap Press of Harvard University Press, 1978), 32; Vol. 8, 1841–1843, ed. William H. Gilman and J. E. Parsons (Cambridge, MA: Belknap Press of Harvard University Press, 1970), 483, 499, 517n; Vol. 13, 1852–1855, ed. Ralph H. Orth and Alfred R. Ferguson (Cambridge, MA: Belknap Press of Harvard University Press, 1977), 16; Vol. 10, 1847–1848, 157; Vol. 9, 1843–1847, ed. Ralph H. Orth and Alfred R. Ferguson (Cambridge, MA: Belknap Press of Harvard University Press, 1971), 371.

19. Kirkham, *The Building of Uncle Tom's Cabin*, 43, 45; Stowe to Henry Ward Beecher, February 1, 1851, in *The Oxford Harriet Beecher Stowe Reader*, ed. Joan D. Hedrick (New York: Oxford University Press, 1994), 65; Rebecca Harding Davis, *Bits of Gossip* (Boston: Houghton, Mifflin, 1904), 1.

20. Stephen Railton, "James Fenimore Cooper," in *Dictionary of Literary Biography* (Detroit: Gale, 1979), 3: 85–86; Cooper to Horatio Hastings Weld, April 4–8(?), 1842, in *The Letters and Journals of James Fenimore Cooper*, ed. James Franklin Beard (Cambridge, MA: Belknap Press of Harvard University Press, 1964), 4: 269, 274; Stephen Railton, *Fenimore Cooper: A Study of His Life and Imagination* (Princeton: Princeton University Press, 1978), 225–31.

21. Brian Higgins and Hershel Parker, "Introduction," in *Herman Melville: The Contemporary Reviews*, ed., Brian Higgins and Hershel Parker (Cambridge: Cambridge University Press, 1995), xx; Parker and Hayford, note in the Norton Critical Edition of *Moby-Dick* (New York: W. W. Norton, 2002), 57.

22. Dana, review of *Typee*, *West Roxbury (Mass.) Harbinger*, April 4, 1846, rpt. in Higgins and Parker, *Herman Melville*, 39–40; Dana's observation about the newspaper's serving as a "daily photograph" is quoted in Emery and Emery, *The Press and America*, 217; review of *Typee*, *New York Morning Courier and New-York Enquirer*, April 17, 1846, rpt. in Higgins and Parker, *Herman Melville*, 46–47; H. C., review of *Typee*, *New York Evangelist*, April 9, 1846, rpt. in ibid., 46; review of *Typee*, *Christian Parlor Magazine*, July 1846, rpt. in ibid., 52, 57; review of *Moby-Dick*, *New York Independent*, November 20, 1851, rpt. in ibid., 380.

23. "Introduction," in ibid., xi; "M.," article in *Albany Argus*, April 21, 1846, rpt. in ibid., 47; Melville's letter to Alexander Bradford is quoted in *Herman Melville: A Biography* (Baltimore: Johns Hopkins

University Press, 1996), 1:418–19. See also reviews in the July 1846 issue of the New Haven *New Englander*, rpt. in ibid., 51–52; and the July 1846 issue of the *Universalist Review*, rpt. in ibid., 51.

24. Ronald Weber, *Hired Pens: Professional Writers in America's Golden Age of Print* (Athens: Ohio University Press, 1997); Doug Underwood, *Journalism and the Novel: Truth and Fiction, 1700–2000* (Cambridge: Cambridge University Press, 2008); Shelley Fisher Fishkin, *From Fact to Fiction: Journalism & Imaginative Writing in America* (Baltimore: Johns Hopkins University Press, 1985); Michael Robertson, *Stephen Crane, Journalism, and the Making of Modern American Literature* (New York: Columbia University Press, 1997); Edgar M. Branch, *The Literary Apprenticeship of Mark Twain* (New York: Russell & Russell, 1950); Joseph J. Kwiat, "The Newspaper Experience: Crane, Norris, and Dreiser," *Nineteenth-Century Fiction* 8 (September 1953): 99–117; Nancy Warner Barrineau, "Introduction" to *Theodore Dreiser's Ev'ry Month* (Athens: University of Georgia Press, 1996), xv–xl.

25. Dwight Thomas and David K. Jackson, *The Poe Log: A Documentary Life of Edgar Allan Poe, 1809–1849* (Boston: G. K. Hall, 1987), 484; Weber, *Hired Pens*, 36; Aleta Feinsod Cane and Susan Alves, "American Women Writers and the Periodical: Creating a Constituency, Opening a Dialogue," in *"The Only Efficient Instrument": American Women Writers & The Periodical, 1837–1916*, ed. Aleta Feinsod Cane and Susan Alves (Iowa City: University of Iowa Press, 2001), 3; Greeley is quoted in Andie Tucher, *Froth and Scum: Truth, Beauty, Goodness, and the Ax Murder in America's First Mass Medium* (Chapel Hill: University of North Carolina Press, 1994), 134; Tucker is quoted in Terence Whalen, *Edgar Allan Poe and the Masses* (Princeton: Princeton University Press, 1999), 81.

26. For a discussion of Poe, Nathaniel Parker Willis and his sister Sara, and other "professional writers," men and women who earned some kind of income contributing to magazines and churning out pulp fiction in the nineteenth and twentieth centuries, see Weber, *Hired Pens*.

27. James Boylan, "William Cullen Bryant," in *American Newspaper Journalists, 1690–1872* (Detroit: Gale, 1985), 83, 85; William Cullen Bryant, "How Abolitionists Are Made," in *Power for Sanity: Selected Editorials of William Cullen Bryant, 1829–1861*, ed. William Cullen Bryant II (New York: Fordham University, 1994), 23; Bryant is quoted in Curtiss S. Johnson, *Politics and a Belly-full: The Journalistic Career of William Cullen Bryant* (Westport, CT: Greenwood, 1962), 87.

28. Boylan, "William Cullen Bryant," 84; Bryant is quoted in ibid., 83, 84.

29. John Lent, "Edgar Allan Poe," in *Dictionary of Literary Biography, Vol. 73* (Detroit: The Gale Group, 1988), 235–51; Poe to Frederick W. Thomas, July 4, 1841, in *The Letters of Edgar Allan Poe*, 172; Whalen, *Edgar Allan Poe and the Masses*, 80; Robert D Richardson, Jr., *Henry*

Thoreau: A Life of the Mind (Berkeley: University of California Press, 1986), 131.

30. Cane and Alves, "American Women Writers and the Periodical," 1; Fanny Fern (Sara Willis), *Ruth Hall*, in *Ruth Hall and Other Writings*, ed. Joyce W. Warren (New Brunswick, NJ: Rutgers University Press, 1986), 115; Joyce W. Warren, "Introduction," in ibid., xi–xx.

31. Cane and Alves, "American Women Writers and the Periodical," 1; Sara Willis, "Family Jars," "Women's Salaries," and "Dull Homes in Bright Places," in *Ruth Hall and Other Writings*, 133, 364, 363; Warren, "Introduction," in ibid., xxxiii. Warren writes, "In addition to women's rights, Fanny Fern wrote often on other social issues of the day: poverty, crime, prostitution, venereal disease, prison reform. She felt strongly about the suffering she saw and believed society had a responsibility to the poor" (xxxiii).

32. Willis, *Ruth Hall*, 143–44.

33. Ibid., 159–60.

34. Sharon M. Harris, *Rebecca Harding Davis and American Realism* (Philadelphia: University of Pennsylvania Press, 1991), 24–25; Rebecca Harding Davis, "The Yares of Black Mountain," in *A Rebecca Harding Davis Reader*, ed. Jean Pfaelzer (Pittsburgh: University of Pittsburgh Press, 1995), 295; Davis to James Fields, March 10(?), 1861, MSS 6109, University of Virginia Libraries; Davis to James Fields, October 25, 1861, MSS 6109, University of Virginia Libraries; Davis, "Women in Literature," in *Rebecca Harding Davis Reader*, 402.

35. Davis, "Two Methods with the Negro," in ibid., 424; Davis, *Bits of Gossip*, 36; Davis, "Some Testimony in the Case" and review of *Undistinguished Americans*, in *A Rebecca Harding Davis Reader*.

36. Walt Whitman, "Is There Any Hope?" Feinberg-Whitman Collection, Container 31, Reel 19, Library of Congress; Walt Whitman, "Sunday Restrictions," in ibid.; Fishkin, *From Fact to Fiction*, 17, 33.

37. Frederick Douglass, *Narrative of the Life of Frederick Douglass*, in *Slave Narratives* (New York: Literary Classics of the United States), 362; Douglass, "Our Paper and Its Prospects," Dec. 3, 1847, The Papers of Frederick Douglass, Container 21, Reel 13, Library of Congress; Wilson J. Moses, "Frederick Douglass and the Constraints of Racialized Writing," in *Frederick Douglass: New Literary and Historical Essays* (Cambridge: Cambridge University Press, 1990), 80; Douglass, "Hints on Journalism," The Papers of Frederick Douglass, Container 32, Reel 20, Library of Congress.

38. *Boston Herald*, February 3, 1897. This article, as well as the ones quoted subsequently, can be found in the Crane scrapbooks housed in the University of Virginia Libraries; *Boston Journal*, April 29, 1897; *New Bedford Journal*, May 15, 1897; *San Francisco Argonaut*, May 17, 1897. The speculation in the *Argonaut* eerily anticipates the experience of *New York Times* reporter Jayson Blair, who was found to have fabricated datelines for stories he actually wrote elsewhere. See "Times Reporter

Who Resigned Leaves Long Trail of Deception," *New York Times*, May 11, 2003, http://www.nytimes.com/2003/05/11/national/11PAPE.html.

39. *Syracuse Standard*, May 14, 1897; *Rochester Post Express*, May 14, 1897; *Los Angeles Express*, May 21, 1897; *Brooklyn Eagle*, May 16, 1897.

40. *Brockton Enterprise*, May 5, 1897; *Boston Herald*, May 4, 1897.

CHAPTER 3

1. Bennett is quoted in William Huntzicker, *The Popular Press, 1833–1865 (The History of American Journalism)* (Westport, CT: Greenwood Press, 1999), 23; Emerson, "The American Scholar," in *The Collected Works of Ralph Waldo Emerson*, ed. Joseph Slater (Cambridge: Harvard University Press, 1971–2007), 1:52.

2. Critiques of science by American authors in the nineteenth century include Poe's "Sonnet—To Science," Whitman's "When I Heard the Learn'd Astronomer," and Hawthorne's "The Artist of the Beautiful."

3. Jack Capps, *Emily Dickinson's Reading* (Cambridge: Harvard University Press, 1966), 133.

4. De Tocqueville, *Democracy in America*, trans. Arthur Goldhammer (New York: Literary Classics of the United States, 2004), 600. Dicken-Garcia summarizes some of the beliefs and hopes in the press in this way: "Among the more glorified functions attributed to the press were those of educator (a constant view across the century); symbol and propellor of progress and civilization; universal reformer; protector of the peace, liberties, and general moral health; the 'brain' of communities; individuals' and humankind's moral guide; an instrument of peace; and a 'companion.'" See Hazel Dicken-Garcia, *Journalistic Standards in Nineteenth-Century America* (Madison: University of Wisconsin Press, 1989), 157–58.

5. Jefferson is quoted in Edwin Emery and Michael Emery, *The Press and America: An Interpretive History of the Mass Media* (Englewood Cliffs, NJ: Prentice-Hall, 1984), 110–11; Farkas, *Journey in North America, 1831*, trans. Arpad Kadarkay (Santa Barbara: American Bibliographical Center—Clio Press, 1978), 93; Emery and Emery, *The Press and America*, 125; J. Herbert Altschull, *From Milton to McLuhan: The Ideas Behind American Journalism* (Baltimore: Johns Hopkins University Press, 1990), 206.

6. Bennett is quoted in ibid., 208; the *Sun* is quoted in Huntzicker, *The Popular Press, 1833–1865*, 2. For other observations on the role of journalism as educator and agent of civilization, see Dicken-Garcia, *Journalistic Standards in Nineteenth-Century America*, 138–39, 155, 158; James Parton, *The Life of Horace Greeley* (New York: Mason Brothers, 1855; rpt. Arno and the *New York Times*, 1970), 138.

7. Dan Schiller, *Objectivity and the News* (Philadelphia: University of Pennsylvania Press, 1981), 48, 53, 76; *The Colored American*, March 4, 1837. See also Huntzicker, *The Popular Press, 1833–1865*, 78–79.

8. David Nord, *Communities of Journalism: A History of American Newspapers and Their Readers* (Urbana: University of Illinois Press, 2001), 99; Altschull, *From Milton to McLuhan*, 209; Dana is quoted in Huntzicker, *The Popular Press, 1833–1865*, 171; William Cullen Bryant, "The Right to Combine vs. Forcible Intimidation," in *Power for Sanity: Selected Editorials of William Cullen Bryant, 1829–1861*, ed. William Cullen Bryant II (New York: Fordham University, 1994), 42; Bryant is quoted in Curtiss S. Johnson, *Politics and a Belly-Full: The Journalistic Career of William Cullen Bryant* (New York: Vantage Press, 1962), 93. See also Dicken-Garcia, *Journalistic Standards in Nineteenth-Century America*, 41.

9. Margaret Fuller, *Papers on Literature and Art* (London: Wiley & Putnam, 1846), 140; Eric Sundquist, "Introduction," in *Frederick Douglass: New Literary and Historical Essays* (Cambridge: Cambridge University Press, 1990), 9; Douglass is quoted in Waldo E. Martin, *The Mind of Frederick Douglass* (Chapel Hill: University of North Carolina Press, 1984), 173–74; Walt Whitman, "The Poor Wretches," *Brooklyn Daily Eagle*, August 1, 1846; Whitman, "Sunday Restrictions," Feinberg-Whitman Collection, Container 32, Reel 19; James Fenimore Cooper, *The American Democrat*, in *Representative Selections*, ed. Robert E. Spiller (Westport, CT: Greenwood Press, 1936), 211–12.

10. Isabelle Lehuu, *Carnival on the Page: Popular Print Media in Antebellum America* (Chapel Hill: University of North Carolina Press, 2000), 132, 148; Emerson is quoted in Lehuu, *Carnival on the Page*, 126.

11. Cooper, *The American Democrat*, 213.

12. Edgar Allan Poe, "The Mystery of Marie Roget," in *Collected Works of Edgar Allan Poe*, ed. Thomas Ollive Mabbott (Cambridge: Belknap Press of Harvard University Press, 1978), 733, 746. Subsequent citations will be noted parenthetically. For a discussion of Poe's feud with H. Hastings Weld, editor of *Brother Jonathan*, see Richard Kopley, *Edgar Allan Poe and the Dupin Mysteries* (New York: Palgrave Macmillan, 2008), 54–63.

13. Cooper, *The American Democrat*, 216; Sara Willis, *Ruth Hall*, in *Ruth Hall and Other Writings*, ed. Joyce W. Warren (New Brunswick, NJ: Rutgers University Press, 1986), 159–60; Henry David Thoreau, "Slavery in Massachusetts," in *Reform Papers*, ed. Wendell Glick (Princeton: Princeton University Press, 1973), 101.

14. Ralph Waldo Emerson, *The Journals and Miscellaneous Notebooks of Ralph Waldo Emerson*, Vol. 7, 1838–1842, ed. A. W. Plumstead and Harrison Hayford (Cambridge, MA: Belknap Press of Harvard University Press, 1969), 179; Cooper, *The American Democrat*, 216. See Chapter 6 for a discussion of Poe's critique in "The Mystery of Marie Roget."

15. Cooper, *The American Democrat*, 214; James Fenimore Cooper, *Home As Found* (New York: Capricorn, 1961), 222, 414, 236; Emerson, *The Journals and Miscellaneous Notebooks of Ralph Waldo Emerson*, Vol. 11, 1848–1851, ed. A. W. Plumstead and William H. Gilman (Cambridge, MA: Belknap Press of Harvard University Press, 1975), 277; Vol. 14, 1854–1861, ed. Susan Sutton Smith and Harrison Hayford (Cambridge, MA: Belknap Press of Harvard University Press, 1978), 204–5.

16. Parke Godwin, "The Able Editor," in *Interpretations of Journalism: A Book of Readings*, ed. Frank Luther Mott and Ralph D. Casey (New York: F.S. Crofts, 1937), 119–20.

17. Everett is quoted in Dicken-Garcia, *Journalistic Standards in Nineteenth-Century America*, 48; Thoreau, "Slavery in Massachusetts," in *Reform Papers*, ed. Wendell Glick (Princeton: Princeton University Press, 1973), 100; Cooper, *The American Democrat*, 212–13, 215; Cooper, *Home As Found*, 238.

18. Michael Schudson, *Discovering the News: A Social History of American Newspapers* (New York: Basic Books, 1978), 19, 25; Papers of Frederick Douglass, page 1 of manuscript on Reel 20, Container 32, Library of Congress. Commercial papers did not entirely replace party organs, and other kinds of publications also existed. Huntzicker explains: "Not all newspapers became penny papers in search of a mass audience. Throughout the nineteenth century, most newspapers continued to rely on political, religious, and other organizations for subsidies. In small frontier towns, for example, newspapers began as town boosters with subsidies from real estate agents and other merchants. . . . Mercantile and partisan newspapers, meanwhile, continued to be among the most influential publications in the nation's major cities" (*The Popular Press, 1833–1865*, 48–49). Even publications not dependent on mass audiences, however, would be inclined to cater to other interests, such as advertisers and politicians.

19. Greeley is quoted in James L. Crouthamel, *Bennett's New York Herald and the Rise of the Popular Press* (Syracuse, NY: Syracuse University Press, 1989), 156.

20. Norma Green, "Concepts of News," in *American Journalism*, ed. W. David Sloan and Lisa Mullikin Parcell (Jefferson, NC: McFarland, 2002), 40–41; Schudson, *Discovering the News*, 27; Crouthamel, *Bennett's New York Herald and the Rise of the Popular Press*, 33–34; "Wedding Extraordinary," *New York Herald*, August 31, 1835; "Winning a Wife," *New York Sun*, September 1, 1835; "El Pedrero Campechano," *New York Herald*, October 24, 1835; "Terrible Story—Seduction, Insanity, and Death," *Brooklyn Daily Eagle*, March 1, 1843; item on parachuting dog in September 1, 1835, issue of *New York Sun*, 2.

21. Bennett is quoted in Crouthamel, *Bennett's New York Herald and the Rise of the Popular Press*, 30, see also p. 31. Crouthamel explains,

"The same gossipy, probing treatment was given to other murders, suicides, seductions, and accidental deaths. In at least eight other murder cases in the next eight years the *Herald* provided coverage as extensive as that of the Robinson-Jewett case, or more so, and usually included an engraving of the victim, the accused, or the scene of the crime."

22. Robin Dunbar, *Grooming, Gossip, and the Evolution of Language* (Cambridge: Harvard University Press, 1997), 79, 115; Lehuu, *Carnival on the Page*, 51; *New York Herald*, August 31, 1835; Hughes is quoted in Crouthamel, *Bennett's New York Herald and the Rise of the Popular Press*, 29. Jewett's actual name was Helen, but the name "Ellen" was also used in reference to her. See Patricia Cline Cohen, *The Murder of Helen Jewett: The Life and Death of a Prostitute in Nineteenth-Century New York* (New York: Vintage, 1999), 9.

23. David S. Reynolds, *Beneath the American Renaissance* (Cambridge: Harvard University Press, 1988), 171; Cooper to Horatio Hastings Weld, April 4–8(?), 1842, in *Letters*, 4: 265; Cooper, *Home As Found*, 187, 325; "Tone of the American Press," *Brooklyn Daily Eagle*, February 26, 1847. This article is not signed, but Reynolds attributes the quoted sentence to Whitman. An item called "Reading" in this same issue concludes with this statement: "It is not the incessant reader that makes the most intelligent person—especially if nothing but the tras[h] of the day is devoured." Andie Tucher, *Froth and Scum: Truth, Beauty, Goodness, and the Ax Murder in America's First Mass Medium* (Chapel Hill: University of North Carolina Press, 1994), 75.

24. Emerson, "Goethe, or the Writer," in *The Collected Works of Ralph Waldo Emerson*, ed. Joseph Slater (Cambridge: Belknap Press of Harvard University Press, 1971–2007), 4:155.

25. Thoreau, "Slavery in Massachusetts," 100–2.

26. Cooper, *Home As Found*, 423, 273.

27. Thoreau, "Slavery in Massachusetts," 99; Emerson, "Self-Reliance," in *Collected Works*, 2:33; Emerson, *Journals*, Vol. 9, 1843–1847, ed. Ralph H. Orth and Alfred R. Ferguson (Cambridge, MA: Belknap Press of Harvard University Press, 1971), 174–75.

28. "The Newspaper and Periodical Press," *Southern Quarterly Review* 1 (1842): 7.

29. Bowles, February 3, 1855 article, in *Interpretations of Journalism*, 116; Dana, "News and Reporting," in *Interpretations of Journalism*, 159; Crouthamel, *Bennett's New York Herald and the Rise of the Popular Press*, 45; Emery and Emery, *The Press and America*, 163, 165; Dicken-Garcia, *Journalistic Standards in Nineteenth-Century America*, 42.

30. Cooper, *Home As Found*, 229, 233, 238; Poe, "The Balloon Hoax," in *Collected Works*, 1068–69; Poe, "Dreams," in ibid., 67–69; Poe, "Dream-Land," in ibid., 344. The theme of escape from reality recurs throughout a number of Poe's works, including "Sonnet—To Science,"

"The Fall of the House of Usher," and "The Masque of the Red Death."

31. Herman Melville, *Moby-Dick*, ed. Hershel Parker and Harrison Hayford (New York: W. W. Norton, 2002), 133. A modern lament about the deluge of news can be heard in Tom Petty's song "Jammin' Me": "Take back your Iranian torture / And the apple in young Steve's eye. / Yeah, take back your losin' streak. / Check your front-wheel drive. / You're jammin' me. / You're jammin' me. / Quit jammin' me."

32. Emerson, "The Poet," 3:11; Emerson, "Self-Reliance, in *Collected Works*, 2:41; Emerson, *The Journals and Miscellaneous Notebooks of Ralph Waldo Emerson*, Vol. 13, 1852–1855, ed. Ralph H. Orth and Alfred R. Ferguson (Cambridge, MA: Belknap Press of Harvard University Press, 1977), 26; Thoreau to Parker Pillsbury, *The Correspondence of Henry David Thoreau*, ed. Walter Harding and Carl Bode (New York: New York University Press, 1958), 611.

33. Dicken-Garcia, *Journalistic Standards in Nineteenth-Century America*, 83. Dicken-Garcia notes that a newspaper of the era might contain some three dozen items relating to events, but few focusing on ideas.

34. Cooper, *Home As Found*, 313; Thoreau to H. G. O. Blake, August 9, 1850, in *Correspondence*, 265; Emerson, "The Poet," 3:3–4. Terence Martin has commented on Poe's elevation of the imagination, especially in contrast to Enlightenment doctrines. He writes, "Poe rejected such doctrines because they granted ultimate authority to facts alone and thus denied the reality of an ideal, mystic, or transcendent truth which was available only to the imagination" (36). See Martin, "Detection, Imagination, and the Introduction to 'The Murders in the Rue Morgue,'" *Modern Language Studies* 19 (1989): 31–45.

35. Walter Lippmann, *Public Opinion* (New York: Macmillan, 1936), 358.

36. Green, "Concepts of News," 35; "Annihilation of Space," in the November 29, 1844, issue of the *Brooklyn Daily Eagle*, reproduces an exchange item from the *Baltimore Patriot*.

37. Poe, *Marginalia*, in *Essays and Reviews*, ed. G. R. Thompson (New York: Literary Classics of the United States, 1984), 1415; Emerson, "Experience," in *Collected Works*, 3:28; Cooper, *Home As Found*, 118.

38. Dicken-Garcia, *Journalistic Standards in Nineteenth-Century America*, 84; Cooper, *Home As Found*, 87.

39. Melville, *Moby-Dick*, 28, 199, 196, 281, 392; Hawthorne, "The Old Manse," in *Tales and Sketches* (New York: Literary Classics of the United States, 1982), 1138.

40. Emerson, "Goethe, or the Writer," 4:151–53.

41. Ibid., 151–53, 162; Emerson, "The Poet," 3:6, 20.

42. In a brief discussion of Thoreau and the press, Leonard writes: "The journal shows us that the function of press opinion was often to inspire such provocative passages, that he saved items and copied the public prints to answer journalism with a higher language" (99).

43. Martin, "The Imagination at Play," *The Naiad Voice: Essays on Poe's Satiric Hoaxing*, ed. Dennis W. Eddings (Port Washington, NY: Associated Faculty Press, 1983), 37–38.

CHAPTER 4

1. Henry David Thoreau, *Walden,* ed. J. Lyndon Shanley (Princeton: Princeton University Press, 1971), 17. Subsequent citations will be noted parenthetically.
2. John Carlos Rowe, "'The Being of Language: The Language of Being,'" in *Henry David Thoreau,* ed. Harold Bloom (New York: Chelsea House, 1987), 146.
3. Henry David Thoreau, "Slavery in Massachusetts," in *Reform Papers,* ed. Wendell Glick (Princeton: Princeton University Press, 1973), 100.
4. Thoreau to Parker Pillsbury, in *The Correspondence of Henry David Thoreau,* ed. Walter Harding and Carl Bode (New York: New York University Press, 1958), 611; Thoreau to H. G. O. Blake, August 9, 1850, in *Correspondence,* 265; Thomas C. Leonard, *News for All: America's Coming-of-Age with the Press* (New York: Oxford University Press, 1995), 94; David S. Reynolds, *Beneath the American Renaissance* (Cambridge: Harvard University Press, 1988), 171.
5. *Walden* appeared in print on August 9, 1854, just a little more than a month after Thoreau delivered "Slavery in Massachusetts" on July 4. Thoreau, however, had been working on *Walden* since 1846. For a discussion of the composition of *Walden,* see Robert Sattelmeyer, "The Remaking of *Walden,*" in *Writing the American Classics,* ed. James Barbour and Tom Quirk (Chapel Hill: University of North Carolina Press, 1990), 53–78.
6. In "Sounds," Thoreau writes: "All day the sun has shone on the surface of some savage swamp, where the double spruce stands hung with usnea lichens, and small hawks circulate above, and the chicadee lisps amid the evergreens, and the partridge and rabbit skulk beneath; but now a more dismal and fitting day dawns, and a different race of creatures awakes to express the meaning of Nature there" (125–26).
7. Remarking on this passage, Rowe writes: "Such deep diving intends to bring to light what is hidden, freeing what has been imprisoned in humans by their faulty methods of perception and cognition" (146). Like a reporter who digs deep into the events he covers to reveal the hidden facts, Thoreau explores the truths inherent in natural facts.
8. Philip F. Gura, "Henry Thoreau and the Wisdom of Words," in *Critical Essays on Henry David Thoreau's Walden,* ed. Joel Myerson (Boston: G. K. Hall, 1988), 204.
9. In "The Pond in Winter," Thoreau asks, "Why is it that a bucket of water soon becomes putrid, but frozen remains sweet forever?" and adds, "It is commonly said that this is the difference between the affections and the intellect" (297). In the following section,

"Spring," he observes: "A single gentle rain makes the grass many shades greener. So our prospects brighten on the influx of better thoughts. We should be blessed if we lived in the present always, and took advantage of every accident that befell us, like the grass which confesses the influence of the slightest dew that falls on it; and did not spend our time in atoning for the neglect of past opportunities, which we call doing our duty" (314).

10. Sattelmeyer, "The Remaking of *Walden*," 73.

11. Jeffrey Cramer, ed., *Walden: A Fully Annotated Edition* (New Haven: Yale University Press, 2004), 17; Kraitsir is quoted in Gura, "Henry Thoreau and the Wisdom of Words," 205; Thoreau, "Slavery in Massachusetts," 99. I am indebted to Gura for the link between Kraitsir and Thoreau.

12. Thoreau referred explicitly to newspaper advertising elsewhere in *Walden*. In the "Sounds" section, he writes, "Here is a hogshead of molasses or brandy directed to John Smith, Cuttingsville, Vermont, some trader among the Green Mountains, who imports for the farmers near his clearing, and now perchance stands over his bulk-head and thinks of the last arrivals on the coast, how they may affect the price for him, telling his customers this moment . . . that he expects some by the next train of prime quality. It is advertised in the Cuttingsville Times" (121).

13. See Mark Canada, "The Critique of Journalism in *Sister Carrie*," *American Literary Realism* 42 (Spring 2010): 227–42.

14. Thoreau to H. G. O. Blake, March 27, 1848, in *Correspondence*, 215.

15. Thomas H. Johnson, "Introduction," in *The Letters of Emily Dickinson* (Cambridge: Belknap Press of Harvard University Press, 1958), xx.

16. Cristanne Miller, *Emily Dickinson: A Poet's Grammar* (Cambridge: Harvard University Press, 1987), 6. Miller explains, "In this role she commands the attention of her family on both sides: she gives the messages of one and receives at least briefly and at a distance the undivided attention of the other."

17. Dickinson to Austin Dickinson, October 1, 1851, in *Letters*, 1: 136–39; Davis to Annie Fields, July 10, [1862?], University of Virginia; Davis, letter to Annie Fields, October 25, 1862, University of Virginia.

18. Dickinson to Austin Dickinson, May 10, 1852, in *Letters*, 1: 204.

19. Robert Weisbuch and Martin Orzeck, "Introduction: Dickinson the Scrivener," in *Dickinson and Audience*, ed. Martin Orzeck and Robert Weisbuch (Ann Arbor: University of Michigan Press, 1996), 4.

20. Miller, *Emily Dickinson: A Poet's Grammar*, 13.

21. The texts of all of Dickinson's poems quoted here come from *The Complete Poems of Emily Dickinson*, ed. Thomas H. Johnson, (Boston: Little, Brown, 1960). Although this book focuses on the antebellum era, I have included analyses of some poems that Dickinson published after 1861.

22. See, for example, L 44, L 48, L 76, L 95, L 114, and L 172.
23. Miller, *Emily Dickinson: A Poet's Grammar*, 76; Sewall, *The Life of Emily Dickinson* (New York: Farrar, Straus and Giroux, 1974), 469–70. Sewall quotes Bowles biographer George Merriam's observation: "Other people were to him sponges out of which he deftly squeezed whatever knowledge they could yield" and adds "knowledge, that is, that could be turned into news items or editorial material."
24. Dickinson, L 229, *Letters* 2: 371; Sewall, *The Life of Emily Dickinson*, 482. I am indebted to Sewall for this reading of Dickinson's letter as a kind of argument for literary language.
25. Thoreau, *Walden*, 297–98.

CHAPTER 5

1. Moira Smith, "Arbiters of Truth at Play: Arbiters of Media April Fools' Day Hoaxes," *Folklore* 120 (December 2009): 274–90; Fred Fedler, *Media Hoaxes* (Ames, IA: Iowa State University Press, 1989); Frank Luther Mott, "Facetious News Writing, 1833–1883," *Mississippi Valley Historical Review* 29 (1942): 35–54.
2. Benjamin Franklin, "A Witch Trial at Mount Holly" and "The Speech of Polly Baker," *Writings*, ed. J. A. Leo Lemay (New York: Literary Classics of the United States, 1987), 155–57, 305–308.
3. William E. Huntzicker, *The Popular Press, 1833–1865* (Westport, CT: Greenwood Press, 1999), 42.
4. Edwin Emery and Michael Emery, *The Press and America: An Interpretive History of the Mass Media* (Englewood Cliffs, NJ: Prentice-Hall, 1984), 197.
5. Fred Fedler, *Media Hoaxes*, 84–96, 98–107, 160–63.
6. Quoted in Shelley Fisher Fishkin, *From Fact to Fiction: Journalism and Imaginative Writing in America* (Baltimore: Johns Hopkins University Press, 1985), 96–97.
7. Mott, writing in the first half of the twentieth century, argues that "tolerance of hoaxes has declined as the ethics of reporting have advanced." In our own day, readers generally expect reputable news organizations to maintain high standards of factual accuracy, but transgressions abound. See Mott, "Facetious News Writing," 46.
8. Ivor Shapiro, "Why They Lie: Probing the Explanations for Journalistic Cheating," *Canadian Journal of Communication* (2006): 261–66; Chris Berdik, "DUPED!" *Quill* 90 (May 2002): 22–26. I return to the subject of fabrication in modern journalism in the epilogue.
9. "Harrington's Great Lunar Panorama," *New York Sun*, September 28, 1835, 2; Andie Tucher, *Froth & Scum: Truth, Beauty, Goodness, and the Ax Murder in America's First Mass Medium* (Chapel Hill: University of North Carolina Press, 1994), 56; "Herschel's Great Discoveries," *New York Sun*, September 1, 1835.

10. G. R. Thompson, "Perspectives on Poe," in *The Naiad Voice : Essays on Poe's Satiric Hoaxing* (Port Washington, NY: Associated Faculty Press, 1983), 101–2; Terence Martin, "The Imagination at Play," in ibid., 30; Daniel Hoffman, *Poe Poe Poe Poe Poe Poe Poe Poe* (Garden City, NY: Doubleday, 1973), 46.

11. Poe later dramatized other aspects of his literary method in "Ligeia" and "The Fall of the House of Usher." See Mark Canada, "The Right Brain in Poe's Creative Process," *The Southern Quarterly* 36 (Summer 1998): 96–105.

12. Pollin, "Introduction: The Contemporary Critical Response," in *The Imaginary Voyages*, ed. Burton R. Pollin (Boston: Twayne, 1981), 372. The text cited here comes from this edition, where the story is called "The Unparalleled Adventure of One Hans Pfaall." References will be cited parenthetically.

13. "The Speculators," *New York Sun*, September 3, 1835, 2.

14. Marcy J. Dinius, "Poe's Moon Shot: 'Hans Phaall' and the Art and Science of Antebellum Print Culture," *Poe Studies/Dark Romanticism: History, Theory, Interpretation* 37 (2004): 5.

15. "Herschel's Great Discoveries"; David Ketterer, "Poe's Usage of the Hoax and the Unity of 'Hans Pfaal,'" in *The Naiad Voice*, 91.

16. Edgar Allan Poe, "The Balloon Hoax," in *Collected Works of Edgar Allan Poe*, ed. Thomas Ollive Mabbott (Cambridge: Belknap Press of Harvard University Press, 1978), 1068–1069. Subsequent references will be cited parenthetically. Poe probably wrote this note.

17. Daniel Burgoyne has argued that hoaxes "rely on and reveal a shift in the public's sense of what is possible." "The Balloon Hoax" may depend on what the public is willing to believe, but I contend that it also pushes the possible into the realm of the real. See Burgoyne, "Coleridge's 'Poetic Faith' and Poe's Scientific Hoax," *Romanticism on the Net* 21 (February 2001): 9 September 2009, http://www. erudit.org/revue/ron/2001/v/n21/005960ar.html.

18. Edgar Allan Poe, *Doings of Gotham* (Pottsville, PA: Jacob E. Spannuth, 1929; reprinted by Norwood Editions, 1977), 33–34. Poe returned to the subject of his hoax's verisimilitude in the June 8 installment of this series, again comparing it favorably with Locke's Moon Hoax. The latter, he notes, "was . . . believed, although abounding in gross errors, which should have caused it to be discredited at once; while, on the other hand, the 'Balloon-Story,' which had *no* error, and which related nothing that might not really have happened, was discredited on account of the frequent previous deceptions, of similar character, perpetrated by the 'Sun'" (53).

19. Bigelow is quoted in Curtiss S. Johnson, *Politics and a Belly-Full: The Journalistic Career of William Cullen Bryant* (New York: Vantage Press, 1962), 177; Julie Hedgepeth Williams, "The Purposes of Journalism," in *American Journalism*, ed. W. David Sloan and Lisa Mullikin Parcell (Jefferson, NC: McFarland, 2002), 4; Aristotle, *Poetics*,

in *Criticism: The Major Texts*, ed. Walter Jackson Bate (New York: Harcourt, Brace, 1952), 25.

20. Edgar Allan Poe, "Von Kempelen and His Discovery," in *Collected Works*, 1364, 1357.

21. Edgar Allan Poe, "The Facts in the Case of M. Valdemar," in *Collected Works*, 1233.

22. Poe, *Doings of Gotham*, 33; Greeley is quoted in Dwight Thomas and David K. Jackson, *The Poe Log: A Documentary Life of Edgar Allan Poe, 1809–1849* (Boston: G. K. Hall, 1987), 603; Collyer is quoted in T. O. Mabbott's introduction to "The Facts in the Case of M. Valdemar," in *Collected Works*, 1230–31; Poe quotes Barrett in a letter to Joseph M. Field (L 233), in *The Collected Letters of Edgar Allan Poe*, ed. John Ward Ostrom, 3rd ed. (New York: Gordian Press, 2008), 581.

23. Burton Pollin, *Discoveries in Poe* (Notre Dame, IN: University of Notre Dame Press, 1970), 167; Poe and Collyer are quoted in Mabbott's introduction to "The Facts in the Case of M. Valdemar," in *Collected Works*, 1230–31.

24. Levine, *Edgar Poe: Seer and Craftsman* (DeLand, FL: Everett/Edwards, 1972), 131; Poe, "Richard Adams Locke," in *Essays and Reviews*, ed. G. R. Thompson (New York: Literary Classics of the United States, 1984), 1215; Allen Tate, "The Angelic Imagination," in *Edgar Allan Poe*, ed. Harold Bloom (New York: Chelsea House, 1985), 44.

CHAPTER 6

A version of "Stowe's Abolitionist Exposé" in this chapter originally appeared in the Ignatius Critical Edition of *Uncle Tom's Cabin* (Mark Canada, "News of Her Own: Harriet Beecher Stowe's Investigative Fiction," in *Uncle Tom's Cabin*, ed. Mary R. Reichardt [San Francisco: Ignatius Press, 2009], 635–53). Used with permission.

1. So far as I know, no authors of the era used the phrase "investigative fiction," but a number of them produced works that could be classed under this heading. What distinguishes these works from other literature designed to expose hidden truths or right wrongs is their response to journalism. In each, the author explicitly mentions news reporters or newspapers, characterizes journalism as a failed medium, and sets up his or her fictional work as an alternative, superior medium for delivering the truth.

2. Walter Lippmann, *Public Opinion* (New York: Macmillan, 1936), 338–40; Paul N. Williams, *Investigative Reporting and Editing* (Englewood Cliffs, NJ: Prentice-Hall, 1978), xi.

3. James Aucoin, *The Evolution of American Investigative Journalism* (Columbia: University of Missouri Press, 2005), 19–21; Hazel Dicken-Garcia, *Journalistic Standards in Nineteenth-Century America* (Madison: University of Wisconsin Press, 1989), 107; J. Herbert Altschull, *From*

Milton to McLuhan: The Ideas Behind American Journalism (New York: Longman, 1990), 157.

4. Edwin Emery and Michael Emery, *The Press and America* (Englewood Cliffs, NJ. Prentice-Hall, 1984), 29–30; Aucoin, *The Evolution of American Investigative Journalism*, 24–25; Hazel Dicken-Garcia, *Journalistic Standards in Nineteenth-Century America* (Madison: University of Wisconsin Press, 1989), 107. See also Mark Feldstein, "A Muckraking Model: Investigative Reporting Cycles in American History," *Harvard International Journal of Press/Politics* 11 (2006): 105–20.

5. Edward Jay Epstein, "The American Press: Some Truths About Truths," in *Ethics and the Press*, ed. John C. Merrill and Ralph D. Barney (New York: Hastings House, 1975), 61; William E. Huntzicker, *The Popular Press, 1833–1865* (Westport, CT: Greenwood Press, 1999), 20–28.

6. Karen Halttunen, *Murder Most Foul* (Cambridge: Harvard University Press, 1998), 2–3.

7. Poe, "The Murders in the Rue Morgue," in *Collected Works of Edgar Allan Poe*, ed. Thomas Ollive Mabbott (Cambridge: Belknap Press of Harvard University Press, 1978), 555, 538, 544. Subsequent references will be cited parenthetically.

8. For a summary of the details surrounding the real murder, as well as the newspaper coverage and Poe's own versions of the story, see John Walsh, *Poe the Detective: The Curious Circumstances Behind "The Mystery of Marie Roget"* (New Brunswick, NJ: Rutgers University Press, 1968). See also Thomas Ollive Mabbott's introduction to "The Mystery of Marie Roget" in *Collected Works of Edgar Allan Poe*, 715–22; William J. Wimsatt, Jr., "Poe and the Mystery of Mary Rogers," *PMLA* 56 (1941): 230–48; Richard Kopley, *Edgar Allan Poe and the Dupin Mysteries* (New York: Palgrave Macmillan, 2008), 45–63. Wimsatt, who examined approximately 60 years' worth of accounts, notes that the authors of these accounts were "almost unanimous in the opinion that Poe contributed little or nothing toward solving the mystery" (230).

9. Merritt's complete affidavit appears in Walsh, *Poe the Detective*, 55. The juicy details reported in the *Tribune* do not appear in Merritt's affidavit. Walsh suggests that workers for the *Tribune* were "eagerly raking in rumors, off-the-record information, and it may be, bits of overheard conversation" (55).

10. Thomas Ollive Mabbott, introduction to "The Mystery of Marie Roget," in *Collected Works*, 720, 722; Edgar Allan Poe, "The Mystery of Marie Roget," in *Collected Works* (Cambridge, MA: Belknap Press of Harvard University Press, 1978), 723. Subsequent references will be cited parenthetically.

11. Walsh, *Poe the Detective*, 61–67. Walsh notes that the new evidence pointing to the involvement of the Loss family—and thus contradicting his own implication of a naval officer—would have severely damaged

Poe's reputation at a time when his dream of establishing a magazine seemed to be nearing fruition. Furthermore, the postponement of the third installment, expected in January, until February might point to Poe's intention to alter his manuscript. Walsh also cites accounts of Poe's presence in New York at or around late 1842, when he could have been conducting his own investigation. Finally, he points to two passages that appear to be have been altered or added to the text. No manuscript of the tale is extant, so scholars can only speculate about any revisions Poe may have made before the publication of the final installment.

12. Poe, "Von Kempelen and His Discovery," in *Collected Works*, 1358.

13. Poe, "The Balloon Hoax," in *Collected Works*, 1068–69.

14. A number of scholars have discussed Dupin's extraordinary reasoning powers, which operate outside the realm of pure logic. See Daniel Hoffman, *Poe Poe Poe Poe Poe Poe Poe* (New York: Doubleday, 1972), 107–10; Merrill Maguire Skaggs, "Poe's Longing for a Bicameral Mind," *The Southern Quarterly: A Journal of the Arts in the South* 19 (1981): 56; Donald Barlow Stauffer, "Poe as Phrenologist: The Example of Monsieur Dupin," in *Papers on Poe: Essays in Honor of John Ward Ostrom*, ed. Richard P. Veler (Springfield, OH: Chantry Music Press, 1972), 122.

15. In extraordinary stories such as the months-long coverage of the Jewett murder, newspapers did indulge in more of this kind of investigation and speculation. Indeed, as Wimsatt has noted, Poe's speculation about a murderer alone with Marie's corpse mirrors a passage that appeared in Bennett's *Herald* (239).

16. A version of this discussion of Stowe and *Uncle Tom's Cabin* originally appeared in the Ignatius Critical Edition of *Uncle Tom's Cabin* (Mark Canada, "News of Her Own: Harriet Beecher Stowe's Investigative Fiction," *Uncle Tom's Cabin*, ed. Mary R. Reichardt [San Francisco: Ignatius Press, 2009], 635–53.). Used with permission.

17. "The True Principle," *Middletown* (Connecticut) *Constitution*, November 6, 1850, 2; untitled article, *New Hampshire Sentinel*, October 10, 1850, 2; "The Fugitive Slave Law," *Amherst* (New Hampshire) *Farmer's Cabinet*, October 10, 1850, 2; "The Slave-Law, and the Union," *New York Independent*, January 16, 1851, 10; "The Case of Long," *New York Evangelist*, January 9, 1851, 6.

18. Harriet Beecher Stowe, undated letter to Henry Ward Beecher, Harriet Beecher Stowe letters, microform from Yale University Library.

19. James M. McPherson, introduction to *Uncle Tom's Cabin*, by Harriet Beecher Stowe (New York: Vintage, 1991), xi; Charles Dudley Warner, "The Story of *Uncle Tom's Cabin*," in *Critical Essays on Harriet Beecher Stowe*, ed. Elizabeth Ammons (Boston: G. K. Hall, 1980), 60–72; Ann Douglas, introduction to *Uncle Tom's Cabin*, by Harriet Beecher Stowe (New York: Penguin, 1981), 13.

20. Elizabeth Ammons, introduction to *Critical Essays on Harriet Beecher Stowe*, xi–xviii.

21. Rodger Streitmatter, *Mightier than the Sword: How the News Media Have Shaped American History* (New York: Westview Press, 1997), 40.

22. E. Bruce Kirkham, *The Building of Uncle Tom's Cabin* (Knoxville: University of Tennessee Press, 1977), 46–47, 43, 49, 62–64.

23. Joan D. Hedrick, *Harriet Beecher Stowe: A Life* (New York: Oxford University Press, 1994), 202.

24. Joan D. Hedrick, ed., *The Oxford Harriet Beecher Stowe Reader* (New York: Oxford University Press, 1994), 64.

25. Ibid., 63.

26. Ibid., 61.

27. Hedrick, *Harriet Beecher Stowe: A Life*, 202.

28. Ibid., 207–8.

29. James Baldwin, "Everybody's Protest Novel," in *Critical Essays on Harriet Beecher Stowe*, 92–97.

30. George Goodin, *The Poetics of Protest: Literary Form and Political Implication in the Victim-of-Society Novel* (Carbondale: Southern Illinois University Press, 1985), 1–3.

31. Harriet Beecher Stowe, *Uncle Tom's Cabin*, ed. Mary R. Reichardt (San Francisco: Ignatius, 2009), 259. Subsequent references will be cited parenthetically.

32. Hedrick, *Harriet Beecher Stowe: A Life*, 205.

33. Anonymous, "The Slave Bills—The Causeway—Political War—Fall Trade, &c.," *New York Tribune*, September 18, 1850, 6.

34. See "The Mystery of Marie Roget," in which the narrator says: "Strange as it may appear, the third week from the discovery of the body had passed, and passed without any light being thrown upon the subject, before even a rumor of the events which had so agitated the public mind, reached the ears of Dupin and myself. Engaged in researches which had absorbed our whole attention, it had been nearly a month since either of us had gone abroad, or received a visitor, or more than glanced at the leading political articles in one of the daily papers." *Poetry and Tales*, 510. See also "The Unparalleled Adventure of One Hans Pfaall," in which the protagonist disparages the public's fascination with current events and finds escape in a balloon. *Poetry and Tales*, 951–1001.

35. Thomas C. Leonard, *News for All: America's Coming-of-Age with the Press* (New York: Oxford University Press, 1995), 10–11, 22.

36. S. Bradley Shaw, "The Pliable Rhetoric of Domesticity," in *The Stowe Debate: Rhetorical Strategies in Uncle Tom's Cabin*, ed. Mason I. Lowance, Jr., Ellen E. Westbrook, and R. C. De Prospo (Amherst: University of Massachusetts Press, 1994), 73–98; Mason I. Lowance. "Biblical Typology and the Allegorical Mode: The Prophetic Strain," in ibid., 159–84; Catharine E. O'Connell, "'The Magic of the Real Presence of Distress': Sentimentality and Competing Rhetorics of Authority," in ibid., 13–36.

37. Hedrick, *Oxford Harriet Beecher Stowe Reader*, 57–58.
38. Harriet Beecher Stowe, "Preface," in *Uncle Tom's Cabin* (New York: Knopf, 1909), 7–8.
39. Harriet Beecher Stowe, *A Key to Uncle Tom's Cabin; Presenting the Original Facts and Documents upon Which the Story Is Founded Together with Corroborative Statements Verifying the Truth of the Work* (Bedford, MA: Applewood, 1998), 5.
40. Douglas, introduction to *Uncle Tom's Cabin*, 13.
41. Rebecca Harding Davis, "Life in the Iron-Mills," in *A Rebecca Harding Davis Reader* (Pittsburgh: University of Pittsburgh Press, 1995), 4. Subsequent references will be cited parenthetically.
42. Sharon M. Harris, *Rebecca Harding Davis and American Realism* (Philadelphia: University of Pennsylvania Press, 1991).
43. Rebecca Harding Davis to Annie Fields, July 10, [1862] and October 25, 1862, MSS 6109, Box 1, Richard Harding Davis Papers, Barrett Library, University of Virginia. Subsequent references to Davis's correspondence are to letters in this same collection.
44. Davis to James Fields, August 9, [1861]; Davis to James Fields, December 30, 1861.
45. Harris, *Rebecca Harding Davis and American Realism*, 9.
46. Rebecca Harding Davis, *Bits of Gossip* (Boston: Houghton, Mifflin, 1904), 36; Davis, "Two Methods with the Negro," in *A Rebecca Harding Davis Reader*, 424; Davis, "Undistinguished Americans," in ibid., 459; "The House on the Beach," in ibid., 383; "Some Testimony in the Case," in ibid., 393–94.
47. Whitney A. Womack, "Reforming Women's Reform Literature: Rebecca Harding Davis's Rewriting of the Industrial Novel," in *Our Sisters' Keepers: Nineteenth-Century Benevolence Literature by American Women* (Tuscaloosa, AL: University of Alabama Press, 2005), 114–15.
48. Davis, *Bits of Gossip*, 166–68.
49. Tillie Olsen, "A Biographical Interpretation," in *Life in the Iron Mills and Other Stories* (New York: The Feminist Press at The City University of New York, 1972), 87.
50. Harris, *Rebecca Harding Davis and American Realism*, 11; Lisa A. Long, "The Postbellum Reform Writings of Rebecca Harding Davis and Elizabeth Stuart Phelps," in *The Cambridge Companion to Nineteenth-Century American Women's Writing*, ed. Dale M. Bauer and Philip Gould (Cambridge: Cambridge University Press, 2001), 262–83. Long has argued that Davis's attitude toward reform was complex, saying, "Rather than offering guides to a better future, Phelps's and Davis's texts seem to express ineffable grief, a sense of surreality, and impotence. . . . Their texts are audience-oriented primarily in that they encourage self-examination of the fragmented, alienated self; social action is a fortuitous by-product of such psychological labors" (268). For the purposes of this book, we need only recognize that Davis shared the press's crusading

spirit, whether that spirit meant only exposure or also calls for action.

51. Harris, *Rebecca Harding Davis and American Realism*, 25.

52. Rebecca Harding Davis, "Women in Literature," in *A Rebecca Harding Davis Reader*, 402.

53. Olsen, "A Biographical Interpretation," 88.

54. Rebecca Harding Davis, "Life in the Iron-Mills," in *A Rebecca Harding Davis Reader*, 5.

55. The content of the news item actually comes through Doctor May, who "was reading to his wife at breakfast from this fourth column of the morning-paper" (25); thus, the quotation may be the story itself, or it may be his summary of the story. A number of details suggest that Doctor May's words constitute the story itself. First, Davis makes no reference to summary and instead uses the words "reading" and "read." Second, Davis uses no ellipsis points to suggest that Doctor May is skipping material or pausing as he reports key details. Finally, similar items can be found in the journalism of the era. The November 19, 1857, issue of the *Weekly Patriot and Union* of Harrisburg, Pennsylvania, contains these items: "Com. vs. Tom Bennet and John H. Jones, both colored. Riot. Guilty." "Com. vs. Jacob Loyer. Riot at the polls. Postponed."

56. David S. Reynolds, *Beneath the American Renaissance: The Subversive Imagination in the Age of Emerson and Melville* (Cambridge: Harvard University Press, 1988), 257.

57. Long, "The Postbellum Reform Writings of Rebecca Harding Davis and Elizabeth Stuart Phelps," 274.

58. Harris, *Rebecca Harding Davis and American Realism*, 154–60, 182–89; Davis, "The Middle-Aged Woman," in *A Rebecca Harding Davis Reader*, 378.

EPILOGUE

1. Other works featuring critiques of journalism and journalists include Henry James's "The Next Time," *The Portrait of a Lady*, and *The Bostonians*; Mark Twain's "Journalism in Tennessee" and *A Connecticut Yankee in King Arthur's Court*; and Rebecca Harding Davis's "The Yares of Black Mountain" and *Earthen Pitchers*. For an analysis of one critique, see Mark Canada, "The Critique of Journalism in *Sister Carrie*," *American Literary Realism* 42 (Spring 2010): 227–42.

2. Shelley Fisher Fishkin, *From Fact to Fiction: Journalism & Imaginative Writing in America* (Baltimore: Johns Hopkins University Press, 1985).

3. "Times Reporter Who Resigned Leaves Long Trail of Deception," *New York Times*, May 11, 2003, http://www.nytimes.com/2003/05/11/national/11PAPE.html; Blake Morrison, "Ex-USA

TODAY reporter faked major stories," March 19, 2004, http://
www.usatoday.com/news/2004-03-18-2004-03-18_kelleymain_x.htm;
Lori Robertson, "Confronting the Culture," *American Journalism
Review* 27 (August/September 2005): 36–37; Rem Rieder, "Falling to
'Pieces,'" *American Journalism Review* 28 (February /March 2006): 6;
Benjamin Hill and Alan Schwarz, "Errors Cast Doubt on a Baseball
Memoir," *New York Times*, March 2, 2009, http://www.nytimes.
com/2009/03/03/sports/baseball/03book.html; "Authorities:
'Balloon boy' incident was a hoax," CNN.com, October 18, 2009,
http://www.cnn.com/2009/US/10/18/colorado.balloon.investi-
gation/index.html; Helene Cooper and Brian Stelter, "Obamas'
Uninvited Guests Prompt Inquiry," *New York Times*, November 26,
2009, http://www.nytimes.com/2009/11/27/us/politics/27party.
html; Roxanne Roberts and Amy Argetsinger, "Surprise 'Housewives'
dinner guests not invited, White House says," *Washington Post*,
November 25, 2009, http://voices.washingtonpost.com/reliable-
source/2009/11/salahi_photos_etc.html.

4. Lori Robertson, "Confronting the Culture," 37–40; Peter Johnson,
"Attacking Deception in the Newsroom," *USA Today*, March 21, 2004,
http://www.usatoday.com/life/columnist/mediamix/2004-03-
21-media-mix_x.htm; Ron F. Smith, *Groping for Ethics in Journalism*
(Malden, MA: Blackwell, 2008), 95–103.

5. Ben Bradlee, *A Good Life: Newspapering and Other Adventures*
(New York: Simon & Schuster, 1995), 437; Margaret Wolf Freivogel, "Newsroom Views," *Journalism Studies* 5 (2004): 571; Rebecca
Leung, "Stephen Glass: I Lied for Esteem," *60 Minutes*, August 17,
2003, http://www.cbsnews.com/stories/2003/05/07/60minutes/
main552819.shtml; Jack Shafer, "Glass Houses," *Slate* (May 15,
1998), http://www.slate.com/id/2074. See also Michael Schudson,
Discovering the News: A Social History of American Newspapers
(New York: Basic Books, 1978), 89.

6. Philip Bennett, interview with Frank Stasio, *The State of Things*,
North Carolina Public Radio, October 12, 2009, http://wunc.org/
tsot/archive/search_media?review_state=published&start.query:
record:list:date=2009-10-12%2023%3A59%3A59&start.
range:record=max&end.query:record:list:date=2009-10-12%
2000%3A00%3A00&end.range:record=min&path=/websites/
wuncplone_webslingerz_com/tsot/archive&month:int=10&
year:int=2009; Peggy Noonan, "Apocalypse No," *The Wall Street
Journal* (October 27, 2007), http://online.wsj.com/article/SB
119343919419073320.html; Mark Twain, "Salutatory," *Buffalo Express*
(August 21, 1869). In a study of ethics in a television newsroom,
Tom Luljak tells of a television reporter who agreed to aid in a police
investigation by interviewing a deputy on camera. To mislead suspects, the deputy would let on that the law enforcement had more

information than it really had. His rationale for taking part in this deceptive practice is revealing. He said, "It's a great story. They get the guys and I get the story" (16). See Tom Luljak, "The Routine Nature of Journalistic Deception," in *Holding the Media Accountable: Citizens, Ethics, and the Law*, ed. David Pritchard (Bloomington: Indiana University Press, 2000), 11–26.

7. In the spirit of full disclosure, this line is an adaptation of Cassius's line in Shakespeare's *Julius Caesar*: "The fault, dear Brutus, is not in our stars, / But in ourselves, that we are underlings" (I.ii.140–41).

Selected Bibliography

Journalism and Literature: Intersections

Cane, Aleta Feinsod, and Susan Alves, eds. *"The Only Efficient Instrument":* *American Women Writers and the Periodical, 1837–1916.* Iowa City: University of Iowa Press, 2001.

Cook, Elizabeth Christine. *Literary Influences in Colonial Newspapers, 1704–1750.* Port Washington, NY: Kennikat Press, 1966.

Davis, Lennard. *Factual Fictions: The Origins of the English Novel.* New York: Columbia University Press, 1983.

Fishkin, Shelley Fisher. *From Fact to Fiction: Journalism & Imaginative Writing in America.* Baltimore: Johns Hopkins University Press, 1985.

Robertson, Michael. *Stephen Crane, Journalism, and the Making of Modern American Literature.* New York: Columbia University Press, 1997.

Roggenkamp, Karen. *Narrating the News: New Journalism and Literary Genre in Late Nineteenth-Century American Newspapers and Fiction.* Kent, OH: Kent State University Press, 2005.

Underwood, Doug. *Journalism and the Novel.* Cambridge: Cambridge University Press, 2008.

Weber, Ronald. *Hired Pens: Professional Writers in America's Golden Age of Print.* Athens: Ohio State University Press, 1997.

Wolfe, Tom. *The New Journalism.* New York: Harper & Row, 1973.

Journalism

Primary Sources

Greeley, Horace. *Recollections of a Busy Life.* New York: J. B. Ford, 1868.

Mott, Frank Luther, and Ralph D. Casey, eds. *Interpretations of Journalism.* New York: F. S. Crofts, 1937.

Newspapers of the era include the *Brooklyn Daily Eagle, Colored American, Emancipator, Liberator, New York Evening Post, New York Herald, New York Sun, New York Tribune, New York Mercury, North Star,* and *Springfield Republican.*

History

Aucoin, James L. *The Evolution of American Investigative Journalism.* Columbia: University of Missouri Press, 2005.

Bradlee, Ben. *A Good Life: Newspapering and Other Adventures.* New York: Simon & Schuster, 1995.

Crouthamel, James L. *Bennett's New York Herald and the Rise of the Popular Press.* Syracuse, NY: Syracuse University Press, 1989.

Dicken-Garcia, Hazel. *Journalistic Standards in Nineteenth-Century America.* Madison: University of Wisconsin Press, 1989.

Emery, Edwin, and Michael Emery. *The Press and America: An Interpretive History of the Mass Media.* Englewood Cliffs, NJ: Prentice-Hall, 1984.

Fedler, Fred. *Media Hoaxes.* Ames, IA: Iowa State University Press, 1989.

Feldstein, Mark. "A Muckraking Model: Investigative Reporting Cycles in American History." *Harvard International Journal of Press/Politics* 11:2 (2006): 105–20.

Grossberger, Lewis. "The Pulitzer Prize Hoax." *Newsweek,* April 27, 1981.

Huntzicker, William E. *The Popular Press, 1833–1865 (The History of American Journalism).* Westport, CT: Greenwood Press, 1999.

Lee, Alfred McClung. *The Daily Newspaper in America: The Evolution of a Social Instrument.* New York: Macmillan, 1947.

Lehuu, Isabelle. *Carnival on the Page.* Chapel Hill: University of North Carolina Press, 2000.

Leonard, Thomas C. *News for All: America's Coming-of-Age with the Press.* New York: Oxford University Press, 1995.

Leung, Rebecca. "Stephen Glass: I Lied for Esteem." *60 Minutes.* http://www.cbsnews.com/stories/2003/05/07/60minutes/main552819.shtml.

Mott, Frank Luther. *American Journalism.* New York: Macmillan, 1962.

———. "Facetious News Writing, 1833–1883." *Mississippi Valley Historical Review* 29 (1942): 35–54.

Nord, David. *Communities of Journalism: A History of American Newspapers and Their Readers.* Urbana: University of Illinois Press, 2001.

Parton, James. *The Life of Horace Greeley.* New York: Mason Brothers, 1855. Reprint, New York: Arno and the *New York Times,* 1970.

Schudson, Michael. *Discovering the News: A Social History of American Newspapers.* New York: Basic Books, 1978.

Smith, Ron F. *Ethics in Journalism.* Malden: Blackwell, 2008.

Streitmatter, Rodger. *Mightier than the Sword: How the News Media Have Shaped American History.* New York: Westview Press, 1997.

Tucher, Andie. *Froth & Scum: Truth, Beauty, Goodness, and the Ax Murder in America's First Mass Medium.* Chapel Hill: University of North Carolina Press, 1994.

Theory and Practice

Altschull, J. Herbert. *From Milton to McLuhan: The Ideas Behind American Journalism.* Baltimore: Johns Hopkins University Press, 1990.

Berdik, Chris. "DUPED!" *Quill* 90 (May 2002): 22–26.

Brown, Fred. "Asking right questions a key to minimizing harm." *Quill* 94 (May 2006): 38.

Brooks, Brian, George Kennedy, Daryl R. Moen, and Don Ranly. *News Reporting and Writing*. Boston: Bedford/St. Martin's, 1999.

Elliott, Deni, and Charles Culver. "Defining and Analyzing Journalistic Deception." *Journal of Mass Media Ethics* 7 (1992): 69–84.

Epstein, Edward J. "The American Press: Some Truth About Truths." In *Ethics and the Press*, edited by John C. Merrill and Ralph D. Barney, 60–68. New York: Hastings House, 1975.

Freivogel, Martha Wolf. "Newsroom Views." *Journalism Studies* 5 (2004): 571–72.

Green, Norma. "Concepts of News." In *American Journalism*, edited by W. David Sloan and Lisa Mullikin Parcell, 34–43. Jefferson, NC: McFarland, 2002.

Hughes, Helen MacGill. *News and the Human Interest Story*. New York: Greenwood Press, 1940.

Lippmann, Walter. *Public Opinion*. New York: Macmillan, 1936.

Luljak, Tom. "The Routine Nature of Journalistic Deception." In *Holding the Media Accountable: Citizens, Ethics, and the Law*, edited by David Pritchard, 11–26. Bloomington: Indiana University Press, 2000.

Love, Robert. "Before Jon Stewart." *Columbia Journalism Review* 45 (March/April 2007): 33–37.

Lule, Jack. *Daily News, Eternal Stories: The Mythological Role of Journalism*. New York: Guilford Press, 2001.

Margolis, Jon. "Pulp Fiction." *Committee of Concerned Journalists*. http://www.concernedjournalists.org/pulp-fiction.

Mencher, Melvin. *News Reporting and Writing*. Madison, WI: Brown & Benchmark, 1994.

"The Newspaper and Periodical Press." *Southern Quarterly Review* 1 (January 1842): 5–66.

Noonan, Peggy. "Apocalypse No." *Wall Street Journal*. October 26, 2007.

Patterson, Philip, and Lee Wilkins. *Media Ethics: Issues and Cases*. 4th ed. Boston: McGraw-Hill, 2001.

Robertson, Lori. "Confronting the Culture." *American Journalism Review* 27 (Aug/Sep 2005): 34–41.

———. "Ethically Challenged." *American Journalism Review* 23 (Mar 2001): 20–29.

Rosen, Jill. "We Mean Business." *American Journalism Review* 26 (Jun/Jul 2004): 22–29.

Schiller, Dan. *Objectivity and the News*. Philadelphia: University of Pennsylvania Press, 1981.

Schwartz, Jerry. *Associated Press Reporting Handbook*. New York: McGraw-Hill, 2002.

Shapiro, Ivor. "Why They Lie: Probing the Explanations for Journalistic Cheating." *Canadian Journal of Communication* 31 (2006): 261–66.

Smith, Moira. "Arbiters of Truth at Play: Arbiters of Media April Fools' Day Hoaxes." *Folklore* 120 (December 2009): 274–90.

The Society of Professional Journalists. "SPJ Code of Ethics." The Society of Professional Journalists. http://www.spj.org/ethicscode.asp.

Weir, David, and Dan Noyes. *Raising Hell: How the Center for Investigative Reporting Gets the Story.* Reading, MA: Addison-Wesley, 1983.

Williams, Paul N. *Investigative Reporting and Editing.* Englewood Cliffs, NJ: Prentice-Hall, 1978.

Williams, Julie Hedgepeth. "The Purposes of Journalism." In *American Journalism,* edited by W. David Sloan and Lisa Mullikin Parcell, 3–13. Jefferson, NC: McFarland, 2002.

LITERATURE

General

Aristotle. *Poetics.* In *Criticism: The Major Texts,* edited by Walter Jackson Bate, 19–39. New York: Harcourt, Brace, 1952.

Goodin, George. *The Poetics of Protest: Literary Form and Political Implication in the Victim-of-Society Novel.* Carbondale: Southern Illinois University Press, 1985.

Gura, Philip F. *The Wisdom of Words: Language, Theology, and Literature in the New England Renaissance.* Middletown, CT: Wesleyan University Press, 1981.

Halttunen, Karen. *Murder Most Foul.* Cambridge, MA: Harvard University Press, 1998.

Irwin, John. *American Hieroglyphics: The Symbol of the Egyptian Hieroglyphics in the American Renaissance.* New Haven: Yale University Press, 1980.

Plato. *Republic. The Collected Dialogues of Plato.* Ed. Edith Hamilton and Huntington Cairns. Princeton, NJ: Princeton University Press, 1961.

Reynolds, David S. *Beneath the American Renaissance.* Cambridge, MA: Harvard University Press, 1988.

Zboray, Ronald J. *A Fictive People: Antebellum Economic Development and the American Reading Public.* New York: Oxford University Press, 1993.

William Cullen Bryant

Bryant, William Cullen. *Power for Sanity: Selected Editorials of William Cullen Bryant, 1829–1861.* Edited by William Cullen Bryant II. New York: Fordham University, 1994.

Johnson, Curtiss S. *Politics and a Belly-Full: The Journalistic Career of William Cullen Bryant.* Westport, CT: Greenwood Press, 1962.

James Fenimore Cooper

Cooper, James Fenimore. *The American Democrat.* In *Representative Selections,* edited by Robert E. Spiller, 182–232. Westport, CT: Greenwood Press, 1936.

———. *Home As Found*. New York: Capricorn, 1961.

Cooper, James Fenimore. *The Letters and Journals of James Fenimore Cooper*. Edited by James Franklin Beard. Cambridge, MA: Belknap Press of Harvard University Press, 1964.

Railton, Stephen. *Fenimore Cooper: A Study of His Life and Imagination*. Princeton: Princeton University Press, 1978.

Rebecca Harding Davis

Davis, Rebecca Harding. *Bits of Gossip*. Boston: Houghton, Mifflin, 1904.

———. *Earthen Pitchers. A Rebecca Harding Davis Reader*. Edited by Jean Pfaelzer. Pittsburgh: University of Pittsburgh Press, 1995.

———. "The House on the Beach." *A Rebecca Harding Davis Reader*. Edited by Jean Pfaelzer. Pittsburgh: University of Pittsburgh Press, 1995.

———. "Life in the Iron-Mills." *A Rebecca Harding Davis Reader*. Edited by Jean Pfaelzer. Pittsburgh: University of Pittsburgh Press, 1995.

———. Papers of Rebecca Harding Davis. Clifton Waller Barrett Library of American Literature. University of Virginia Libraries.

———. "Review of *Undistinguished Americans*." *A Rebecca Harding Davis Reader*. Edited by Jean Pfaelzer. Pittsburgh: University of Pittsburgh Press, 1995.

———. "Some Testimony in the Case." *A Rebecca Harding Davis Reader*. Edited by Jean Pfaelzer. Pittsburgh: University of Pittsburgh Press, 1995.

———. "Two Methods with the Negro." *A Rebecca Harding Davis Reader*. Edited by Jean Pfaelzer. Pittsburgh: University of Pittsburgh Press, 1995.

———. "Women in Literature." *A Rebecca Harding Davis Reader*. Edited by Jean Pfaelzer. Pittsburgh: University of Pittsburgh Press, 1995.

———. "The Yares of Black Mountain." *A Rebecca Harding Davis Reader*. Edited by Jean Pfaelzer. Pittsburgh: University of Pittsburgh Press, 1995.

Harris, Sharon M. *Rebecca Harding Davis and American Realism*. Philadelphia: University of Pennsylvania Press, 1991.

Long, Lisa A. "The Postbellum Reform Writings of Rebecca Harding Davis and Elizabeth Stuart Phelps." In *The Cambridge Companion to Nineteenth-Century American Women's Writing*, edited by Dale M. Bauer and Philip Gould, 262–83. Cambridge: Cambridge University Press, 2001.

Olsen, Tillie. "A Biographical Interpretation." In *Life in the Iron Mills and Other Stories*, edited by Tillie Olsen, 69–174. New York: The Feminist Press at the City University of New York, 1972.

Womack, Whitney A. "Reforming Women's Reform Literature: Rebecca Harding Davis's Rewriting of the Industrial Novel." In *Our Sisters' Keepers: Nineteenth-Century Benevolence Literature by American Women*, edited by Jill Bergman and Debra Bernardi, 105–31. Tuscaloosa: University of Alabama Press, 2005.

Emily Dickinson

Buckingham, Willis J. "Emily Dickinson and the Reading Life." In *Dickinson and Audience*, edited by Martin Orzeck and Robert Weisbuch, 233–54. Ann Arbor: University of Michigan Press, 1996.

Capps, Jack. *Emily Dickinson's Reading*. Cambridge, MA: Harvard University Press, 1966.

Dandurand, Karen. "Dickinson and the Public." In *Dickinson and Audience*, edited by Martin Orzeck and Robert Weisbuch, 255–77. Ann Arbor: University of Michigan Press, 1996.

Dickinson, Emily. *The Letters of Emily Dickinson*. Edited by Thomas H. Johnson. Cambridge, MA: Belknap Press of Harvard University, 1958.

———. *The Complete Poems*. Edited by Thomas H. Johnson. Boston: Little, Brown, 1960.

Kirkby, Joan. "Dickinson Reading." *Emily Dickinson Journal* 5 (Fall 1996): 246–54.

Leyda, Jay. *Years and Hours of Emily Dickinson*. New Haven: Yale University Press, 1960.

Miller, Cristanne. *Emily Dickinson: A Poet's Grammar*. Cambridge, MA: Harvard University Press, 1987.

Sewall, Richard. *The Life of Emily Dickinson*. New York: Farrar, Straus and Giroux, 1974.

Weisbuch, Robert, and Martin Orzeck. "Introduction: Dickinson the Scrivener." In *Dickinson and Audience*, edited by Martin Orzeck and Robert Weisbuch, 1–8. Ann Arbor: University of Michigan Press, 1996.

Whicher, George Frisbie. *This Was a Poet: A Critical Biography*. Philadelphia: Dufour, 1952.

Frederick Douglass

Douglass, Frederick. "Colored National Press." *North Star*, January 14, 1848.

———. "Men of Color, To Arms!" *Douglass Monthly*, March 21, 1863.

———. *Narrative of the Life of Frederick Douglass*. In *Slave Narratives*, 267–368. New York: Literary Classics of the United States, 2000.

———. *The Papers of Frederick Douglass*. Library of Congress.

Martin, Waldo E. *The Mind of Frederick Douglass*. Chapel Hill: University of North Carolina Press, 1984.

Moses, Wilson J. "Frederick Douglass and the Constraints of Racialized Writing." In *Frederick Douglass: New Literary and Historical Essays*, edited by Eric J. Sundquist, 66–83. Cambridge: Cambridge University Press, 1990.

Sundquist, Eric J. Introduction to *Frederick Douglass: New Literary and Historical Essays*, edited by Eric J. Sundquist, 1–22. Cambridge: Cambridge University Press, 1990.

Ralph Waldo Emerson

Emerson, Ralph Waldo. "The American Scholar." In *The Collected Works of Ralph Waldo Emerson*, edited by Robert E. Spiller and Alfred R. Ferguson, 1:52–70. Cambridge, MA: Belknap Press of Harvard University Press, 1971.

———. "Experience." In *The Collected Works of Ralph Waldo Emerson*, edited by Joseph Slater, Alfred R. Ferguson, and Jean Ferguson Carr, 3:27–49. Cambridge, MA: Belknap Press of Harvard University Press, 1983.

———. "Goethe, or the Writer." In *The Collected Works of Ralph Waldo Emerson*, edited by Wallace E. Williams and Douglas Emory Wilson, 151–66. Cambridge, MA: Belknap Press of Harvard University Press, 1987.

———. *The Journals and Miscellaneous Notebooks of Ralph Waldo Emerson*, edited by William H. Gilman and others. Cambridge, MA: Belknap Press of Harvard University Press, 1960–1982.

———. "The Poet." In *The Collected Works of Ralph Waldo Emerson*, edited by Joseph Slater, 3:3–24. Cambridge, MA: Belknap Press of Harvard University Press, 1983.

———. "Self-Reliance." In *The Collected Works of Ralph Waldo Emerson*, edited by Joseph Slater, Alfred R. Ferguson, and Jean Ferguson Carr, 2:25–51. Cambridge, MA: Belknap Press of Harvard University Press, 1979.

Richardson, Robert D., Jr. *Emerson: The Mind on Fire*. Berkeley: University of California Press, 1995.

Margaret Fuller

Fuller, Margaret. *Papers on Literature and Art*. London: Wiley & Putnam, 1846.

Nathaniel Hawthorne

Hawthorne, Nathaniel. Preface to *The House of the Seven Gables*. In *Complete Novels*, 351–53. New York: Literary Classics of the United States, 1983.

———. "Old News." In *Tales and Sketches*, 251–75. New York: Literary Classics of the United States, 1982.

———. "Wakefield." In *Tales and Sketches*, 290–98. New York: Literary Classics of the United States, 1982.

Scholnick, Robert J. "'The Ultraism of the Day': Greene's *Boston Post*, Hawthorne, Fuller, Melville, Stowe, and Literary Journalism in Antebellum America." *American Periodicals* 18 (2008): 163–91.

Herman Melville

Higgins, Brian, and Hershel Parker, eds. *Herman Melville: The Contemporary Reviews*. Cambridge: Cambridge University Press, 1995.

Melville, Herman. *The Confidence-Man*. New York: Russell & Russell, 1963.
———. *Moby-Dick*. Edited by Hershel Parker and Harrison Hayford. New York: W. W. Norton, 2002.
———. *Pierre*. New York: Russell & Russell, 1963.

Edgar Allan Poe

Burgoyne, Daniel. "Coleridge's 'Poetic Faith' and Poe's Scientific Hoax." *Romanticism on the Net* 21 (February 2001), http://www.erudit.org/revue/ron/2001/v/n21/005960ar.html.
Canada, Mark. "The Right Brain in Poe's Creative Process." *The Southern Quarterly* 36 (Summer 1998): 96–105.
Dinius, Marcy. "Poe's Moon Shot: 'Hans Phaall' and the Art and Science of Antebellum Print Culture." *Poe Studies/Dark Romanticism: History, Theory, Interpretation* 37 (2004): 1–10.
Hoffman, Daniel. *Poe Poe Poe Poe Poe Poe Poe*. Garden City, NY: Doubleday, 1973.
Ketterer, David. "Poe's Usage of the Hoax and the Unity of 'Hans Pfaal.'" In *The Naiad Voice: Essays on Poe's Satiric Hoaxing*, edited by Dennis W. Eddings. Port Washington, NY: Associated Faculty Press, 1983.
Kopley, Richard. *Edgar Allan Poe and the Dupin Mysteries*. New York: Palgrave Macmillan, 2008.
Levine, Stuart. *Edgar Poe: Seer and Craftsman*. DeLand, FL: Everett/Edwards, 1972.
———. "The Imagination at Play: Edgar Allan Poe." In *The Naiad Voice: Essays on Poe's Satiric Hoaxing*, edited by Dennis W. Eddings, 29–40. Port Washington, NY: Associated Faculty Press, 1983. Originally published in *Kenyon Review* 28 (1966): 194–209.
Poe, Edgar Allan. "The Balloon Hoax." In *Collected Works of Edgar Allan Poe*, edited by Thomas Ollive Mabbott, 1068–82. Cambridge, MA: Belknap Press of Harvard University Press, 1978.
———. *Doings of Gotham*. Pottsville, PA: Jacob E. Spannuth, 1929. Reprint, Norwood, PA: Norwood Editions, 1977.
———. "The Facts in the Case of M. Valdemar." In *Collected Works of Edgar Allan Poe*, edited by Thomas Ollive Mabbott, 1233–43. Cambridge, MA: Belknap Press of Harvard University Press, 1978.
———. "The Fall of the House of Usher." In *Collected Works of Edgar Allan Poe*, edited by Thomas Ollive Mabbott, 397–417. Cambridge, MA: Belknap Press of Harvard University Press, 1978.
———. *The Collected Letters of Edgar Allan Poe*, edited by John Ward Ostrom. Revised, corrected, and expanded by Burton R. Pollin and Jeffrey A. Savoye. New York: Gordian, 2008.
———. "Ligeia." In *Collected Works of Edgar Allan Poe*, edited by Thomas Ollive Mabbott, 310–30. Cambridge, MA: Belknap Press of Harvard University Press, 1978.

―――. "The Literati of New York City." In *Essays and Reviews*, edited by G. R. Thompson, 1118–222. New York: Literary Classics of the United States, 1984.

―――. "The Man of the Crowd." In *Collected Works of Edgar Allan Poe*, edited by Thomas Ollive Mabbott, 506–14. Cambridge, MA: Belknap Press of Harvard University Press, 1978.

―――. "Marginalia." In *Essays and Reviews*, edited by G. R. Thompson, 1445–72. New York: Literary Classics of the United States, 1984.

―――. "The Murders in the Rue Morgue." In *Collected Works of Edgar Allan Poe*, edited by Thomas Ollive Mabbott, 527–68. Cambridge, MA: Belknap Press of Harvard University Press, 1978.

―――. "The Mystery of Marie Roget." In *Collected Works of Edgar Allan Poe*, edited by Thomas Ollive Mabbott, 723–74. Cambridge, MA: Belknap Press of Harvard University Press, 1978.

―――. "The Philosophy of Composition." In *Essays and Reviews*, edited by G. R. Thompson, 13–25. New York: Literary Classics of the United States, 1984.

―――. "The Unparalleled Adventure of One Hans Pfaall." In *The Imaginary Voyages*, edited by Burton R. Pollin, 387–433. Boston: Twayne, 1981.

―――. "Von Kempelen and His Discovery." In *Collected Works of Edgar Allan Poe*, edited by Thomas Ollive Mabbott, 1357–64. Cambridge, MA: Belknap Press of Harvard University Press, 1978.

Pollin, Burton. *Discoveries in Poe*. Notre Dame, IN: University of Notre Dame Press, 1970.

―――. Introduction to "The Unparalleled Adventures of One Hans Pfaall." In *Imaginary Voyages*, edited by Burton R. Pollin, 366–79. Boston: Twayne, 1981.

Thomas, Dwight, and David K. Jackson. *The Poe Log: A Documentary Life of Edgar Allan Poe, 1809–1849*. Boston: G. K. Hall, 1987.

Thompson, G. Richard. "Perspectives on Poe." In *The Naiad Voice: Essays on Poe's Satiric Hoaxing*, edited by Dennis W. Eddings, 97–111. Port Washington, NY: Associated Faculty Press, 1983.

Walsh, John. *Poe the Detective: The Curious Circumstances Behind "The Mystery of Marie Roget."* New Brunswick, NJ: Rutgers University Press, 1968.

Whalen, Terence. *Edgar Allan Poe and the Masses: The Political Economy of Literature in Antebellum America*. Princeton: Princeton University Press, 1999.

Wimsatt, William J., Jr. "Poe and the Mystery of Mary Rogers." *PMLA* 56 (1941): 230–48.

Harriet Beecher Stowe

Ammons, Elizabeth. Introduction to *Critical Essays on Harriet Beecher Stowe*, edited by Elizabeth Ammons, xi–xviii. Boston: G. K. Hall, 1980.

Baldwin, James. "Everybody's Protest Novel." In *Critical Essays on Harriet Beecher Stowe*, edited by Elizabeth Ammons, 92–97. Boston: G. K. Hall, 1980.

Douglas, Ann. Introduction. *Uncle Tom's Cabin.* New York: Penguin, 1981.

Hedrick, Joan D. *Harriet Beecher Stowe: A Life.* New York: Oxford University Press, 1994.

Kirkham, E. Bruce. *The Building of Uncle Tom's Cabin.* Knoxville: University of Tennessee Press, 1977.

Lowance, Mason I. "Biblical Typology and the Allegorical Mode: The Prophetic Strain." In *The Stowe Debate: Rhetorical Strategies in Uncle Tom's Cabin,* edited by Mason I. Lowance, Jr., Ellen E. Westbrook, and R. C. De Prospo, 159–84. Amherst: University of Massachusetts Press, 1994.

O'Connell, Catharine. "'The Magic of the Real Presence of Distress': Sentimentality and Competing Rhetorics of Authority." In *The Stowe Debate: Rhetorical Strategies in Uncle Tom's Cabin,* 13–36. Edited by Mason I. Lowance, Jr., Ellen E. Westbrook, and R. C. De Prospo. Amherst: University of Massachusetts Press, 1994.

Shaw, S. Bradley. "The Pliable Rhetoric of Domesticity." In *The Stowe Debate: Rhetorical Strategies in Uncle Tom's Cabin,* edited by Mason I. Lowance, Jr., Ellen E. Westbrook, and R. C. De Prospo, 73–98. Amherst: University of Massachusetts Press, 1994.

Stowe, Harriet Beecher. Letter to Catharine Beecher. In *The Oxford Harriet Beecher Stowe Reader,* edited by Joan Hedrick, 61–62. New York: Oxford University Press, 1994.

———. Letter to Henry Ward Beecher. In *The Oxford Harriet Beecher Stowe Reader,* edited by Joan Hedrick, 63–65. New York: Oxford University Press, 1994.

———. *Uncle Tom's Cabin.* Edited by Mary R. Reichardt. San Francisco: Ignatius, 2009.

Warner, Charles Dudley. "The Story of *Uncle Tom's Cabin.*" In *Critical Essays on Harriet Beecher Stowe,* edited by Elizabeth Ammons, 60–72. Boston: G. K. Hall, 1980.

Henry David Thoreau

Gura, Philip F. "Henry Thoreau and the Wisdom of Words." In *Critical Essays on Henry David Thoreau's Walden,* edited by Joel Myerson, 203–15. Boston: G. K. Hall, 1988.

Richardson, Robert D., Jr. *Henry Thoreau: A Life of the Mind.* Berkeley: University of California Press, 1986.

Rowe, John Carlos. "The Being of Language: The Language of Being." In *Henry David Thoreau,* edited by Harold Bloom, 145–71. New York: Chelsea House, 1987.

Sattelmeyer, Robert. "The Remaking of *Walden.*" In *Writing the American Classics,* edited by James Barbour and Tom Quirk, 53–78. Chapel Hill: University of North Carolina Press, 1990.

Thoreau, Henry David. *The Correspondence of Henry David Thoreau.* Edited by Walter Harding and Carl Bode. New York: New York University Press, 1958.

———. "Slavery in Massachusetts." In *Reform Papers*, edited by Wendell Glick, 91–109. Princeton: Princeton University Press, 1973.

———. *Walden*. Edited by J. Lyndon Shanley. Princeton: Princeton University Press, 1971.

Walt Whitman

Whitman, Walt. *The Collected Writings of Walt Whitman*. Edited by Gay Wilson Allen and Sculley Bradley. 17 volumes. New York: New York University Press, 1961–1984.

———. Feinberg-Whitman Collection. Library of Congress.

Sara Willis ("Fanny Fern")

Warren, Joyce W. "Introduction." In *Ruth Hall and Other Writings*, edited by Joyce W. Warren, xi–xx. New Brunswick, NJ: Rutgers University Press, 1986.

Willis, Sara. "Dull Homes in Bright Places." In *Ruth Hall and Other Writings*, edited by Joyce W. Warren, 362–64. New Brunswick, NJ: Rutgers University Press, 1986.

———. *Ruth Hall*. In *Ruth Hall and Other Writings*, edited by Joyce W. Warren, 1–211. New Brunswick, NJ: Rutgers University Press, 1986.

———. "Women's Salaries." In *Ruth Hall and Other Writings*, edited by Joyce W. Warren, 364–66. New Brunswick, NJ: Rutgers University Press, 1986.

OTHER

Dunbar, Robin. *Grooming, Gossip, and the Evolution of Language*. Cambridge, MA: Harvard University Press, 1997.

Farkas, Sandor. *Journey in North America, 1831*. Trans. Arpad Kadarkay. Santa Barbara: American Bibliographic Center-Clio Press, 1978.

Locke, John. *Essay Concerning Human Understanding*. New York: Dover, 1959.

Miller, Cynthia. "Introduction: At Play in the Fields of the Truth." *Post Script* 28 (Summer 2009): 3–8.

Tocqueville, Alexis de. *Democracy in America*. New York: Literary Classics of the United States, 2004.

INDEX